1P @ 1650 #825
4/96
D0041647

Reading and Writing
JAPANESE

EDITORIAL STAFF

FLORENCE SAKADE: *General Editor*

KENJI EMORI: *Associate Editor (Japanese Language)*

RALPH FRIEDRICH: *Associate Editor (English Language)*

SUSUMU OHASHI: *Assistant Editor*

A Guide to READING & WRITING JAPANESE

当用漢字

The 1,850 Basic Characters and the Kana Syllabaries

Revised Edition

CHARLES E. TUTTLE COMPANY
Rutland, Vermont & Tokyo, Japan

Representatives

For Continental Europe:
BOXERBOOKS, INC., *Zurich*

For the British Isles:
PRENTICE-HALL INTERNATIONAL, INC., *London*

For Australasia:
BOOK WISE (AUSTRALIA) PTY. LTD.
104-108 Sussex Street, Sydney 2000

Published by the Charles E. Tuttle Co., Inc.
of Rutland, Vermont and Tokyo, Japan
with editorial offices at
Suido 1-chome, 2-6, Bunkyo-ku, Tokyo, Japan

© *1959 by Charles E. Tuttle Co., Inc.*

All rights reserved

Library of Congress Catalog Card No. 59-10412

International Standard Book No. 0-8048-0226-2

First edition, 1959
Four reprintings
Second edition (revised), 1961
Fifty-sixth printing, 1986

PRINTED IN JAPAN

TABLE OF CONTENTS

Introduction 7

1. The 881 Essential Characters 15

2. The 1,850 General-Use Characters 192

3. Proposed Changes 279

   Characters to Be Added 279

   Additional Readings and Simplified Writings 280

   Characters to Be Dropped 281

4. Syllabary: Katakana and Hiragana 283

5. Index of Readings 288

INTRODUCTION

THIS BOOK is designed for those who are eager to acquaint themselves with the written Japanese language and to acquire an elementary ability to read and write it. It has been the purpose of the editor to produce, in as practical a form as possible, a handbook that will furnish the beginner in written Japanese with the knowledge of sufficient characters to enable him to read and write the language in its everyday style. Specifically, the book presents the 1,850 characters prescribed by the Japanese Ministry of Education and adopted by law as those most essential for common use and everyday communication. Since Japanese publications in general now limit themselves to the use of these 1,850 characters (except in the case of proper names), it is no longer a formidable task for the student of the written language to learn to read ordinary books and periodicals and to write in reasonably fluent style. It should be noted that the editor has made a positive effort to include in this volume only the most useful definitions of the *kanji* themselves and the most practical examples of their use in everyday words.

The book is divided into two major sections. The first of these presents the 881 characters designated by the Ministry of Education as the basic requirement for the six years of elementary school. The choice of these characters and their order of appearance in the list were determined by the Ministry through careful research into the frequency of their use, and the resulting selection thus represents the minimum of characters considered essential for common use. Similarly, the majority of the compounds given are those which the Ministry's most recent research shows to be of high frequency in everyday use.

The second major section of the book presents the 1,850 characters designated as "standard" for general everyday use in the publishing world. They include, of course, the 881 basic characters, and the total represents the most significant measure taken to date to simplify the written Japanese language. Not only do these 1,850 characters represent a major reduction in the number formerly in general use; they also represent a simplification of readings and, in a number of cases, of written forms. It should be of considerable interest to foreign students of Japanese to know that many words formerly written with *kanji* (characters) are now written with *kana* (phonetic symbols), that numerous abstruse readings of individual characters have been discarded, and that many of the characters themselves have been simplified from their earlier complex forms. The editor of this book has further assisted the process of simplification for the foreign student by omitting occasional readings that are considered too specialized or too uncommon for the beginner in *kanji*.

It is pertinent to note that the process of simplification is being continued in Japan. In the "Proposed Changes" section of this book will be found one group of 28 characters destined for probable elimination from the standard list and another group of 28 considered for inclusion. These proposed changes, although not yet legally sanctioned, have already been adopted by publishers. In the same section of the book will be found a list of new readings and writings proposed for adoption. It should be added that *kana* usage, particularly as it affects *okurigana* (word endings written in phonetic symbols), is still undergoing revision. These matters notwithstanding, the contents of the present volume are as up-to-date as it has been possible to make them.

The 881 essential characters are given with their *on-yomi* (readings taken from Chinese), *kun-yomi* (native Japanese readings), definitions, and number of strokes. Each character is accompanied by a chart showing the proper order of strokes in its writing. The listing of characters follows that of the graded list established by the Ministry of Education. The readings are those designated for use in the elementary grades. Each character is followed by compounds that illustrate its use in the formation of everyday words.

The 1,850 general-use characters are presented with their *on-yomi*, *kun-yomi*, and definitions, but without illustrative compounds. In many cases, however, they may be found in compound form in examples given for the 881 essential characters. The order of listing for the general-use characters is that of the number of strokes, in accordance with the latest Ministry of Education list. Since it would be superfluous to repeat the readings and definitions of the 881 essential characters when they appear in the general-use list, each is indicated only by its proper number in the list and the number of the page where it may be found in the list of essential characters.

It should be mentioned here that in 1951 the Ministry of Education found it necessary to supplement the list of 1,850 characters with a list of 92 characters approved for use in personal names. Although this supplementary list is not included in the present volume, the story of its adoption is of interest. After the original standard list had been approved by law, it was discovered that a number of characters traditionally used in personal names had been excluded. The situation that resulted had its amusing side. Parents who had chosen among the excluded characters in selecting names for their newborn children were met with refusal when they sought to register the births at government offices, since the characters were missing from the approved list. Because the majority of these parents countered with a refusal on their own part to substitute characters from the approved list, a sizable number of young Japanese citizens remained legally nameless. To provide an escape from this intolerable predicament, the Ministry of Education came to the rescue by issuing its supplementary list of 92 name characters.

In an effort to include as many useful words as possible, the editor has largely excluded proper nouns and has attempted to avoid duplication among the examples of words given. Some repetitions were inevitable, however, because of the limited use of certain *kanji*. As far as possible, three examples of combinations have been provided for each of the 881 essential *kanji*, but in some cases—either because the *kanji* are limited in use or because fewer examples suffice (as with numerals)—fewer examples are given. It should be noted that a few of the *kanji*, including those of Japanese rather than Chinese origin, have no *on-yomi* (e.g., Nos. 302 and 749), while certain others have no *kun-yomi* (e.g., Nos. 155 and 444).

A few words regarding romanization and pronunciation are in

order. The Hepburn system of romanization has been followed throughout, for the simple reason that it is the least confusing to foreign students of Japanese and is the most frequently used. The change of *n* to *m* before *b*, *m*, and *p* in spoken Japanese is indicated by the use of *m* in the romanized spellings, e.g., *sambyaku* (three hundred), *sammyaku* (mountain range), *dempō* (telegram). Where correct pronunciation and word-meaning require a careful distinction between syllables, a hyphen indicates the proper separation, e.g., *sen-en* (one thousand yen), *kao-iro* (complexion), *i-in* (committee member), *ashi-ato* (footprint), *shin-ya* (midnight). The hyphen is also used to mark off the honorific *o* and the prefix *ō* meaning "large" or "great," e.g., *o-kane* (money), *ō-ame* (heavy rain). The change from an unvoiced to a voiced consonant (*dakuon*) in word combinations is shown, wherever possible, in brackets in the readings for the 881 essential *kanji*.

The following examples explain the typographical arrangements used in giving the readings and definitions of the characters:

KEN; *mi(ru)*, to see, to look

On-yomi in capitals, *kun-yomi* in italics, definitions in roman.

Okurigana of *kun-yomi* in parentheses.

SAN [ZAN]; *yama*, mountain

Vocalized (*dakuon*) form of *on-yomi* in brackets, *kun-yomi* in italics.

SHIN; *kokoro* [*gokoro*], heart, spirit, mind

Vocalized (*dakuon*) form of *kun-yomi* in brackets.

GEN, GAN; *moto*, beginning, foundation

Two *on-yomi* of same meaning.

KATSU (energy)

No *kun-yomi*. Original meaning of character given in parentheses.

I (easy); EKI, divination

Two *on-yomi* of different meaning. Original meaning of character given in parentheses. No *kun-yomi*.

HI, ratio, comparison; *kura(beru)*, to compare

Definitions immediately following *on-yomi* indicate that it is used either independently or in compounds.

Okurigana of *kun-yomi* in parentheses.

Although there are exceptions to the rule, *on-yomi* are usually used in compounds. In cases where *on-yomi* can be used either independently or in compounds, effort has been made to distinguish this fact insofar as possible by placing the definition of the *on-yomi* immediately after it, preceded by a comma.

A few basic rules will suffice to explain the proper method of writing Japanese characters. In general, the basic rule in the order of strokes is from

1. top to bottom:

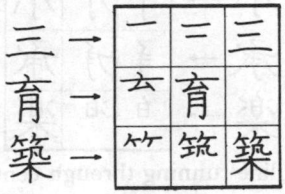

2. left to right:

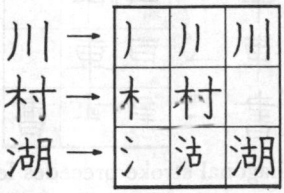

Other rules are

3. When two or more strokes cross, horizontal strokes usually precede perpendicular ones:

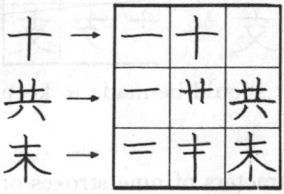

4. Sometimes perpendicular strokes precede horizontal ones:

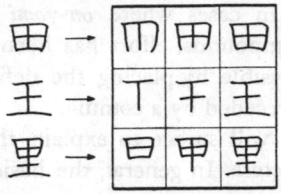

5. Center first, then left and right:

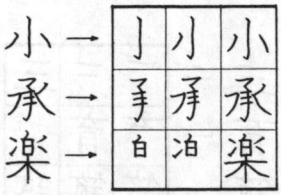

6. Perpendicular line running through center written last:

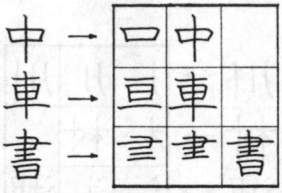

7. Right-to-left diagonal stroke precedes left-to-right:

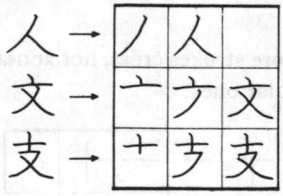

8. Constant effort should be made to keep the characters of uniform size.

In this book, characters of nine strokes or less are drawn stroke by stroke. For purposes of simplification, characters requiring more than nine strokes are shown with one or more of their component elements already drawn, e.g., No. 370, in which the terminal "mouth" simply reproduces in smaller size the character *kuchi* (No. 27). In these cases, an element already drawn is shown in small type under the compounds along with the number of the original character. If the element already drawn is not a character itself, it is shown in small type along with a character in which its stroke order has been previously shown.

It should be noted, however, that when one character (usually in reduced size) is used to form part of a more complex character, the shape of the former sometimes changes. Thus No. 15, for example, changes from 木 to 扌 when it becomes a part of No. 107 村. Other examples are the change of 人 to 亻 in 休 and of 手 to 扌 in 打. Changes of this kind are also shown in small type under the compounds. Although there are partial differences in the accepted writings of *kanji*, the forms shown in this book are those approved for use in textbooks; in 1961 these forms will become universal for all textbooks. Printed forms, of course, may differ somewhat from written forms.

The book concludes with instructions for writing the two *kana* syllabaries, *hiragana* (phonetic symbols in cursive style, used principally for native words and word endings) and *katakana* (phonetic symbols in angular style, used chiefly for transcribing foreign words). The syllabaries are accompanied by a chart listing sound changes and *kana* combinations with their romanized forms.

The models for the writing of the characters are the work of Mr. Kenji Emori, expert calligrapher and official of the Elementary and Secondary Education Division, Ministry of Education. In addition to his responsibility for assessing the calligraphic and art content of all school textbooks submitted for the Ministry's approval, he has been engaged in an intensive study of the form, style, and stroke order of *kanji*. Valuable assistance in the preparation of the book was also given by Mr. Susumu Ōhashi and Mr. Ralph Friedrich, who participated in selecting the English definitions and checking the accuracy of the manuscript. The editor further acknowledges her indebtedness to the following texts compiled by the Ministry of Education: *Hitsujun no Tebiki*, *Shōgakkō Gakushū Shidō Yōryō*, *Kokugo Series Nos. 21 and 33*, and *Kyōiku Kanji no Gakunen Haitō*.

NOTE TO THE REVISED EDITION

IN RESPONSE to requests from many users of this book who have wanted to use it for a dictionary as well as for a study guide, an index of the Japanese readings of the characters has been added at the end. So the book now has two dictionary uses: (1) If the character is known, look for it by stroke-count in the list of 1,850 general-use characters (including the 881 essential characters) beginning on page 192. (2) If the reading but not the character is known, consult the index beginning on page 288. As it has proved impractical to include an index of English equivalents, if neither the character nor the reading is known, recourse must be had to one of the many English-Japanese dictionaries.

Keep in mind that the following 881 characters are not arranged in an order suitable for dictionary use (they can, however, be found easily by either of the steps described above) but in an order determined by the Japanese Ministry of Education after careful research into the frequency of their use and recommended for teaching in elementary schools. This order is most valuable in indicating the relative importance of the characters and a suggested priority to be followed in their study. They are divided by school grades as follows:

School Grade	Character Numbers
1	1–46
2	47–151
3	152–338
4	339–543
5	544–737
6	738–881

The 881
ESSENTIAL CHARACTERS

一	一			ICHI, *hito(tsu)*, one 一月 *ichigatsu*, January 一番 *ichiban*, first, best 一冊 *issatsu*, one (book, magazine)
1 1 stroke				
二	一	二		NI, *futa(tsu)*, two 二月 *nigatsu*, February 二か月 *nikagetsu*, two months 二回 *nikai*, twice
2 2 strokes				
三	一	二	三	SAN, *mi*, *mit(tsu)*, three 三月 *sangatsu*, March 三人 *sannin*, three people 三日 *mikka*, three days, the third day
3 3 strokes				
四	丿	冂	冂	SHI, *yon*, *yo*, *yot(tsu)*, four 四月 *shigatsu*, April 四日 *yokka*, four days, the fourth day 四十 *shijū*, *yonjū*, forty
4 5 strokes	四	四		

五	一	丆	五	GO, *itsu(tsu)*, five 五月 *gogatsu*, May 五人 *gonin*, five people 五十 *gojū*, fifty
	五			
5 4 strokes				
六	丶	亠	六	ROKU, *mut(tsu)*, six 六月 *rokugatsu*, June 六か月 *rokkagetsu*, six months 六十 *rokujū*, sixty
	六			
6 4 strokes				
七	一	七		SHICHI, *nana(tsu)*, seven 七月 *shichigatsu*, July 七か月 *nanakagetsu*, seven months 七十 *shichijū*, *nanajū*, seventy
7 2 strokes				
八	ノ	八		HACHI, *yat(tsu)*, eight 八月 *hachigatsu*, August 八か月 *hachikagetsu*, eight months 八十 *hachijū*, eighty
8 2 strokes				
九	ノ	九		KU, KYŪ, *kokono(tsu)*, nine 九月 *kugatsu*, September 九十 *kujū*, *kyūjū*, ninety 九時 *kuji*, nine o'clock
9 2 strokes				

十 10 2 strokes	一 十	JŪ, *tō*, ten 十月 *jūgatsu*, October 十日 *tōka*, ten days, the tenth day 十回 *jikkai*, ten times
日 11 4 strokes	丨 冂 日 日	NICHI, JITSU; *hi* [*bi*], day, sun; ~*ka*, suffix for counting days 日曜日 *nichiyōbi*, Sunday 昨日 *sakujitsu*, yesterday 朝日 *asahi*, morning sun
月 12 4 strokes	丿 冂 月 月	GETSU, GATSU; *tsuki* [*zuki*], month, moon 月曜日 *getsuyōbi*, Monday 来月 *raigetsu*, next month 三日月 *mikazuki*, new moon
火 13 4 strokes	丶 丶丿 火 火	KA; *hi* [*bi*], fire 火曜日 *kayōbi*, Tuesday 火ばち *hibachi*, charcoal brazier 火事 *kaji*, fire, conflagration 灬
水 14 4 strokes	丿 刀 水 水	SUI; *mizu*, water 大水 *ō-mizu*, flood, inundation 水力 *suiryoku*, water power 水兵 *suihei*, sailor

木 15 4 strokes	一 十 才 木	MOKU, BOKU; *ki* [*gi*], tree, wood 木曜日 *mokuyōbi*, Thursday 材木 *zaimoku*, lumber 木製 *mokusei*, made of wood 木
金 16 8 strokes	ノ 八 ⺅ 今 ⺅ 今 金 金	KIN, gold; KON (gold); *kane*, money 金曜日 *kin-yōbi*, Friday お金 *o-kane*, money 金魚 *kingyo*, goldfish 金
土 17 3 strokes	一 十 土	DO, TO; *tsuchi*, earth, soil 土曜日 *doyōbi*, Saturday 土地 *tochi*, ground, plot of land 土人 *dojin*, native 土
左 18 5 strokes	一 ナ 𠂇 𠂇 左	SA; *hidari*, left 左派 *saha*, leftist (political), left wing 左側 *sasoku*, *hidarigawa*, left side 左手 *hidarite*, left hand
右 19 5 strokes	ノ ナ 𠂇 右 右	YŪ, U; *migi*, right 左右 *sayū*, left and right 右派 *uha*, right wing (political) 右側 *usoku*, *migigawa*, right side

上	丨	卜	上	JŌ; *ue*, top, above, on; *kami*, upper; *nobo(ru)*, to go up, to go toward Tōkyō; *a(geru)*, to raise; *a-(garu)*, to rise 上流 *jōryū*, upstream, upper class 海上 *kaijō*, on the sea, maritime 川上 *kawakami*, upstream
20 3 strokes				
下	一	丅	下	KA, GE; *shita*, bottom, under, beneath; *moto*, base; *shimo*, lower; *kuda(ru)*, to go down, to go away from Tōkyō; *sa(geru)*, to hang (v.t.), to lower; *sa(garu)*, to hang down 川下 *kawashimo*, downstream 下品 *gehin*, vulgar, coarse 地下鉄 *chikatetsu*, subway
21 3 strokes				
大	一	𠂇	大	DAI, TAI; *ō(kii)*, big, large, great 大学 *daigaku*, university, college 大変 *taihen*, tremendous, serious 大広間 *o-hiroma*, grand hall
22 3 strokes				
中	丨	冂	口	CHŪ; *naka*, middle, within, inside 中学校 *chūgakkō*, middle school 中心 *chūshin*, center, heart (of a city, etc.) 集中 *shūchū*, concentration
23 4 strokes	中			
小	亅	小	小	SHŌ; *ko*, *o*, *chii(sai)*, small, minor 小学校 *shōgakkō*, primary school 小屋 *koya*, hut 小説 *shōsetsu*, novel (fiction)
24 3 strokes				

目 25 5 strokes	丨 冂 冃 目 目 目	MOKU; *me*, eye; also used as an ordinal suffix 横目 *yokome*, side glance 目的 *mokuteki*, purpose 目標 *mokuhyō*, mark, target
耳 26 6 strokes	一 丆 下 耳 耳 耳	JI; *mimi*, ear 早耳 *hayamimi*, keen of hearing 耳鳴り *miminari*, ringing in the ears 耳が遠い *mimi ga tōi*, deaf 耳
口 27 3 strokes	丨 冂 口	KŌ, KU; *kuchi* [*guchi*], mouth 口ひげ *kuchihige*, mustache 入口 *iriguchi*, entrance 口論 *kōron*, dispute 口
手 28 4 strokes	ノ 二 三 手	SHU; *te*, hand 握手 *akushu*, handshake 手袋 *tebukuro*, gloves 手紙 *tegami*, letter 扌
足 29 7 strokes	丨 口 口 足 足 足 足	SOKU [ZOKU]; *ashi*, foot, leg; *ta(riru)*, to be sufficient 足跡 *ashi-ato*, footprint 満足 *manzoku*, satisfaction 不足 *fusoku*, insufficiency

人	丿 人	NIN, JIN; *hito* [*bito*], person 人類 *jinrui*, human race 人間 *ningen*, human being 人口 *jinkō*, population
30 2 strokes		
子	了 子	SHI, SU; *ko* [*go*], child 子ども *kodomo*, child, children 原子 *genshi*, atom 様子 *yōsu*, the state of things, appearance
31 3 strokes		
女	乂 女	JO, NYO; *onna*, woman, girl 女中 *jochū*, maid 少女 *shōjo*, maiden 女王 *joō*, queen
32 3 strokes		
先	丿 ㇂ 牛 生 生 先	SEN; *saki*, previous, ahead 先生 *sensei*, teacher 先日 *senjitsu*, the other day 行き先 *yukisaki*, destination
33 6 strokes		
生	丿 ㇂ 牛 牛 生	SEI, SHŌ; birth, life; *u*(*mareru*), to be born; *u*(*mu*), to give birth; *i*(*kiru*), to live; *ki*, pure, genuine; *nama*, raw 一生 *isshō*, one's (whole) life 生活 *seikatsu*, livelihood 大学生 *daigakusei*, college student
34 5 strokes		

赤 35 7 strokes	一 十 土 ナ 赤 赤 赤	SEKI, SHAKU; *aka*, *aka(i)*, red 赤ちゃん *akachan*, baby, infant 赤十字 *sekijūji*, Red Cross 赤銅 *shakudō*, alloy of copper and gold
青 36 8 strokes	一 十 ⺾ 主 主 青 青 青	SEI, SHŌ; *ao*, *ao(i)*, blue, green, inexperienced 青年 *seinen*, youth 青白い *aojiroi*, pale 青空 *aozora*, blue sky
白 37 5 strokes	ノ 亻 白 白 白	HAKU, BYAKU; *shiro* [*jiro*], *shiro(i)*, white 白人 *hakujin*, Caucasian 白状 *hakujō*, confession 白鳥 *hakuchō*, swan
山 38 3 strokes	丨 山 山	SAN [ZAN]; *yama*, mountain 山道 *sandō*, *yamamichi*, mountain path 山脈 *sammyaku*, mountain range 登山 *tozan*, mountain climbing
川 39 3 strokes	丿 川 川	SEN; *kawa* [*gawa*], river 谷川 *tanigawa*, mountain stream 川ばた *kawabata*, riverside 川口 *kawaguchi*, mouth of a river

田 40 5 strokes	丨 冂 冃 田 田	DEN; *ta* [*da*], rice field 田園 *den-en*, fields and gardens, rural districts 稲田 *inada*, rice field 田植 *taue*, rice planting
森 41 12 strokes	一 十 才 木 木 木 森 森 森	SHIN; *mori*, forest, grove 森林 *shinrin*, forest 森閑 *shinkan*, silent 森厳 *shingen*, solemn, awe-inspiring
雨 42 8 strokes	一 一 冂 而 而 雨 雨 雨	U; *ame*, rain 大雨 *ō-ame*, heavy rain 雨戸 *amado*, rain door, shutter 梅雨 *baiu*, rainy season of early summer
花 43 7 strokes	一 十 艹 艹 艹 花 花	KA; *hana*, flower 花屋 *hanaya*, flower shop, florist 花びん *kabin*, vase 花火 *hanabi*, fireworks
石 44 5 strokes	一 厂 不 石 石	SEKI, KOKU, SHAKU; *ishi*, stone 小石 *ko-ishi*, pebble 石炭 *sekitan*, coal 磁石 *jishaku*, magnet

本	一 十 才 木 本	HON [BON, PON], book, suffix for counting long, slender objects 一本 *ippon*, one (bottle, rod, etc.) 本箱 *hombako*, bookcase 日本 *Nihon*, *Nippon*, Japan
45 5 strokes		
正	一 丅 下 正 正	SEI, SHŌ; *tada*(*shii*), correct, right 正直 *shōjiki*, honesty 正方形 *seihōkei*, square (geometrical figure) 正月 *shōgatsu*, New Year's
46 5 strokes		
雲	一 冖 冖 雨 雨 雨 雲 雲 雲	UN; *kumo* [*gumo*], cloud 雲状 *unjō*, cloudlike, nebulous 入道雲 *nyūdōgumo*, gigantic clouds 星雲 *seiun*, nebula (雨 42)
47 12 strokes		
円	丨 冂 冂 円	EN, circle, yen (Japanese monetary unit) 円満 *emman*, perfection, satisfaction 千円札 *sen-ensatsu*, thousand-yen bill 円盤 *emban*, disc
48 4 strokes		
王	一 丅 干 王	Ō, king 王様 *ōsama*, king 王子 *ōji*, prince 王国 *ōkoku*, kingdom, monarchy 王
49 4 strokes		

音 50 9 strokes	一 亠 亠 立 立 音 音 音 音	ON, IN; *ne*, *oto*, sound 音楽 *ongaku*, music 発音 *hatsuon*, pronunciation 母音 *boin*, vowel
何 51 7 strokes	ノ 亻 亻 亻 何 何 何	KA; *nani*, (*nan*), what, how many (interrogative prefix) 何人 *nannin*, how many people? 何時間 *nanjikan*, how much time? 何時 *nanji*, what time?
夏 52 10 strokes	一 丆 丆 百 百 百 夏 夏 夏	KA; *natsu*, summer 夏休み *natsuyasumi*, summer vacation 初夏 *shoka*, early summer 真夏 *manatsu*, midsummer (目 25)
家 53 10 strokes	丶 丶 宀 宀 宀 家 家 家 家	KA, KE; *ya*, *ie*, house 家主 *yanushi*, owner of a house, landlord 家族 *kazoku*, family 農家 *nōka*, farmhouse
会 54 6 strokes	ノ 人 亼 亼 会 会	KAI, E, meeting; *a*(*u*), to meet 会場 *kaijō*, place of meeting, site 会長 *kaichō*, president (of a society), chairman (of a committee) 会話 *kaiwa*, conversation

海 55 9 strokes		KAI; *umi*, sea, ocean 海岸 *kaigan*, seacoast, seaside 海水浴 *kaisuiyoku*, sea bathing 海外 *kaigai*, overseas, abroad
外 56 5 strokes	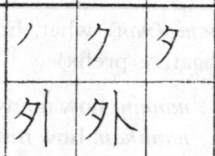	GAI, GE (outside, foreign); *hoka*, other; *soto*, outside 外国 *gaikoku*, foreign country 外国人 *gaikokujin*, foreigner 外科 *geka*, surgery
学 57 8 strokes	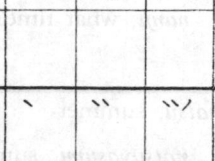	GAKU, learning, science; *mana-(bu)*, to learn 学校 *gakkō*, school 医学 *igaku*, medicine 科学 *kagaku*, science
間 58 12 strokes	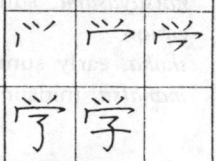	KAN, KEN; *aida*, interval, space; *ma*, interval, room, time 時間 *jikan*, time 二時間 *nijikan*, two hours 昼間 *hiruma*, daytime (II 11)
気 59 6 strokes	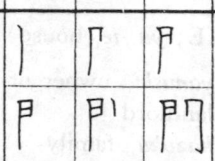	KI, KE, spirit, energy, mind 天気 *tenki*, weather 元気 *genki*, good spirits, health 病気 *byōki*, sickness

汽	丶	氵	氵	KI (steam, vapor) 汽車 *kisha*, steam-driven train 汽笛 *kiteki*, steam whistle 汽船 *kisen*, steamship, steamboat
	氵	氵	汽	
60 7 strokes	汽			
休	丿	亻	亻	KYŪ; *yasu(mi)*, rest, vacation; *yasu(mu)*, to rest 休憩 *kyūkei*, rest, intermission 休日 *kyūjitsu*, holiday 休養 *kyūyō*, relaxation, recreation
	亻	休	休	
61 6 strokes				
牛	丿	𠂉	𠂉	GYŪ; *ushi*, cow, bull 小牛 *ko-ushi*, calf 牛乳 *gyūnyū*, milk 牛肉 *gyūniku*, beef
	牛			
62 4 strokes				
京	丶	亠	亠	KYŌ, capital; KEI 東京 *Tōkyō*, capital of Japan 京都 *Kyōto*, ancient capital of Japan 上京 *jōkyō*, going to Tōkyō
	亠	亠	亨	
63 8 strokes	亨	京		
玉	一	丅	干	GYOKU; *tama* [*dama*], jewel, round object 水玉 *mizutama*, drop of water 目玉 *medama*, eyeball
	王	玉		
64 5 strokes				

空 65 8 strokes	丶 丶 宀 空 空 空 空 空	KŪ; *sora* [*zora*], sky 青空 *aozora*, blue sky 空気 *kūki*, air 空港 *kūkō*, airport
犬 66 4 strokes	一 ナ 大 犬	KEN; *inu*, dog 小犬 *ko-inu*, puppy 番犬 *banken*, watchdog 狂犬病 *kyōkembyō*, rabies
見 67 7 strokes	丨 冂 月 目 目 目 見	KEN; *mi*(*ru*), to see, to look 見せる *miseru*, to show 見物 *kembutsu*, sightseeing 見本 *mihon*, sample
元 68 4 strokes	一 二 テ 元	GEN, GAN; *moto*, beginning, foundation 根元 *kongen*, root, origin, source 元来 *ganrai*, originally, primarily 元日 *ganjitsu*, New Year's
戸 69 4 strokes	一 ヲ ヨ 戸	KO; *to* [*do*], door 戸外 *kogai*, outdoors 木戸 *kido*, gate, door 江戸 *Edo*, old name for Tōkyō

古 70 5 strokes	一 十 十 古 古	KO; *furu(i)*, old, ancient 古代 *kodai*, ancient times 古今 *kokon*, past and present 考古学 *kōkogaku*, archeology
工 71 3 strokes	一 丅 工	KŌ, KU (worker, construction) 工夫 *kōfu*, workman, laborer 工事中 *kōjichū*, under construction 工学 *kōgaku*, engineering
光 72 6 strokes	丨 小 小 业 光 光	KŌ; *hikari*, light, ray; *hika(ru)*, to shine 光年 *kōnen*, light-year 光波 *kōha*, light wave 観光 *kankō*, sightseeing
行 73 6 strokes	丿 彳 彳 彳 行 行	KŌ, GYŌ, AN; *i(ku)*, *yu(ku)*, to go; *oko(nau)*, to hold, to conduct 行列 *gyōretsu*, procession, queue 急行 *kyūkō*, express 銀行 *ginkō*, bank
考 74 6 strokes	一 十 土 耂 耂 考	KŌ; *kanga(e)*, thought, idea, opinion; *kanga(eru)*, to think 参考 *sankō*, reference 考案 *kōan*, idea, plan, scheme 考査 *kōsa*, examination

校 75 10 strokes	一 十 木 木 杩 校 校 校 校	KŌ (school; to correct, to investigate, to compare, to think) 校正 *kōsei*, proofreading 校舎 *kōsha*, school building 校友 *kōyū*, alumnus (木 15)
高 76 10 strokes	亠 亠 高 高 高 高	KŌ; *taka(i)*, high, costly 高等学校 *kōtōgakkō*, high school 最高 *saikō*, highest 高台 *takadai*, elevated land (口 27)
合 77 6 strokes	丿 亼 亼 合 合 合	GŌ; *a(u)*, to be together, to fit 合図 *aizu*, signal, sign 都合 *tsugō*, circumstances, convenience 組合 *kumiai*, union
谷 78 7 strokes	丿 八 八 八 谷 谷 谷	KOKU; *tani*, valley 谷間 *tanima*, valley 谷底 *tanizoko*, bottom of a ravine
国 79 8 strokes	丨 冂 冂 冂 国 国 国 国	KOKU; *kuni* [*guni*], country 国語 *kokugo*, national language (Japanese) 国会 *kokkai*, the National Diet 全国 *zenkoku*, national

黒 80 11 strokes		KOKU; *kuro* [*guro*], *kuro*(*i*), black 黒人 *kokujin*, negro 黒板 *kokuban*, blackboard 暗黒 *ankoku*, darkness, blackness
今 81 4 strokes	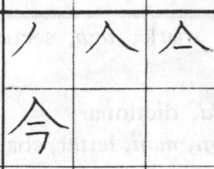	KON, KIN; *ima*, now, the present 今月 *kongetsu*, this month 今度 *kondo*, next time 今夜 *kon-ya*, tonight
作 82 7 strokes	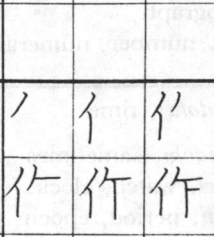	SAKU, SA; *tsuku*(*ru*), to make 作文 *sakubun*, (literary) composition 名作 *meisaku*, masterpiece 作曲 *sakkyoku*, musical composition
糸 83 6 strokes	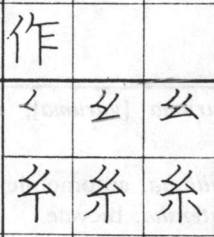	SHI; *ito*, thread 毛糸 *keito*, woolen yarn 糸口 *itoguchi*, clue 糸巻 *itomaki*, spool for thread
思 84 9 strokes		SHI; *omo*(*u*), to think, to recall 思想 *shisō*, thought, idea 不思議 *fushigi*, strange 思い出 *omoide*, remembrance, recollection

紙	85 10 strokes	SHI; *kami* [*gami*], paper ボール紙 *bōrugami*, cardboard 表紙 *hyōshi*, cover, binding 紙くず *kamikuzu*, wastepaper (糸 83)
字	86 6 strokes	JI, letter, mark; *aza*, section (of a village) 字引 *jibiki*, dictionary 文字 *monji*, *moji*, letter, character, ideograph 数字 *sūji*, number, numeral
時	87 10 strokes	JI; *toki* [*doki*], time 時々 *tokidoki*, sometimes 時計 *tokei*, watch, clock 時代 *jidai*, period, epoch
車	88 7 strokes	SHA; *kuruma* [*guruma*], wheel, vehicle 自動車 *jidōsha*, automobile 自転車 *jitensha*, bicycle 発車 *hassha*, departure of a vehicle
秋	89 9 strokes	SHŪ; *aki*, fall, autumn 初秋 *shoshū*, early autumn 秋風 *akikaze*, autumn breeze 秋分 *shūbun*, autumnal equinox

出 90 5 strokes	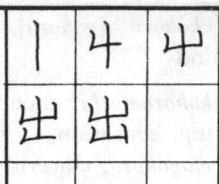	SHUTSU, SUI; *de(ru)*, to come out, to go out; *da(su)*, to put out, to take out, to bring out, to draw out 出発 *shuppatsu*, setting out, departure, starting 出版 *shuppan*, publishing 出口 *deguchi*, exit
春 91 9 strokes		SHUN; *haru*, spring 春風 *harukaze*, spring breeze 青春 *seishun*, springtime of life 晩春 *banshun*, late spring
書 92 10 strokes		SHO; *ka(ku)*, to write 辞書 *jisho*, dictionary 書物 *shomotsu*, book, volume 教科書 *kyōkasho*, textbook
少 93 4 strokes		SHŌ; *suko(shi)*, *suku(nai)*, few, little, scarce 少年 *shōnen*, boy, lad 多少 *tashō*, more or less, somewhat 少佐 *shōsa*, major (army), lieutenant commander (navy)
色 94 6 strokes	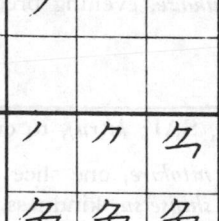	SHIKI, SHOKU; *iro*, color 顔色 *kao-iro*, complexion 天然色 *tennenshoku*, natural color, technicolor 色彩 *shikisai*, color, hue

心 95 4 strokes	心	SHIN; *kokoro* [*gokoro*], spirit, heart, mind 心持ち *kokoromochi*, mood, feeling, sensation 真心 *magokoro*, sincerity, devotion 一心 *isshin*, whole-heartedness
西 96 6 strokes	西	SEI, SAI; *nishi*, west 西洋 *seiyō*, the West, the Occident 大西洋 *Taiseiyō*, Atlantic Ocean 東西 *tōzai*, east and west, Orient and Occident
声 97 7 strokes	声	SEI; *koe* [*goe*], voice 泣き声 *nakigoe*, crying voice 音声学 *onseigaku*, phonetics 声帯 *seitai*, the vocal cords
夕 98 3 strokes		SEKI; *yū*, evening 夕方 *yūgata*, evening 夕飯 *yūhan*, supper 夕風 *yūkaze*, evening breeze
切 99 4 strokes	切	SETSU, SAI; *ki*(*ru*), to cut 一切れ *hitokire*, one slice 親切 *shinsetsu*, kindness 一切 *issai*, all, everything

雪 100 11 strokes	一 一 冖 冂 冂 冂 雪 雪 雪	SETSU; *yuki*, snow 雪だるま *yukidaruma*, snowman 雪解け *yukidoke*, thaw 積雪 *sekisetsu*, snowdrift (雨 42)
千 101 3 strokes	ノ 二 千	SEN [ZEN], *chi*, thousand 千円 *sen-en*, a thousand yen 三千 *sanzen*, three thousand 五千 *gosen*, five thousand
前 102 9 strokes	丶 丷 亠 亠 亠 亠 前 前 前	ZEN; *mae*, before, in front of, previous 午前 *gozen*, morning, A.M. 前後 *zengo*, before and after, context 以前 *izen*, ago, since, before
組 103 11 strokes	乂 乂 乂 糸 糸 糸 組 組 組	SO; *kumi* [*gumi*], class, group, set; *ku*(*mu*), to join, to unite 組み立て *kumitate*, construction, structure 一組 *hitokumi*, one set, one class 番組 *bangumi*, program (糸 83)
早 104 6 strokes	丨 冂 日 日 旦 早	SŌ; *haya* [*baya*], *haya*(*i*), early, fast 早口 *haya-guchi*, quick speaking 早春 *sōshun*, early spring 手早い *tebayai*, quick, nimble

走	一 十 土	SŌ; *hashi(ru)*, to run
	十 十 走	競走 *kyōsō*, race, running match
105 7 strokes	走	走り書き *hashirigaki*, hasty writing 走り去る *hashirisaru*, to run away
草	一 十 艹	SŌ; *kusa* [*gusa*], grass, vegetation
	艹 艹 草	草原 *kusahara* (*kusawara*), grassy plain
106 9 strokes	草 草 草	草案 *sōan*, draft (of a manuscript) 草取り *kusatori*, weeding
村	一 十 才	SON; *mura*, village
	木 木 村	村民 *sonmin*, villager 村長 *sonchō*, village mayor 農村 *nōson*, a farm village
107 7 strokes	村	
多	ノ ク 夕	TA; *ō(i)*, many, much, abundant
	夕 多 多	多数 *tasū*, large number 多分 *tabun*, perhaps 多量 *taryō*, great quantity
108 6 strokes		
男	丨 冂 冂	DAN, NAN; *otoko*, man, male
	田 田 男	男性 *dansei*, male sex, male 男子 *danshi*, male, boy 長男 *chōnan*, eldest son
109 7 strokes	男	

池 110 6 strokes	丶 氵 氵 氵 氵 池	CHI; *ike*, pond, lake 電池 *denchi*, electric cell, battery 池畔 *chihan*, side of a pond, around a pond 用水池 *yōsuichi*, reservoir
地 111 6 strokes	一 十 土 土 扌 扌 地	CHI, JI, earth, ground 地上 *chijō*, on the ground 地下 *chika*, underground 地面 *jimen*, surface of the earth
知 112 8 strokes	丿 ㇂ 𠂉 𠂉 矢 矢 知 知	CHI; *shi*(*ru*), to know; *shi*(*raseru*), to inform 知識 *chishiki*, knowledge 知人 *chijin*, an acquaintance 承知 *shōchi*, assent, agreement
竹 113 6 strokes	丿 ㇂ 𠂉 竹 竹 竹	CHIKU; *take* [*dake*], bamboo 竹やぶ *takeyabu*, bamboo grove 竹細工 *takezaiku*, bamboo ware 竹かご *takekago*, bamboo basket ⺮
虫 114 6 strokes	丶 冂 冂 中 虫 虫	CHŪ; *mushi*, insect, bug, worm 害虫 *gaichū*, harmful insect 虫歯 *mushiba*, decayed tooth こん虫 *konchū*, insect, bug

町	115 7 strokes	CHŌ; *machi*, town 町はずれ *machihazure*, outskirts of a town 町内 *chōnai*, the neighborhood 町長 *chōchō*, mayor of a town
長	116 8 strokes	CHŌ, head of an institution or organization; *naga(i)*, long 細長い *hosonagai*, long and narrow 長ぐつ *nagagutsu*, boots 校長 *kōchō*, principal of a school
鳥	117 11 strokes	CHŌ; *tori* [*dori*], bird 鳥類 *chōrui*, birds (as a species) 小鳥 *kotori*, small bird 渡り鳥 *wataridori*, migratory bird
朝	118 12 strokes	CHŌ; *asa*, morning 朝刊 *chōkan*, morning paper 朝食 *chōshoku*, breakfast 毎朝 *mai-asa*, every morning (月 12)
天	119 4 strokes	TEN, *ame*, sky, heaven 天気 *tenki*, weather 天井 *tenjō*, ceiling 天才 *tensai*, genius

冬 120 5 strokes	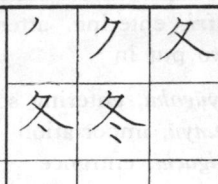	TŌ; *fuyu*, winter 冬休み *fuyuyasumi*, winter vacation 冬眠 *tōmin*, hibernation 冬期 *tōki*, winter season
東 121 8 strokes		TŌ; *higashi*, east 東側 *higashigawa*, east side 東洋 *tōyō*, the East, the Orient 北東 *hokutō*, northeast
道 122 12 strokes	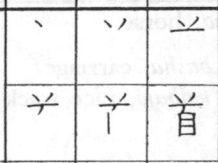	DŌ; *michi*, road, path 水道 *suidō*, waterworks 道具 *dōgu*, tool 鉄道 *tetsudō*, railroad (日 25)
読 123 14 strokes		DOKU, TOKU; *yo(mu)*, to read 読者 *dokusha*, reader (person) 読書 *dokusho*, reading 読み返す *yomikaesu*, to reread (口 27, 土 410)
南 124 9 strokes	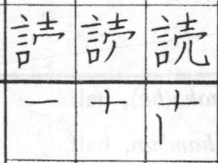	NAN; *minami*, south 南部 *nambu*, southern part 南極 *Nankyoku*, South Pole 西南 *seinan*, southwest

入 125 2 strokes	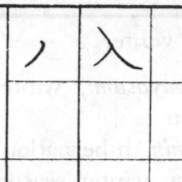	NYŪ; *iri*, entering, attendance; *i*(*reru*), to put in 入学 *nyūgaku*, entering school 輸入 *yunyū*, importation 入口 *iriguchi*, entrance
年 126 6 strokes	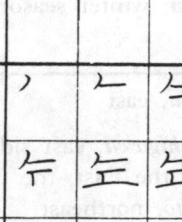	NEN; *toshi*, year 六年生 *rokunensei*, sixth-grade pupil 年寄り *toshiyori*, old person 青年 *seinen*, youth
馬 127 10 strokes	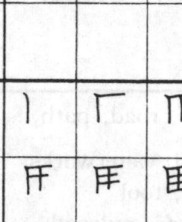	BA; *uma*, horse 馬車 *basha*, carriage 競馬場 *keibajō*, race track
麦 128 7 strokes	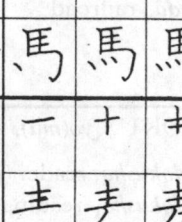	BAKU; *mugi*, barley, wheat 麦わら *mugiwara*, (barley) straw 麦刈り *mugikari*, mowing barley 小麦 *komugi*, wheat
半 129 5 strokes	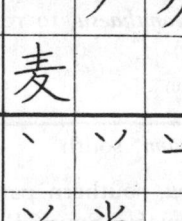	HAN; *naka*(*ba*), half 半分 *hambun*, half 一時半 *ichiji-han*, one-thirty, half-past one 半島 *hantō*, peninsula

百 130 6 strokes	一 ア 丆 百 百 百	HYAKU [BYAKU], hundred 二百 *nihyaku*, two hundred 三百 *sambyaku*, three hundred 百貨店 *hyakkaten*, department store
父 131 4 strokes	ノ 八 ⺈ 父	FU; *chichi*, father 父兄会 *fukeikai*, parents' association 祖父 *sofu*, grandfather 父母 *fubo*, parents
風 132 9 strokes	ノ 几 凡 凡 凡 凡 風 風 風	FŪ; *kaze*, wind 風景 *fūkei*, scenery 台風 *taifū*, typhoon 南風 *minamikaze*, south wind
分 133 4 strokes	ノ 八 分 分	FUN [PUN], minute; BUN, BU, part, share; *wa*(*keru*), to divide, to separate (v.t.); *wa*(*kareru*), to be divided, to branch off 自分 *jibun*, self 二分 *nifun*, two minutes 十分 *jippun*, ten minutes
文 134 4 strokes	丶 亠 ナ 文	BUN, writings, a sentence; MON, ancient unit of money 文化 *bunka*, culture 文学 *bungaku*, literature 文部省 *Mombushō*, Ministry of Education

米 135 6 strokes	丶 丶 ⺍ ⺍ 米 米	BEI (America, rice), MAI (rice); *kome*, rice 米国 *Beikoku*, America, the United States 米作 *beisaku*, rice-growing (crop) 白米 *hakumai*, polished rice
歩 136 8 strokes	丨 ⺊ 止 止 歩 歩 歩 歩	HO [PO], BU; *ayu(mu)*, *aru(ku)*, to walk, to step 第一歩 *dai-ippo*, the first step 進歩 *shimpo*, progress 散歩 *sampo*, a walk, a stroll
母 137 5 strokes	乂 ⺕ ⺕ ⺕ 母	BO; *haha*, mother 母の日 *Haha-no-hi*, Mother's Day 母国 *bokoku*, mother country 母親 *haha-oya*, mother
方 138 4 strokes	丶 亠 方 方	HŌ [PŌ], direction, side; *kata* [*gata*], side, way of ~ing, person 両方 *ryōhō*, both sides 作り方 *tsukurikata*, way of making 夕方 *yūgata*, evening
北 139 5 strokes	一 丨 ⺊ ⺊ 北	HOKU [BOKU]; *kita*, north 北極 *Hokkyoku*, North Pole 南北 *namboku*, north and south 北風 *kitakaze*, north wind

名 140 6 strokes	一 ク タ タ 名 名	MEI, MYŌ (name, fame); *na*, name 名まえ *namae*, name 有名 *yūmei*, famous, well-known 名人 *meijin*, an expert
明 141 8 strokes	丨 冂 日 日 明 明 明 明	MEI, MYŌ (bright); *aka*(*rui*), light, bright; *aki*(*raka*), bright; *a*(*keru*), to dawn, to break (day) 夜明け *yoake*, dawn 説明 *setsumei*, explanation 発明 *hatsumei*, invention
毛 142 4 strokes	一 二 三 毛	MŌ; *ke*, hair 毛糸 *keito*, woolen thread, yarn 毛虫 *kemushi*, caterpillar 毛布 *mōfu*, blanket
門 143 8 strokes	丨 冂 門 門 門 門 門 門	MON, gate; *kado*, gate 校門 *kōmon*, school gate 専門 *semmon*, specialty 門口 *kadoguchi*, door, entrance
夜 144 8 strokes	丶 亠 亠 亠 夜 夜 夜 夜	YA; *yo*, *yoru*, evening, night 夜中 *yonaka*, midnight 十五夜 *jūgoya*, night of the full moon 今夜 *kon-ya*, tonight

友	一 ナ 方 友	YŪ; *tomo*, friend 友だち *tomodachi*, friend 友人 *yūjin*, friend 友情 *yūjō*, friendship
145 4 strokes		
用	丿 冂 月 用	YŌ, business; *mochi(iru)*, to use 用意 *yōi*, preparation 用心 *yōjin*, heed, care, caution 用事 *yōji*, business
146 5 strokes		
来	一 丶 冫 平 来	RAI; *ku(ru)*, to come; *ki(masu)*, come (present tense); *ko(i)*, come (imperative) 来年 *rainen*, next year 以来 *irai*, since, from that time 将来 *shōrai*, the future
147 7 strokes	来	
力	力	RIKI, RYOKU; *chikara*, strength, power 力持 *chikaramochi*, strong person 協力 *kyōryoku*, co-operation 努力 *doryoku*, endeavor
148 2 strokes		
立	丶 亠 立	RITSU; *ta(tsu)*, *tachi* [*dachi*], to stand 独立 *dokuritsu*, independence 役立つ *yakudatsu*, useful 立場 *tachiba*, standpoint
149 5 strokes		

林 150 8 strokes	一 十 才 木 杢 杜 材 林	RIN; *hayashi* [*bayashi*], woods 植林 *shokurin*, reforestation 密林 *mitsurin*, thick forest 農林 *nōrin*, agriculture and forestry
話 151 13 strokes	丶 亠 言 言 言 言 訁 舌 話	WA; *hanashi* [*banashi*], story; *hana*(*su*), to speak 世話 *sewa*, aid 電話 *denwa*, telephone 会話 *kaiwa*, conversation (口 27)
悪 152 11 strokes	一 丅 亞 亞 亜 亜 亜 悪	AKU, badness, evil; *waru*(*i*), bad, evil 悪口 *warukuchi*, evil talk, gossip 悪人 *akunin*, bad man, villain 悪路 *akuro*, bad road (心 95)
安 153 6 strokes	丶 丶 宀 宀 安 安	AN; *yasu*(*i*), cheap, inexpensive 安心 *anshin*, peace of mind 安全 *anzen*, safe 不安 *fuan*, uneasiness
暗 154 13 strokes	丨 冂 日 日 日 立 日立 暗 暗	AN; *kura*(*i*), dark まっ暗 *makkura*, pitch dark 暗号 *angō*, code, cryptograph 暗記 *anki*, memorization (音 50)

意	立 音 音 意	I, mind, heart, attention, care 注意 *chūi*, care, attention 意見 *iken*, opinion, admonition 意味 *imi*, meaning (立 149, 心 95)
155 13 strokes		
引	引	IN; *hiki* [*biki*], pulling; *hi*(*ku*), to pull, to draw 福引き *fukubiki*, lottery 引用 *in-yō*, quotation, citation 引き立て *hikitate*, favor, patronage
156 4 strokes		
運	冒 宣 軍 運	UN, luck; *hako*(*bu*), to carry, to transport 運よく *un-yoku*, luckily 運動 *undō*, exercise, motion 運命 *ummei*, fate (車 88)
157 12 strokes		
駅	馬 馬 馬 駅	EKI, station 駅前 *ekimae*, in front of the station 駅長 *ekichō*, station master 駅員 *eki-in*, station employee (馬 127)
158 14 strokes		
園	囗 園 園 園	EN; *sono* [*zono*], garden 公園 *kōen*, public park 花園 *hanazono*, flower garden 動物園 *dōbutsu-en*, zoo (土 17, 囗 27)
159 13 strokes		

遠	土 吉 亨	EN, ON; *tō(i)*, far, distant
	亨 亨 袁	遠足 *ensoku*, excursion, long walk 遠方 *empō*, long distance 永遠 *eien*, eternity
160 13 strokes	袁 遠 遠	(土 17, 口 27)
屋	一 ㄱ 尸	OKU; *ya*, shop
	尸 屋 屋	屋根 *yane*, roof 時計屋 *tokeiya*, watch shop 屋上 *okujō*, housetop, roof
161 9 strokes	屋 屋 屋	
温	氵 氵 氵	ON (warm)
	氵 氵 氵	温度 *ondo*, temperature 温泉 *onsen*, hot spring 体温 *taion*, body temperature
162 12 strokes	温 温 温	(氵 汽 60)
化	ノ 亻 亻	KA, KE; *ba(keru)*, to take the form of; *ba(kasu)*, to bewitch
	化	変化 *henka*, change, variation, alteration 化学 *kagaku*, chemistry 化粧 *keshō*, make-up
163 4 strokes		
科	丿 二 千	KA, course, branch
	禾 禾 禾	学科 *gakka*, a school subject 教科書 *kyōkasho*, textbook 科学 *kagaku*, science
164 9 strokes	科 科 科	

荷	一 艹 艹	KA; *ni*, a load, burden
	艹 艹 艹	荷物 *nimotsu*, baggage 荷船 *nibune*, freighter 荷作り *nizukuri*, packing
165 10 strokes	荷 荷 荷	
歌	一 ㇇ 可	KA; *uta*, song; *uta(u)*, to sing
	可 哥 哥	国歌 *kokka*, national anthem 歌劇 *kageki*, opera 歌手 *kashu*, singer
166 14 strokes	歌 歌 歌	(口 27)
画	一 ㇇ 亠	GA (a picture); KAKU, stroke (of a Japanese character)
	亩 亩 画	図画 *zuga*, a drawing 映画 *eiga*, moving picture 計画 *keikaku*, plan
167 8 strokes	画 画	
回	丨 冂 冂	KAI, a turn; *mawa(su)*, to turn (v.t.); *mawa(ru)*, to turn (v.i.)
	冋 回 回	何回 *nankai*, how many times? 回転 *kaiten*, revolution, rotation 回数 *kaisū*, number of times, frequency
168 6 strokes		
貝	丨 冂 月	*kai* [*gai*], sea shell
	月 目 貝	貝がら *kaigara*, shell 貝拾い *kaihiroi*, shell gathering 真珠貝 *shinjugai*, pearl oyster
169 7 strokes	貝	

界	一 冂 冊	KAI (world)
	冊 田 甲	世界 *sekai*, world 世界一 *sekai-ichi*, best in the world
170 9 strokes	甲 界 界	限界 *genkai*, boundary, limits
開	戸 戸 門	KAI; *hira(ku)*, to open (v. t. & i.)
	門 門 問	開会 *kaikai*, opening a meeting 満開 *mankai*, full bloom 開発 *kaihatsu*, development, exploitation
171 12 strokes	問 開 開	(門 143)
絵	丿 幺 糸	KAI; E, picture
	糸 糸 糸	浮世絵 *ukiyoe*, Japanese print 絵葉書 *ehagaki*, picture postcard さし絵 *sashie*, illustration
172 12 strokes	絵 絵 絵	(糸 83)
角	丿 ク 角	KAKU, angle; *tsuno*, horn (of an animal)
	角 角 角	三角 *sankaku*, triangle 四角 *shikaku*, square 角度 *kakudo*, angle
173 7 strokes	角	
活	丶 氵 氵	KATSU (energy)
	氵 氵 汗	生活 *seikatsu*, life 活動 *katsudō*, activity 活字 *katsuji*, printer's type
174 9 strokes	汗 活 活	

寒 175 12 strokes	KAN, the coldest season of the year; *samu(i)*, cold 極寒 *gokkan*, bitter cold 寒中 *kanchū*, cold season 寒流 *kanryū*, cold current	
感 176 13 strokes	KAN, feeling, thought 感想 *kansō*, thoughts, impressions 感心 *kanshin*, admiration 感覚 *kankaku*, sensation (心 95, 口 27)	
岸 177 8 strokes	GAN; *kishi* [*gishi*], bank, shore 海岸 *kaigan*, seashore 岸壁 *gampeki*, quay, wharf 川岸 *kawagishi*, riverbank	
岩 178 8 strokes	GAN; *iwa*, rock, crag 花こう岩 *kakōgan*, granite 岩石 *ganseki*, rock 岩屋 *iwaya*, cavern	
顔 179 18 strokes	GAN; *kao*, face 顔面 *gammen*, face 顔色 *kao-iro*, complexion 顔付 *kaotsuki*, face, look, countenance (立 149, 貝 169)	

記	180 10 strokes	KI (chronicle) 日記 *nikki*, diary 記念 *kinen*, remembrance, souvenir 記者 *kisha*, journalist (口 27)
起	181 10 strokes	KI; *o*(*kiru*), to rise, to get up; *o*(*kosu*), to raise, to awaken (v.t.) 早起き *hayaoki*, early rising 起原 *kigen*, origin 起重機 *kijūki*, crane, derrick (土 17)
帰	182 10 strokes	KI; *kae*(*ru*), to return, to leave 帰り道 *kaerimichi*, (on) one's way back 帰化人 *kikajin*, naturalized person 帰国 *kikoku*, return to one's native country
期	183 12 strokes	KI, GO (period, term) 学期 *gakki*, school term 期待 *kitai*, expectation 時期 *jiki*, the times, season (月 12)
客	184 9 strokes	KYAKU, KAKU, guest お客さん *o-kyaku-san*, guest 客車 *kyakusha*, railroad passenger car 客船 *kyakusen*, passenger boat

究 185 7 strokes	宀 穴 穴 究 究 究	KYŪ (study) 研究 *kenkyū*, research 研究会 *kenkyūkai*, research society 研究家 *kenkyūka*, researcher
急 186 9 strokes	ノ 勹 勹 急 急 急	KYŪ; *iso(gu)*, to hurry 急病 *kyūbyō*, sudden illness 急行 *kyūkō*, express 大急ぎ *ō-isogi*, great haste
級 187 9 strokes	〈 糸 糸 糸 糸 級 級	KYŪ, rank, grade 学級 *gakkyū*, school class 上級 *jōkyū*, high class 同級生 *dōkyūsei*, classmate
球 188 11 strokes	丁 王 王 玨 玨 球 球 球	KYŪ, sphere, globe 野球 *yakyū*, baseball 地球 *chikyū*, the earth, the globe 電球 *denkyū*, electric light bulb (王 49)
去 189 5 strokes	一 十 土 去 去	KYO, KO (past); *sa(ru)*, to leave, to depart 去年 *kyonen*, last year 過去 *kako*, the past, past tense

魚	190 11 strokes	GYO; *uo*, fish 金魚 *kingyo*, goldfish 魚市場 *uo-ichiba*, fish market 魚つり *uotsuri*, fishing (灬 点 285)
教	191 11 strokes	KYŌ; *oshi(eru)*, to teach 教室 *kyōshitsu*, classroom 教育 *kyōiku*, education 教会 *kyōkai*, church (土 17)
強	192 11 strokes	KYŌ, GŌ; *tsuyo(i)*, strong 勉強 *benkyō*, study 強弱 *kyōjaku*, strength and weakness 強情 *gōjō*, obstinacy (虫 114)
橋	193 16 strokes	KYŌ; *hashi* [*bashi*], bridge さん橋 *sambashi*, pier 土橋 *dobashi*, earthen bridge 鉄橋 *tekkyō*, iron bridge (木 15, 口 27)
局	194 7 strokes	KYOKU, bureau, board, office, department 放送局 *hōsōkyoku*, broadcasting station 編集局 *henshūkyoku*, editorial department 郵便局 *yūbinkyoku*, post office

近 195 7 strokes	丿 ノ 斤 斤 沂 沂 近	KIN; *chika(i)*, near 近道 *chikamichi*, shortcut 近所 *kinjo*, neighborhood 最近 *saikin*, recently
銀 196 14 strokes	人 今 金 釒 釒 釒 銀 銀 銀	GIN, silver 銀行 *ginkō*, bank 銀色 *gin-iro*, silver color 銀貨 *ginka*, silver coin (金 16)
苦 197 8 strokes	一 十 艹 艹 艹 艹 苦 苦	KU, pain, anxiety; *kuru(shii)*, painful; *niga(i)*, bitter 苦労 *kurō*, troubles, toil 苦心 *kushin*, pains, hard work 苦戦 *kusen*, hard fighting
君 198 7 strokes	𠂇 ヲ ヲ 尹 尹 君 君	KUN, Mister, Master; *kimi*, you (familiar form) 佐藤君 *Satō-kun*, Mr. Satō 貴君 *kikun*, you (lit., masc.) 諸君 *shokun*, gentlemen, ladies and gentlemen, you
兄 199 5 strokes	丶 口 口 尸 兄	KEI, KYŌ; *ani*, older brother 兄弟 *kyōdai*, brothers (and sisters) 父兄 *fukei*, guardians (of pupils)

形	一 二 干	KEI, GYŌ; *katachi*, ~*gata*, shape, form
	开 开 形	人形 *ningyō*, doll 長方形 *chōhōkei*, rectangle 半円形 *han-enkei*, semicircle
200 7 strokes	形	
計	丶 亠 言	KEI; *haka*(*ru*), to measure
	言 言 言	合計 *gōkei*, sum, total 寒暖計 *kandankei*, weather thermometer 体温計 *taionkei*, clinical thermometer
201 9 strokes	言 計 計	
決	丶 氵 氵	KETSU; *ki*(*maru*), to be decided; *ki*(*meru*), to decide
	氵 氵 決	決心 *kesshin*, making up one's mind 決定 *kettei*, decision 解決 *kaiketsu*, solution
202 7 strokes	決	
県	丨 冂 冂	KEN, prefecture
	目 目 県	県道 *kendō*, prefectural road 県庁 *kenchō*, prefectural office 県知事 *kenchiji*, prefectural governor
203 9 strokes	県 県 県	
研	一 丆 丆	KEN (study)
	石 石 石	研究 *kenkyū*, study, research 研究室 *kenkyūshitsu*, laboratory 研究所 *kenkyūjo*, research institute
204 9 strokes	研 研 研	

原 205 10 strokes	一 厂 厂 厂 厂 厂 厂 厚 原	GEN (original); *hara* (*wara*), field, meadow 原因 *gen-in*, cause 高原 *kōgen*, plateau 草原 *kusawara*, grassy plain (小 24)
庫 206 10 strokes	丶 亠 广 广 广 后 后 庫 庫	KO (warehouse) 書庫 *shoko*, library 倉庫 *sōko*, warehouse 冷蔵庫 *reizōko*, icebox, refrigerator (車 88)
午 207 4 strokes	ノ 𠂉 𠂉 午	GO (noon) 午前 *gozen*, morning, A.M. 午後 *gogo*, afternoon, P.M. 正午 *shōgo*, noon
後 208 9 strokes	丿 彳 彳 彳 彳 彳 彳 後 後	GO, KŌ; *ushi*(*ro*), behind; *nochi*, after 食後 *shokugo*, after a meal 最後 *saigo*, last 前後 *zengo*, before and after, context
語 209 14 strokes	丶 亠 言 言 言 訂 訂 語 語	GO, word, speech; *katari* [*gatari*], narration; *kata*(*ru*), to tell, to speak 外国語 *gaikokugo*, foreign language 英語 *eigo*, English language 物語 *monogatari*, tale (口 27)

公 210 4 strokes	丿 八 公 公	KŌ; *ōyake*, public 主人公 *shujinkō*, hero, heroine 公園 *kōen*, public park 公転 *kōten*, revolution, turning
広 211 5 strokes	丶 亠 广 広 広	KŌ; *hiro(i)*, wide; *hiro(geru)*, to spread (v.t.); *hiro(garu)*, to spread (v.i.); *hiro(maru)*, to be spread 広場 *hiroba*, open space, plaza 広告 *kōkoku*, advertisement 広大 *kōdai*, vast
交 212 6 strokes	丶 亠 亠 六 交 交	KŌ; *ma(jiru)*, to be mixed; *maji-(waru)*, to associate with 交際 *kōsai*, intercourse, association 交番 *kōban*, police box 交通 *kōtsū*, traffic
向 213 6 strokes	丿 冂 冂 向 向 向	KŌ; *mu(ku)*, to turn toward, to be suited for; *mu(kau)*, to face, to head for 向こう *mukō*, opposite 向こう側 *mukōgawa*, opposite side 方向 *hōkō*, direction, course
黄 214 11 strokes	一 廿 廿 艹 艹 苗 黄 黄 黄	KŌ, Ō; *ki*, yellow 黄色 *ki-iro* yellow 黄金 *ōgon*, gold 黄熱病 *ōnetsubyō*, yellow fever (艹 草 106)

号 215 5 strokes	丶 口 口 口 号	GŌ, number, issue (of a magazine) 番号 *bangō*, number 記号 *kigō*, symbol 信号 *shingō*, signal, code
根 216 10 strokes	一 十 木 木ㄱ 木コ 木ヨ 根 根 根	KON, root (math.), perseverance; *ne*, root 根気 *konki*, patience, perseverance 大根 *daikon*, giant white radish 根本 *kompon*, basis
才 217 3 strokes	一 十 才	SAI, talent, suffix for counting age 十六才 *jūroku-sai*, sixteen years old 天才 *tensai*, genius 才能 *sainō*, talent
細 218 11 strokes	丿 乡 幺 糸 糸 糸 紀 細 細 細	SAI; *hoso(i)*, slender, narrow; *koma(kai)*, minute, fine, detailed 細道 *hosomichi*, narrow road 細工 *saiku*, work, craftsmanship 細菌 *saikin*, bacillus, germ (糸 83)
算 219 14 strokes	丿 ⺈ 𥫗 ⺈⺈ ⺈⺈ 竹 算 算 算	SAN [ZAN] (reckoning) 算数 *sansū*, arithmetic, calculation 計算 *keisan*, computation, figuring 予算 *yosan*, budget (目 25)

止 220 4 strokes	丨 卜 止 止	SHI; *to(maru)*, to stop (v.i.); *to-(meru)*, to bring to a stop; *tome* [*dome*], stop 中止 *chūshi*, discontinuation 禁止 *kinshi*, prohibition 通行止 *tsūkōdome*, suspension of traffic
仕 221 5 strokes	ノ 亻 仁 什 仕	SHI (work); *tsuka(eru)*, to serve 仕事 *shigoto*, work 給仕 *kyūji*, office boy, waiter 仕方 *shikata*, way of doing
市 222 5 strokes	丶 亠 亠 亠 市	SHI, city; *ichi*, market 市役所 *shiyakusho*, city office 市場 *ichiba*, *shijō*, market 都市 *toshi*, cities
死 223 6 strokes	一 ア 歹 歹 歹 死	SHI, death; *shi(nu)*, to die 死体 *shitai*, corpse 死傷者 *shishōsha*, dead and injured, casualties 必死 *hisshi*, certain death, desperation
使 224 8 strokes	ノ 亻 仁 仁 仁 仁 使 使	SHI; *tsuka(u)*, to use 使い *tsukai*, errand, messenger 使命 *shimei*, mission, errand 使用 *shiyō*, use

始 225 8 strokes	𠂉 𠂉 女 𡿨 𡿨 始 始 始	SHI; *haji(maru)*, to begin (v.i.); *haji(meru)*, to begin (v.t.) 開始 *kaishi*, commencement, start 始末 *shimatsu*, circumstances, the particulars; management 始業 *shigyō*, beginning of work or class
指 226 9 strokes	一 扌 扌 扌 扌 指 指 指 指	SHI; *yubi*, finger 親指 *oyayubi*, thumb 指輪 *yubiwa*, ring 指揮者 *shikisha*, conductor, commander
次 227 6 strokes	丶 冫 冫 冫 次 次 	SHI, JI; *tsugi*, next; *tsu(gu)*, to rank next to 次第 *shidai*, order, reason, as soon as 次官 *jikan*, vice-minister 目次 *mokuji*, table of contents
寺 228 6 strokes	一 十 土 土 寺 寺 	JI; *tera* [*dera*], temple 寺院 *ji-in*, Buddhist temple 山寺 *yamadera*, mountain temple
自 229 6 strokes	丿 亻 𠂉 𠂉 自 自 	JI, SHI; *mizuka(ra)*, self, in person 自分 *jibun*, self 自信 *jishin*, confidence 自由 *jiyū*, freedom

事 230 8 strokes	一 丶 冂 冂 亐 亨 亨 事	JI; *koto*, thing, action, affair, fact 仕事 *shigoto*, work 用事 *yōji*, business 大事 *daiji*, great matter, serious affair, importance
持 231 9 strokes	一 丨 扌 扌一 扌十 扌土 扌寺 持 持	JI; *mo(chi)*, durability; *mo(tsu)*, to have, to hold 気持 *kimochi*, feeling 持参 *jisan*, bringing 支持 *shiji*, support
室 232 9 strokes	丶 丶 宀 宀 宀 宀 宀 室 室	SHITSU, room; *muro*, storeroom, cave 教室 *kyōshitsu*, classroom 室内 *shitsunai*, indoors 温室 *onshitsu*, hothouse, greenhouse
実 233 8 strokes	丶 丶 宀 宀 宀 宣 実 実	JITSU, reality; *mi*, nut, fruit; *mino(ru)*, to bear fruit 実際 *jissai*, actual state, reality 真実 *shinjitsu*, truth 果実 *kajitsu*, fruit
社 234 7 strokes	丶 ㇇ 礻 礻 礻一 礻十 社	SHA [JA], a company; *yashiro*, Shintō shrine 社会 *shakai*, society, the world, the community 会社 *kaisha*, (business) company 神社 *jinja*, shrine

者	一 十 土	SHA; *mono*, person
	耂 者 者	若者 *wakamono*, young man 医者 *isha*, doctor 学者 *gakusha*, scholar
235 8 strokes	者 者	
弱	弓 弓 弓	JAKU; *yowa(i)*, weak; *yowa(ru)*, to grow weak, to be perplexed
	弓 弓 弱	弱虫 *yowamushi*, weakling 弱音 *yowane*, complaints 貧弱 *hinjaku*, scantiness, meagerness
236 10 strokes	弱 弱 弱	
主	丶 亠 亠	SHU, SU; *nushi*, master, owner
	主 主	主人 *shujin*, master 民主主義 *minshushugi*, democracy 持主 *mochinushi*, owner
237 5 strokes		
取	一 丅 下	SHU; *to(ru)*, to take
	下 耳 耳	取り出す *toridasu*, to take out 取材 *shuzai*, choice of subject 取扱い *toriatsukai*, treatment, handling
238 8 strokes	取 取	
首	丶 丷 亠	SHU; *kubi*, neck
	亠 亠 首	首輪 *kubiwa*, collar (dog) 手首 *tekubi*, wrist 首府 *shufu*, capital
239 9 strokes	首 首 首	

受	240 8 strokes	JU; *u(ke)*, popularity, receptacle; *u(keru)*, to receive 受持 *ukemochi*, charge, matter in hand 受付 *uketsuke*, receptionist, information desk 受話機 *juwaki*, telephone receiver
終	241 11 strokes	SHŪ; *o(wari)*, end; *o(waru)*, to come to an end; *o(eru)*, to finish 終戦 *shūsen*, end of a war 終業 *shūgyō*, end of work 最終 *saishū*, the last (糸 83)
週	242 11 strokes	SHŪ, week 週刊誌 *shūkanshi*, weekly magazine 来週 *raishū*, next week 今週 *konshū*, this week (辶 27)
集	243 12 strokes	SHŪ; *atsu(meru)*, to collect (v.t.); *atsu(maru)*, to gather together (v.i.) 編集 *henshū*, editing 詩集 *shishū*, anthology of poems 文集 *bunshū*, literary anthology (木 15)
住	244 7 strokes	JŪ, dwelling; *su(mu)*, to dwell, to live 住所 *jūsho*, address 衣食住 *i-shoku-jū*, necessities of life (clothing, food, shelter) 住宅 *jūtaku*, dwelling, living quarters

重 245 9 strokes		JŪ, CHŌ; *omo(i)*, heavy; *kasa-(neru)*, to pile (things) up; *kasa-(naru)*, to be piled up; *~e*, ~fold 体重 *taijū*, weight (of the body) 厳重 *genjū*, strictness 二重 *futae*, *nijū*, duplicate, double, twofold
所 246 8 strokes		SHO (JO); *tokoro* [*dokoro*], place 台所 *daidokoro*, kitchen 場所 *basho*, place 近所 *kinjo*, neighborhood
暑 247 12 strokes	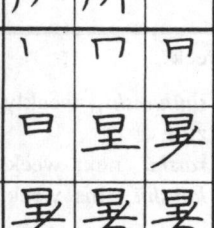	SHO; *atsu(i)*, hot 残暑 *zansho*, lingering summer heat 避暑 *hisho*, summering, going to a summer resort 暑中 *shochū*, midsummer (土 17)
助 248 7 strokes		JO; *tasu(karu)*, to be aided, to be rescued; *tasu(keru)*, to aid, to rescue; *~suke*, suffix for masculine names 助手 *joshu*, assistant 補助 *hojo*, assistance 助力 *joryoku*, help, aid
昭 249 9 strokes		SHŌ (bright) 昭和 *Shōwa*, p.n., name of the present era in Japan

勝	月 月 月 月 月 月 月 月 月 月 月 月	SHŌ; *ka(tsu)*, to win 勝負 *shōbu*, victory or defeat, match 勝敗 *shōhai*, the issue (of a battle) 勝手 *katte*, selfish, willful (月 12)
250 12 strokes		
乗	一 二 三 乗 乗 乗 乗 乗 乗 乗 乗 乗	JŌ; *no(ru)*, to ride; *no(seru)*, to give a ride to, to place upon 乗り物 *norimono*, vehicle 乗客 *jōkyaku*, passenger 遠乗り *tōnori*, a long ride
251 9 strokes		
場	一 十 土 場 場 場 場 場 場 場 場 場	JŌ; *ba*, place 工場 *kōjō*, *kōba*, factory 場所 *basho*, place 仕事場 *shigotoba*, place of work (日 11)
252 12 strokes		
食	丿 人 人 食 食 食 食 食 食 食 食 食	SHOKU, food; *ta(beru)*, to eat; *ku(u)*, to eat 食物 *shokumotsu*, food, edibles 食堂 *shokudō*, dining hall 食事 *shokuji*, a meal (食)
253 9 strokes		
申	丨 冂 冂 申 申 申 申	SHIN; *mō(su)*, to say 申し込み *mōshikomi*, application, proposal 申告 *shinkoku*, report, filing a return 申し合わせ *mōshiawase*, arrangement
254 5 strokes		

身 255 7 strokes	丿 亻 冂 自 自 身 身	SHIN; *mi*, body 身体 *shintai*, body 身長 *shinchō*, height (of the body) 身分 *mibun*, social position
新 256 13 strokes	立 立 辛 辛 辛 新 新 新 新	SHIN; *atara(shii)*, new; *ara(tani)*, newly, afresh 新聞 *shimbun*, newspaper 新年 *shinnen*, the New Year 新学期 *shingakki*, new school term (立 149)
神 257 9 strokes	丶 ㇇ 礻 礻 礻 礻 礻 神 神	SHIN, JIN; *kami* [*gami*], god 神経質 *shinkeishitsu*, nervous temperament 精神 *seishin*, soul, spirit 神様 *kamisama*, god
深 258 11 strokes	丶 氵 氵 氵 氵 氵 氵 深 深 深 深	SHIN; *fuka(i)*, deep, profound, thick (fog), close (connection); *fuka(sa)*, depth, profundity 深夜 *shin-ya*, midnight 深呼吸 *shinkokyū*, deep breath 深刻 *shinkoku*, serious, significant (木 15)
進 259 11 strokes	亻 亻 亻 隹 隹 隹 隹 隹 隹 進 進	SHIN; *susu(mu)*, to advance, to proceed 進行 *shinkō*, progress, advance 進級 *shinkyū*, promotion 行進 *kōshin*, march, parade (隹 集 243)

親 260 16 strokes	立 亲 亲 新 新 新 親 親 親	SHIN; *oya*, parent; *shita*(*shimu*), to make friends with, to take kindly to; *shita*(*shii*), intimate, familiar 両親 *ryōshin*, parents 親切 *shinsetsu*, kindness 親類 *shinrui*, relative, relation (立 149, 木 15)
図 261 7 strokes	丨 冂 冂 冈 冈 冈 図	ZU, drawing, plan; TO; *haka*(*ru*), to devise 図画 *zuga*, drawing, a picture 地図 *chizu*, map 図書館 *toshokan*, library
数 262 13 strokes	亠 米 米 娄 娄 娄 娄 娄 数	SŪ [ZŪ]; *kazu*, number; *kazo*-(*eru*), to count 数字 *sūji*, figure, numeral 数学 *sūgaku*, mathematics 人数 *ninzū*, the number of people (米 135)
世 263 5 strokes	一 十 廿 廿 世	SE, SEI; *yo*, world, age, reign 世界 *sekai*, the world 世紀 *seiki*, century 世間 *seken*, the world, society, life
星 264 9 strokes	丨 冂 日 日 日 旦 旦 旱 星	SEI, JŌ; *hoshi* [*boshi*], star 星座 *seiza*, constellation 火星 *kasei*, Mars 明星 *myōjō*, Venus

晴	265 12 strokes	SEI ; *ha*(*re*), fine weather ; *ha*(*reru*), to clear (weather), to be dispelled 秋晴れ *akibare*, clear autumn weather 晴れ着 *haregi*, one's best clothes 晴天 *seiten*, fine weather (月 12)
船	266 11 strokes	SEN ; *fune* [*bune*], *funa*, boat, ship 渡し船 *watashi-bune*, ferry 船員 *sen-in*, sailor 汽船 *kisen*, steamboat, steamship (口 27)
全	267 6 strokes	ZEN (whole) ; *matta*(*ku*), entirely 全体 *zentai*, the whole 全部 *zembu*, all, the whole 完全 *kanzen*, perfect
送	268 9 strokes	SŌ ; *oku*(*ru*), to send 放送 *hōsō*, (radio) broadcast 輸送 *yusō*, transportation 送金 *sōkin*, sending money
太	269 4 strokes	TAI, TA ; *futo*(*i*), big, deep (voice), bold (lines), shameless ; *futo*(*ru*), to grow fat 太陽 *taiyō*, sun 丸太 *maruta*, log 太平洋 *Taiheiyō*, Pacific Ocean

体 270 7 strokes	亻 亻 亻 什 什 休 体	TAI, TEI (body) 体育 *tai-iku*, physical education 団体 *dantai*, a group 車体 *shatai*, body of a vehicle
待 271 9 strokes	亻 彳 彳 彳 彳 往 往 待 待	TAI; *ma(tsu)*, to wait for 待合室 *machiaishitsu*, waiting room 接待 *settai*, reception 招待 *shōtai*, invitation
台 272 5 strokes	厶 厶 厶 台 台	TAI; DAI, a stand 台風 *taifū*, typhoon 舞台 *butai*, stage 燈台 *tōdai*, lighthouse
第 273 11 strokes	丿 𠂉 𠂉 ⺮ ⺮ 笒 笒 第 第	DAI (grade), prefix for ordinal numbers 第一回 *dai-ikkai*, the first time 及第 *kyūdai*, passing an examination 落第 *rakudai*, failure (in an examination), rejection
炭 274 9 strokes	丶 山 山 山 屮 屮 屮 炭 炭	TAN; *sumi*, charcoal 炭坑 *tankō*, coal mine 石炭 *sekitan*, coal 木炭 *mokutan*, charcoal

茶 275 9 strokes	一 十 廿 艹 艾 芝 茶 茶 茶	CHA, tea, tea plant 茶色 *cha-iro*, light brown 茶の湯 *cha-no-yu*, tea ceremony 茶わん *chawan*, teacup, rice bowl
着 276 12 strokes	丶 丶 ⺍ ⺍ 羊 羊 羊 羊 着	CHAKU; *ki(ru)*, to wear; *tsu(ku)*, to reach, to arrive 着物 *kimono*, Japanese robe 一着 *itchaku*, first arrival, a suit (of clothes) 上着 *uwagi*, coat (目 25)
注 277 8 strokes	丶 丶 丶 氵 氵 汁 汁 注	CHŪ; *soso(gu)*, to pour, to concentrate on 注意 *chūi*, attention, care, warning, advice 注目 *chūmoku*, attention, observation 注文 *chūmon*, order, request, demand
柱 278 9 strokes	一 十 才 木 木 杙 杙 柱 柱	CHŪ; *hashira* [*bashira*], post, pillar 帆柱 *hobashira*, mast 柱時計 *hashiradokei*, wall clock 電柱 *denchū*, telegraph (electric) pole
昼 279 9 strokes	㇇ ㇇ 尸 尺 尺 尽 尽 昼 昼	CHŪ; *hiru*, noon, daytime 昼間 *hiruma*, daytime 昼夜 *chūya*, day and night 昼食 *chūshoku*, noon meal, lunch

追	280 9 strokes	TSUI; *o(u)*, to run after, to drive away 追いかける *oikakeru*, to chase 追求 *tsuikyū*, pursuit 追放 *tsuihō*, banishment, exile, purge
通	281 10 strokes	TSŪ; *tō(ru)*, to go along, to pass; *kayo(u)*, to go to and from (a place) 大通り *ō-dōri*, main street 通信 *tsūshin*, correspondence, communication 通訳 *tsūyaku*, interpreter (用 146)
弟	282 7 strokes	TEI, DAI; *otōto*, younger brother 兄弟 *kyōdai*, brothers 弟妹 *teimai*, younger brothers and sisters
鉄	283 13 strokes	TETSU, iron, steel 鉄道 *tetsudō*, railroad 地下鉄 *chikatetsu*, subway 鉄橋 *tekkyō*, iron bridge, railway bridge (金 16)
店	284 8 strokes	TEN; *mise*, store 店番 *miseban*, tending a store 商店 *shōten*, store (shop) 売店 *baiten*, stand, stall

点 285 9 strokes	丨 卜 卜 占 占 占 占 占 占	TEN, point, marks, dot 点数 *tensū*, merit marks 点字 *tenji*, braille points 決勝点 *kesshōten*, goal
電 286 13 strokes	一 冖 冖 雨 雨 雨 雨 雨 電	DEN (lightning, electricity) 電気 *denki*, electricity 電話 *denwa*, telephone 電報 *dempō*, telegram (雨 42)
都 287 11 strokes	土 耂 耂 者 者 者 者 都 都	TO, TSU; *miyako*, capital, metropolis 都会 *tokai*, city 首都 *shuto*, capital 都合 *tsugō*, circumstances, conditions (土 17)
度 288 9 strokes	丶 亠 广 广 庀 庀 庐 度 度	DO, degree, time, times 一度 *ichido*, once 速度 *sokudo*, speed 程度 *teido*, degree, level, extent
刀 289 2 strokes	刀 刀	TŌ; *katana* [*gatana*], sword 小刀 *kogatana*, pocketknife 大刀 *daitō*, long sword 軍刀 *guntō*, sabre

当	丶	小	小	TŌ; *a*(*taru*), to hit, to be equal to, to win (v.i.); *a*(*teru*), to hit, to apply, to guess (v.t.) 見当 *kentō*, guess 手当 *teate*, treatment, allowance 当然 *tōzen*, justly, naturally
	当	当	当	
290 6 strokes				
投	一	扌	扌	TŌ; *na*(*geru*), to throw, to give up 投票 *tōhyō*, voting 投資 *tōshi*, investment 投書 *tōsho*, contribution (to a magazine, newspaper, etc.)
	扌	扌	投	
291 7 strokes	投			
島	丿	冂	冂	TŌ; *shima* [*jima*], island 半島 *hantō*, peninsula 群島 *guntō*, group of islands 島国 *shimaguni*, island country (山 38)
	冂	自	鳥	
292 10 strokes	鳥	島	島	
答	ノ	丿	𠂉	TŌ [DŌ]; *kota*(*e*), answer; *kota*(*eru*), to answer 答案 *tōan*, examination paper 問答 *mondō*, questions and answers 解答 *kaitō*, answer, solution (竹 113, 口 27)
	𠂉	𠂉	𠂉	
293 12 strokes	𠂉	答	答	
頭	一	冖	冖	TŌ [DŌ], ZU; *atama*, head, top, brain 先頭 *sentō*, leader, head 教頭 *kyōtō*, head teacher 頭痛 *zutsū*, headache (頁 169)
	豆	豆	豆	
294 16 strokes	豆	頭	頭	

同 295 6 strokes	一 冂 冂 冋 同 同	DŌ; *ona(ji)*, same 同時 *dōji*, the same time 同情 *dōjō*, sympathy 一同 *ichidō*, all (of us, them), all the persons concerned
動 296 11 strokes	二 旨 重 重 重 動 動	DŌ; *ugo(ku)*, to move 動物 *dōbutsu*, animal 自動車 *jidōsha*, automobile 運動 *undō*, motion, physical exercise, athletic sports (重 245)
肉 297 6 strokes	一 冂 内 内 肉 肉	NIKU, meat, flesh 牛肉 *gyūniku*, beef 筋肉 *kinniku*, muscles 肉屋 *nikuya*, butcher, butcher shop
波 298 8 strokes	丶 氵 氵 氵 氵 沪 波 波	HA; *nami*, wave 大波 *ō-nami*, big wave 防波堤 *bōhatei*, breakwater 電波 *dempa*, electric wave
配 299 10 strokes	一 冂 冂 西 西 酉 酉 酉 配	HAI [PAI]; *kuba(ru)*, to distribute, to deliver 配給 *haikyū*, ration, distribution (of food or goods) 配達 *haitatsu*, delivery 心配 *shimpai*, worry

買 300 12 strokes	丶 冂 罒 罒 罒 罒 買 買	BAI; *ka(u)*, to buy, to purchase 売買 *baibai*, purchase and sale, buying and selling 買い物 *kaimono*, shopping 買い手 *kaite*, buyer (貝 169)
売 301 7 strokes	一 十 士 十 声 売 売	BAI; *u(ri)*, sale; *u(ru)*, to sell 売り出し *uridashi*, opening sale, bargain sale 商売 *shōbai*, business 発売 *hatsubai*, sale
畑 302 9 strokes	丶 丶 少 火 灬 灬 灬 灬 畑	*hata*, *hatake* [*batake*], field, farm, cultivated field 田畑 *tahata*, fields 麦畑 *mugibatake*, wheat (barley) field 花畑 *hanabatake*, flower garden
発 303 9 strokes	フ ヲ ヲ 癶 癶 癶 癶 癶 発	HATSU [PATSU] (to expose, to open, to shoot, to happen) 発音 *hatsuon*, pronunciation 発表 *happyō*, announcement 出発 *shuppatsu*, departure
坂 304 7 strokes	一 十 土 圷 圷 坂 坂	HAN; *saka* [*zaka*], slope, hill 坂道 *sakamichi*, sloping road 上り坂 *noborizaka*, ascent, uphill road 急坂 *kyūhan*, steep slope

板 305 8 strokes		HAN [BAN]; *ita*, board (of wood) 板の間 *ita-no-ma*, wooden floor 掲示板 *keijiban*, notice-board 看板 *kamban*, poster, signboard, shingle
番 306 12 strokes	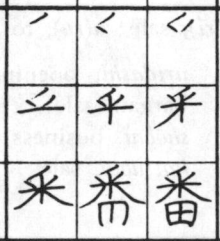	BAN, number, guard, order, (one's) turn 番組 *bangumi*, program 交番 *kōban*, police-box 順番 *jumban*, order, one's turn (田 40)
皮 307 5 strokes		HI; *kawa* [*gawa*], skin, leather 毛皮 *kegawa*, fur 皮肉 *hiniku*, irony 皮膚 *hifu*, skin
美 308 9 strokes		BI, beauty; *utsuku*(*shii*), beautiful 美術 *bijutsu*, fine arts 美人 *bijin*, a beauty, pretty girl, beautiful woman 美術館 *bijutsukan*, art museum
表 309 8 strokes		HYŌ [PYŌ], list, table, schedule; *omote*, the outside, surface; *ara-*(*wasu*), to show, to indicate, to expose, to express, to represent 表紙 *hyōshi*, cover of a book 表面 *hyōmen*, surface 時間表 *jikanhyō*, schedule, time-table

病	一 广 疒 疒 疒 疒 病 病 病	BYŌ; *yamai*, illness; *ya(mu)*, to fall ill 病気 *byōki*, illness, sickness 病院 *byōin*, hospital 病人 *byōnin*, sick person
310 10 strokes		
品	丶 口 口 口 口 口 丶 品 品	HIN, elegance, dignity; *shina*, goods 品物 *shinamono*, article, goods 手品 *tejina*, jugglery, sleight of hand 作品 *sakuhin*, work, works
311 9 strokes		
負	ノ 勹 勹 角 角 角 負 負 負	FU [BU]; *o(u)*, to bear, to be indebted to; *ma(ke)*, a defeat; *ma(keru)*, to lose, to be defeated, to reduce in price, to make cheaper 勝負 *shōbu*, victory or defeat, game 負傷 *fushō*, wound 背負う *se-ou*, to carry on one's back
312 9 strokes		
物	ノ 丿 牛 牛 牛 物 物 物	BUTSU, MOTSU; *mono*, thing, article, object 食べ物 *tabemono*, food 名物 *meibutsu*, noted product, special product 貨物 *kamotsu*, freight
313 8 strokes		
聞	丨 門 門 門 門 門 門 聞 聞	BUN; *ki(ku)*, to hear, to listen to, to ask, to obey; *ki(koeru)*, to be heard 新聞 *shimbun*, newspaper 新聞社 *shimbunsha*, newspaper office 見聞 *kembun*, information, experience (耳 26)
314 14 strokes		

平 315 5 strokes	一 ⺈ 丆 ⺈ 平	HEI, BYŌ; *tai(ra)*, evenness, flatness; *hira(tai)*, even, level, simple 平和 *heiwa*, peace 平気 *heiki*, calmness, indifference 平等 *byōdō*, equality
返 316 7 strokes	一 厂 万 反 反 返 返	HEN; *kae(su)*, to return, to give back; *kae(shi)* [*gae(shi)*] 返事 *henji*, answer 繰り返す *kurikaesu*, to repeat 恩返し *ongaeshi*, repayment of a favor, returning a favor
勉 317 10 strokes	ノ ク 冂 冂 冂 免 免 勉	BEN (to exert oneself, to make efforts) 勉強 *benkyō*, study 勤勉 *kimben*, diligence 勉強家 *benkyōka*, studious person (カ 148)
毎 318 6 strokes	ノ 𠂉 乞 ⺈ 毎 毎	MAI, every (prefix) 毎日 *mainichi*, every day 毎朝 *mai-asa*, every morning 毎週 *maishū*, every week
妹 319 8 strokes	く 乂 女 女一 女二 妹 妹 妹	MAI; *imōto*, younger sister 弟妹 *teimai*, younger brothers and sisters 姉妹 *shimai*, sisters

万 320 3 strokes	一 丿 万	MAN, ten thousand; BAN 万年筆 *mannenhitsu*, fountain pen 万一 *man-ichi*, if by any chance 万国 *bankoku*, all countries
鳴 321 14 strokes	口 口′ 吖 吖 吖 唧 唧 唧 鳴 鳴 鳴	MEI; *na(ku)*, to sing (birds), to cry (animals), to howl (animals), to chirp (insects) 鳴き声 *nakigoe*, cry (of animals) 悲鳴 *himei*, scream, cry of distress 鳴動 *meidō*, rumbling (口 27, 灬 点 285)
面 322 9 strokes	一 ㇇ 丆 丆 丆 而 而 而 面	MEN, side, phase, mask; *omote*, face, outside, front, surface; *omo* (lit.), face, surface 表面 *hyōmen*, surface 正面 *shōmen*, the front 場面 *bamen*, scene
野 323 11 strokes	丨 口 日 甲 里 野 野 野 野	YA; *no*, field, plain 野原 *nohara*, field 野球 *yakyū*, baseball 野外 *yagai*, outdoors
役 324 7 strokes	丿 彳 彳 彳 役 役 役	YAKU, office, duty, role, use, service; EKI (lit.), war 役所 *yakusho*, public office 役人 *yakunin*, government official 役者 *yakusha*, actor, actress

由 325 5 strokes	丨 冂 巾 由 由	YŪ, YU; *yoshi*, a reason, significance 自由 *jiyū*, liberty, freedom 不自由 *fujiyū*, inconvenience, discomfort 理由 *riyū*, reason
遊 326 12 strokes	丶 亠 方 方 方 旂 旂 旂 遊	YŪ; *aso(bu)*, to play, to be idle 遊星 *yūsei*, planet 遊戯 *yūgi*, game, sports, children's play 遊覧 *yūran*, excursion, sightseeing (子 31, 辶 近 195)
葉 327 12 strokes	一 艹 艹 艹 艹 艹 艹 世 葉	YŌ; *ha* [*ba*], leaves, foliage 葉緑素 *yōryokuso*, chlorophyll 落ち葉 *ochiba*, fallen leaves 葉巻 *hamaki*, cigar (木 15)
様 328 14 strokes	木 木 木 木 様 様 様 様 様	YŌ, way, style, manner; *sama*, Mr., Mrs., Miss, etc. (polite suffix for personal names); state, way, form, condition 神様 *kamisama*, god 様子 *yōsu*, appearance, manner, state (木 15)
曜 329 18 strokes	丨 冂 日 日 日 日 日 日 曜	YŌ (term used for days of the week) 木曜日 *mokuyōbi*, Thursday 土曜日 *doyōbi*, Saturday 水曜日 *suiyōbi*, Wednesday (隹 集 243)

落 330 12 strokes		RAKU; *o(chiru)*, to fall (v.i.), to be omitted, to be inferior to; *o(tosu)*, to let drop, to lose (v.t.), to omit, to make worse 落第 *rakudai*, failure (in an examination), rejection 落成 *rakusei*, completion (building, etc.) (艹 27)
楽 331 13 strokes		GAKU, music; RAKU, comfort, ease; *tano(shii)*, pleasant 楽しみ *tanoshimi*, pleasure 音楽会 *ongakukai*, concert, musicale 気楽 *kiraku*, ease, comfort (木 15)
里 332 7 strokes	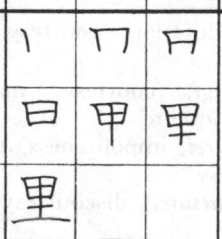	RI, Japanese linear unit (2.44 miles); *sato* [*zato*], village, country, one's native home (usually as viewed by a woman married into another family) 郷里 *kyōri*, one's native place, home 村里 *murazato*, village 一里 *ichiri*, one ri
理 333 11 strokes	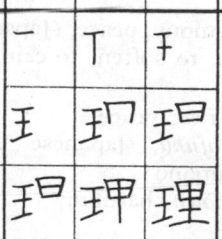	RI, reason, logic 理解 *rikai*, understanding 整理 *seiri*, arrangement, adjustment 料理 *ryōri*, cooking (里 332)
流 334 10 strokes		RYŪ, RU; *naga(re)*, stream, current, flow; *naga(reru)*, to flow (v.i.); *naga(su)*, to set afloat, to wash away, to pour (v.t.) 流れ星 *nagareboshi*, shooting star 流行 *ryūkō*, fashion, vogue 電流 *denryū*, electric current

旅 335 10 strokes	亠 方 方 方 旂 旅 旅 旅 旅	RYO; *tabi*, travel, journey 旅人 *tabibito*, traveler 旅行 *ryokō*, trip, travel 旅館 *ryokan*, inn, hotel (方 138)
両 336 6 strokes	一 一 冂 冂 両 両	RYŌ, old Japanese monetary unit, (two, both) 両手 *ryōte*, both hands 両方 *ryōhō*, both, both sides 両親 *ryōshin*, parents, father and mother
礼 337 5 strokes	丶 ㇇ 礻 礻 礼	REI, salutation, courtesy, bow, thanks 礼儀 *reigi*, courtesy, manners, etiquette 無礼 *burei*, impoliteness, discourtesy 失礼 *shitsurei*, discourtesy, rude-「ness
和 338 8 strokes	丿 二 千 禾 禾 和 和 和	WA, harmony, peace, (Japan); *yawa(ragu)*, to soften, to calm down (v.i.) 平和 *heiwa*, peace 和服 *wafuku*, Japanese clothes, kimono 調和 *chōwa*, harmony
愛 339 13 strokes	丿 ⺤ ⺤ ⺤ 爫 愛 愛 愛 愛	AI, love; *ai(suru)*, to love 愛情 *aijō*, love, affection 愛国心 *aikokushin*, patriotism 愛児 *aiji*, one's beloved child (心 95, ⺤ 受 240)

案 340 10 strokes	丶 丶 宀 宀 安 安 安 宰 案	AN, plan, idea; *an(jiru)*, to be anxious about, to be concerned about 案外 *angai*, unexpectedly 案内 *annai*, guide, guidance 名案 *meian*, good idea, good plan (木 15)
衣 341 6 strokes	丶 亠 ナ 衣 衣 衣	I; *koromo*, clothes, garment, priest's robe 衣類 *irui*, clothing 衣食住 *i-shoku-jū*, clothing, food and shelter 衣替え *koromogae*, change of dress
以 342 5 strokes	丨 ㇇ ㇇ 以 以	I (with, through, on account of) 以上 *ijō*, above, more than 以外 *igai*, besides, outside of 以前 *izen*, before, formerly
囲 343 7 strokes	丨 冂 冂 囗 囲 囲 囲	I; *kako(mu)*, to surround 胸囲 *kyōi*, girth of the chest, chest measurement 周囲 *shūi*, circumference, surroundings 範囲 *han-i*, extent, sphere, limits
位 344 7 strokes	丿 亻 亻 仁 位 位 位	I; *kurai*, rank, position, grade; about (approximately) 地位 *chi-i*, rank, social standing 位置 *ichi*, location, situation 学位 *gaku-i*, academic degree

医 345 7 strokes		I (to heal, to cure) 医者 *isha*, physician, doctor 医学 *igaku*, medical science 医院 *i-in*, medical practitioner's office
委 346 8 strokes		I (to entrust with) 委員 *i-in*, committee, delegate 委員長 *i-inchō*, chairman of a committee 委任 *i-nin*, charge, trust, commission
育 347 8 strokes		IKU; *soda(teru)*, to bring up, to educate, to raise 教育 *kyōiku*, education 体育 *tai-iku*, physical education 育児 *ikuji*, upbringing of a child
印 348 6 strokes		IN, seal, stamp; *shirushi* [*jirushi*], sign, symbol, trace 印刷 *insatsu*, printing 矢印 *yajirushi*, arrow sign 目印 *mejirushi*, mark
員 349 10 strokes	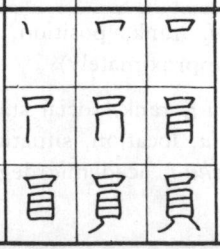	IN (member, official, personnel) 満員 *man-in*, no vacancy, full house 一員 *ichi-in*, (one) member 職員 *shokuin*, staff, personnel

院 350 10 strokes	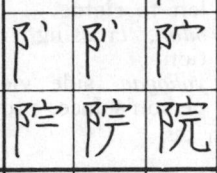	IN (temple, academy, board), suffix for "institution" 病院 *byōin*, hospital 美容院 *biyōin*, beauty shop 下院 *ka-in*, House of Representatives, Lower House (元 68)
飲 351 12 strokes	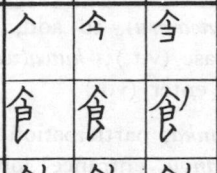	IN; *no*(*mu*) to drink 飲料水 *inryōsui* drinking water 飲み水 *nomimizu*, drinking water 飲み物 *nomimono*, drinks (食 253)
泳 352 8 strokes	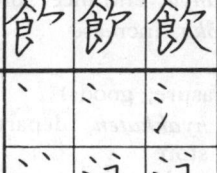	EI; *oyo*(*gu*), to swim 水泳 *suiei*, swimming 平泳ぎ *hira-oyogi*, breast stroke 水泳大会 *suiei taikai*, swimming meet
英 353 8 strokes	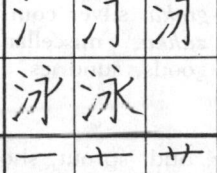	EI (England, excellent) 英語 *eigo*, English language 英雄 *eiyū*, hero 日英 *Nichi-Ei*, Japan and England
塩 354 13 strokes	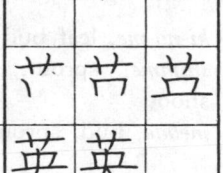	EN; *shio*, salt 塩水 *shiomizu*, salt water 塩田 *enden*, salt bed 食塩 *shokuen*, table salt (土 17, 田 27)

横 355 15 strokes		Ō; *yoko*, the side, the width 横書き *yokogaki*, writing from left to right 横断 *ōdan*, crossing, intersection 横顔 *yokogao*, side view of a person's face, profile (木 15, 由 325)
加 356 5 strokes		KA; *kuwa(eru)*, to add, to join, to increase (v.t.); *kuwa(waru)*, to join, to enter (v.i.) 参加 *sanka*, participation 加入 *kanyū*, entrance, joining 増加 *zōka*, increase
貨 357 11 strokes		KA (treasure, goods) 百貨店 *hyakkaten*, department store 銀貨 *ginka*, silver coin 雑貨 *zakka*, miscellaneous goods, sundries (貝 169)
芽 358 7 strokes		GA; *me*, bud, sprout, shoot 木の芽 *ki-no-me*, leaf bud 新芽 *shimme*, sprout, bud, shoot 芽ばえ *mebae*, bud, sprout
改 359 7 strokes		KAI; *arata(meru)*, to change, to reform, to revise; *arata(maru)*, to be reformed 改良 *kairyō*, improvement 改心 *kaishin*, conversion, reform 改札口 *kaisatsuguchi*, ticket gate

械 360 11 strokes		KAI (shackles) 機械 *kikai*, machine 器械 *kikai*, instrument, apparatus
階 361 12 strokes		KAI [GAI], story of a building, floor, grade 階段 *kaidan*, stairs, stairway 階級 *kaikyū*, class, caste 三階 *sangai*, 3rd floor (白 37)
害 362 10 strokes	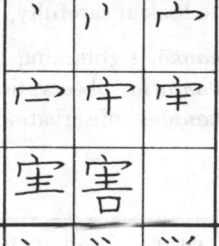	GAI, harm, calamity 害虫 *gaichū*, harmful insect 損害 *songai*, loss, damage 障害 *shōgai*, obstacle, hindrance (口 27)
覚 363 12 strokes		KAKU; *obo(eru)*, to remember, to understand 覚え書 *oboegaki*, memorandum, note 感覚 *kankaku*, sensation, sense, feeling 自覚 *jikaku*, consciousness, self-consciousness (目 25)
官 364 8 strokes		KAN, government, government position 官庁 *kanchō*, government office 裁判官 *saibankan*, judge 警官 *keikan*, policeman, police officer

関 365 14 strokes		KAN; *seki*, barrier 関心 *kanshin*, concern, interest 玄関 *genkan*, entrance hall, entrance 機関車 *kikansha*, engine, locomotive (門 143)
館 366 16 strokes		KAN (building, hall) 図書館 *toshokan*, library 映画館 *eigakan*, movie theater 旅館 *ryokan*, inn, hotel (食 253, 官 364)
観 367 18 strokes	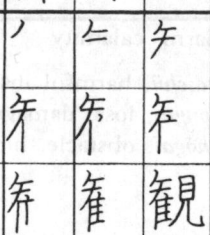	KAN (to look at carefully, to show) 観光 *kankō*, sightseeing 観察 *kansatsu*, observation 観測 *kansoku*, observation, survey (見 67)
願 368 19 strokes		GAN; *nega(i)*, wish, petition, request; *nega(u)*, to ask, to request, to wish, to beg 願書 *gansho*, written application 志願 *shigan*, volunteering, desire, application (原 205, 貝 169)
季 369 8 strokes		KI, season 季節 *kisetsu*, season 四季 *shiki*, the four seasons 雨季 *uki*, rainy season

喜	一	十	士	KI; *yoroko(bi)*, joy, happy event, congratulation; *yoroko(bu)*, to rejoice, to be glad 大喜び *ō-yorokobi*, great joy, great delight 喜劇 *kigeki*, comedy 歓喜 *kanki*, joy, ecstasy (口 27)
	吉	吉	壴	
370 12 strokes	壴	喜		
旗	方	方一	方十	KI; *hata*, flag 国旗 *kokki*, national flag 校旗 *kōki*, school flag 星条旗 *seijōki*, the Stars and Stripes (方 138)
	方丼	方丼	方旨	
371 14 strokes	旌	旗	旗	
器	口	口口	口口	KI; *utsuwa*, vessel, utensil, capacity, caliber 食器 *shokki*, tableware 陶器 *tōki*, pottery, ceramics 洗面器 *semmenki*, wash basin (口 27)
	哭	哭	哭	
372 15 strokes	器			
機	木	杦	杦幺	KI; *hata*, loom 機械 *kikai*, machine, mechanism 機会 *kikai*, opportunity, chance 危機 *kiki*, crisis, emergency (木 15, 幺 糸 83)
	杦幾	杦幾	杦幾	
373 16 strokes	機	機	機	
宮	宀	宀	宀	KYŪ, GŪ, KU; *miya*, shrine, prince (of the blood) 宮殿 *kyūden*, palace 神宮 *jingū*, Shintō shrine 宮様 *miya-sama*, royal prince (宀 27)
	宮	宮	宮	
374 10 strokes				

375 10 strokes		KYO (to conduct, to perform) 選挙 *senkyo*, election 挙行 *kyokō*, performance 挙手 *kyoshu*, raising one's hand, a show of hands (手 28)
376 6 strokes		KYŌ; *tomo*, both, as well as, together 共通 *kyōtsū*, commonness 共和国 *kyōwakoku*, republic 共産党 *kyōsantō*, Communist Party
377 8 strokes	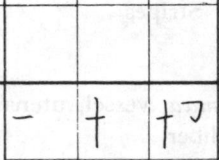	KYŌ (to be in harmony) 協力 *kyōryoku*, cooperation 協会 *kyōkai*, society, association 協議 *kyōgi*, conference, consultation
378 19 strokes	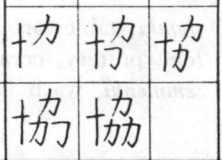	KYŌ; *kagami*, mirror 鏡台 *kyōdai*, dressing table, mirror stand 双眼鏡 *sōgankyō*, binoculars 顕微鏡 *kembikyō*, microscope (金 16, 立 149)
379 20 strokes	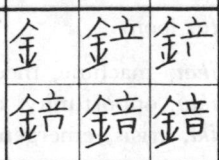	KYŌ, KEI; *kiso(u)*, to rival, to compete 競争 *kyōsō*, competition 競技 *kyōgi*, match, tournament, sporting events 競馬 *keiba*, horse race (立 149, 口 27)

業 380 13 strokes		GYŌ, occupation, business, industry, studies; GŌ, karma 職業 *shokugyō*, occupation, profession 産業 *sangyō*, industry 工業 *kōgyō*, industry, manufacturing industry
曲 381 6 strokes		KYOKU, melody; *ma(garu)*, to bend, to twist, to turn (v.i.); *ma(geru)*, to bend, to twist, to turn (v.t.) 曲線 *kyokusen*, curved line 作曲 *sakkyoku*, musical composition 曲がり道 *magarimichi*, crooked road, winding lane
極 382 12 strokes		KYOKU, terrestrial poles, magnetic poles, zenith; GOKU (very, extremely) 極端 *kyokutan*, extremity 北極 *hokkyoku*, North Pole 至極 *shigoku*, very, quite (木 15, 口 27)
具 383 8 strokes		GU, tool, utensil; ingredients 道具 *dōgu*, tool, utensil, instrument 具合 *guai*, condition, state 具体的 *gutaiteki*, concrete, definite
郡 384 10 strokes	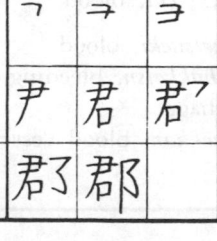	GUN, county, district; *kōri* (lit.), county, district 郡部 *gumbu*, rural district, counties 郡長 *gunchō*, head of a county (口 27)

係 385 9 strokes	KEI; *kakari* [*gakari*], charge, duty, in charge (of); *kaka(ru)*, to affect, to concern 係員 *kakari-in*, clerk in charge 関係 *kankei*, relation, connection, participation, implication 記録係 *kirokugakari*, person in charge of records, recorder
景 386 12 strokes	KEI, KE (view, scene) 風景 *fūkei*, scenery, view 不景気 *fukeiki*, bad times, depression 光景 *kōkei*, spectacle, scene (日 27)
軽 387 12 strokes	KEI; *karu* [*garu*], *karu(i)* light (in weight), slight, easy 軽卒 *keisotsu*, rashness, hastiness 軽音楽 *kei-ongaku*, light music 気軽 *kigaru*, light-hearted (車 88)
芸 388 7 strokes	GEI, arts, accomplishments 芸術 *geijutsu*, art 民芸 *mingei*, folk art 芸者 *geisha*, Japanese singing and dancing girl
血 389 6 strokes	KETSU; *chi*, blood 血液 *ketsueki*, blood 出血 *shukketsu*, bleeding, hemorrhage 血管 *kekkan*, blood vessel

結	390 12 strokes	KETSU; *musu(bi)*, end, knot; *musu(bu)*, to tie, to bind, to conclude, to link; *yu(u)*, to dress (the hair) 結果 *kekka*, result 結婚 *kekkon*, marriage 連結 *renketsu*, coupling, connection, linking (糸 83, 口 27)
建	391 9 strokes	KEN; *ta(teru)*, to build, to establish; *ta(tsu)*, to be built; ~*date*, ~-storied building 建物 *tatemono*, a building 建築 *kenchiku*, construction, architecture, building 二階建 *nikaidate*, two-storied building
言	392 7 strokes	GEN, GON, speech, statement; *koto*, word, speech, expression; *i(u)*, to say 方言 *hōgen*, dialect 無言 *mugon*, silence, muteness 言葉 *kotoba*, word, language
固	393 8 strokes	KO; *kata(meru)*, to harden, to make hard (v.t.); *kata(maru)*, to become hard; *kata(i)*, hard, firm 固有 *koyū*, peculiar, one's own 固体 *kotai*, a solid (body) 強固 *kyōko*, firmness, solidity, stability
湖	394 12 strokes	KO; *mizu-umi*, lake 湖水 *kosui*, lake 湖岸 *kogan*, shore of a lake 湖畔 *kohan*, border of a lake (口 27, 月 12)

幸	一 十 土	KŌ; *saiwa(i)*, blessings, good luck, happiness, fortune
	十 十 十	不幸 *fukō*, unhappiness, misfortune
395 8 strokes	十 幸	幸福 *kōfuku*, happiness 幸運 *kōun*, good fortune
航	丿 亻 舟	KŌ (to sail on the water)
	舟 舟 舟	航海 *kōkai*, voyage, navigation 航路 *kōro*, sea route, air route 航空 *kōkū*, aviation, air voyage
396 10 strokes	航 航 航	
港	氵 氵 氵	KŌ; *minato*, harbor
	氵 氵 氵	港町 *minatomachi*, port town 入港 *nyūkō*, entry into port 空港 *kūkō*, airport
397 12 strokes	港 港 港	(→ 汽 60)
告	ノ 亠 牛	KOKU; *tsu(geru)*, to tell, to inform
	牛 牛 告	報告 *hōkoku*, report 広告 *kōkoku*, advertisement 忠告 *chūkoku*, advice
398 7 strokes	告	
差	丶 ⺍ 𠂉	SA, difference, remainder (math.); *sa(su)*, to thrust, to insert
	𠂉 羊 差	差別 *sabetsu*, distinction, discrimination 大差 *taisa*, great difference 差出人 *sashidashinin*, sender, addresser
399 10 strokes	差 差 差	

祭	400 11 strokes	SAI; *matsu(ri)*, festival; *matsu(ru)*, to deify, to worship as a god, to offer prayers for the sake of 村祭り *muramatsuri*, village festival 祭日 *saijitsu*, national holiday 文化祭 *bunkasai*, cultural festival (示 622)
菜	401 11 strokes	SAI; *na*, greens, rape (vegetable) 野菜 *yasai*, vegetables 菜の花 *na-no-hana*, rape blossoms 菜園 *saien*, vegetable garden (木 15)
最	402 12 strokes	SAI, prefix for forming superlatives; *motto(mo)*, most 最初 *saisho*, the first, beginning 最後 *saigo*, the last 最善 *saizen*, the best (日 旱 104)
材	403 7 strokes	ZAI, material (for work), timber, ability, talent 木材 *mokuzai*, lumber, wood 材料 *zairyō*, raw material, ingredients 人材 *jinzai*, capable man
昨	404 9 strokes	SAKU (yesterday, ancient times) 昨日 *sakujitsu*, yesterday 昨年 *sakunen*, last year 昨夜 *sakuya*, last night

刷	405 8 strokes	SATSU; *su*(*ru*), to print; ~*zuri*, suffix for "printing" 印刷 *insatsu*, printing 校正刷り *kōseizuri*, proofs (printing) 謄写版刷り *tōshaban-zuri*, mimeographed copy
察	406 14 strokes	SATSU; *sas*(*suru*), to guess, to perceive, to sympathize with 観察 *kansatsu*, observation 視察 *shisatsu*, inspection 警察 *keisatsu*, police (祭 400)
散	407 12 strokes	SAN; *chi*(*ru*), to fall (leaves), to be scattered (v.i.); *chi*(*rasu*), to scatter, to disperse (v.t.); ~*san*, suffix for "powder" (medicine) 散歩 *sampo*, walk, stroll 解散 *kaisan*, breakup, dissolution 胃散 *isan*, medical powder for the stomach
産	408 11 strokes	SAN, childbearing, product, fortune; *u*(*mu*), to give birth to, to produce 産物 *sambutsu*, products 産地 *sanchi*, place of production 産業 *sangyō*, industry (生 34)
残	409 10 strokes	ZAN; *noko*(*ri*), remainder; *noko*(*ru*), to be left over, to remain; *noko*(*su*), to leave, to save 残念 *zannen*, regret, disappointment 残金 *zankin*, balance, money left over 残り物 *nokorimono*, remains, leftovers

士	一 十 士	SHI (man, figure) 武士 *bushi*, samurai 紳士 *shinshi*, gentleman 勇士 *yūshi*, brave man, hero
410 3 strokes		
史	丶 ㇇ ㇇ 屮 史	SHI (annals, history, chronicles) 歴史 *rekishi*, history 女史 *joshi*, Madame, Mrs., Miss 史上 *shijō*, in history, in the annals
411 5 strokes		
司	冂 司 司 司 司	SHI (to rule, to manage) 司会者 *shikaisha*, master of ceremonies, moderator, chairman 司令 *shirei*, order, command 司令部 *shireibu*, headquarters
412 5 strokes		
姉	乂 女 女 女丶 女亡 女亡	SHI ; *ane*, elder sister 姉妹 *shimai*, *ane-imōto*, sisters 姉娘 *anemusume*, elder daughter 姉婿 *anemuko*, elder sister's husband
413 8 strokes	姉 姉	
歯	丨 卜 卜 止 歩 歩	SHI ; *ha* [*ba*], tooth 虫歯 *mushiba*, decayed tooth 歯医者 *ha-isha*, dentist 歯車 *haguruma*, gear, cogwheel
414 12 strokes	歩 歯 歯	(米 135)

詩 415 13 strokes	言 言 言 言 言 詩 詩 詩 詩 詩	SHI, poetry, poem 詩人 *shijin*, poet 詩集 *shishū*, anthology of poetry 叙事詩 *jojishi*, epic poem (口 27, 土 17)
試 416 13 strokes	言 言 言 言 言 試 試 試 試 試	SHI; *kokoro(mi)*, trial, test; *kokoro(miru)*, to try 試験 *shiken*, examination 試運転 *shi-unten*, test driving, trial run 試合 *shiai*, match, contest (言 392)
式 417 6 strokes	一 二 工 式 式	SHIKI, ceremony, form, model; *~shiki*, ~-style (suffix for "style," "type") 式場 *shikijō*, ceremonial hall 卒業式 *sotsugyō-shiki*, graduation ceremony, commencement 旧式 *kyūshiki*, old-style
失 418 5 strokes	丿 ⺈ 夫 失	SHITSU; *ushina(u)*, to lose, to miss 失礼 *shitsurei*, impoliteness 失敗 *shippai*, failure 失望 *shitsubō*, despair, disappointment
写 419 5 strokes	丿 冖 冖 写 写	SHA; *utsu(su)*, to copy, to imitate, to take (a photograph) 写真 *shashin*, photograph 写生 *shasei*, sketch, drawing from nature 映写 *eisha*, projection

借 420 10 strokes	亻 亻 亻 什 借 借 借 借 借	SHAKU; *ka(ri)*, borrowing, debt; *ka(riru)*, to borrow, to rent, to substitute temporarily, to obtain (help) 借金 *shakkin*, debt, loan 借り物 *karimono*, borrowed thing 拝借 *haishaku*, loan, borrowing (日 11)
守 421 6 strokes	宀 宀 宀 宀 守 守	SHU, SU; *mamo(ru)*, to protect, to guard, to defend, to obey (the law), to keep (a promise) お守り *o-mamori*, amulet, charm 留守 *rusu*, absence 保守 *hoshu*, conservatism
酒 422 10 strokes	氵 氵 氵 氵 酒 酒 酒 酒	SHU; *sake* (*saka*), rice wine, liquor ぶどう酒 *budōshu*, wine 酒飲み *sakenomi*, drinker 酒屋 *sakaya*, liquor shop (酉 60)
種 423 14 strokes	丿 ⺈ 千 禾 禾 秊 稙 稙 種	SHU (kind, sort); *tane*, seed 種まき *tanemaki*, sowing seed 種類 *shurui*, sort, kind 人種 *jinshu*, human race (重 245)
州 424 6 strokes	丿 丿 州 州 州 州	SHŪ, province, state (U.S.A.) 本州 *Honshū* (main island of Japan) 九州 *Kyūshū* (Japan's third largest island) ユタ州 *Yuta-shū*, State of Utah

拾 425 9 strokes	一 扌 扌 扌 扌 扌 拾 拾 拾	SHŪ; JŪ, ten (used in legal documents); *hiro(u)*, to pick up 拾い物 *hiroimono*, something picked up, windfall, bargain 命拾い *inochibiroi*, narrow escape (from death) 拾弐円 *jūni-en*, 12 yen
習 426 11 strokes	冂 习 习 羽 羽 羽 習 習 習	SHŪ; *nara(u)*, to learn, to study 練習 *renshū*, practice 習字 *shūji*, penmanship 習慣 *shūkan*, habit, custom
順 427 12 strokes	丿 川 川 川 川 川 順 順 順	JUN, order, turn 順序 *junjo*, order, procedure, method 順番 *jumban*, order, turn 順調 *junchō*, normal condition, smooth progress (目 25)
初 428 7 strokes	丶 ラ 礻 礻 礻 初 初	SHO; *hatsu*, first; *haji(me)*, beginning 初秋 *shoshū*, early autumn 初雪 *hatsuyuki*, first snow of the year 初期 *shoki*, first stage
消 429 10 strokes	氵 氵 氵 氵 氵 消 消 消	SHŌ; *ki(eru)*, to vanish, to go out, to melt away; *ke(su)*, to extinguish, to switch off, to put out (a light) 消しゴム *keshigomu*, eraser 消防 *shōbō*, fire fighting 消毒 *shōdoku*, disinfection (氵 汽 60)

唱	430 11 strokes	SHŌ; *tona(eru)*, to chant, to recite, to say 独唱 *dokushō*, vocal solo 合唱 *gasshō*, chorus 唱歌 *shōka*, song, singing
商	431 11 strokes	SHŌ; *akina(u)*, to sell, to deal in 商人 *shōnin*, merchant 商売 *shōbai*, business, trade, transaction 商業 *shōgyō*, commerce, trade (口 27)
章	432 11 strokes	SHŌ, chapter 文章 *bunshō*, sentence 記章 *kishō*, medal, badge 勲章 *kunshō*, decoration, order (for honors) (立 149)
照	433 13 strokes	SHŌ; *te(rasu)*, to shine on, to compare with, to shed light on; *te(ru)*, to shine 日照り *hideri*, drought 照明 *shōmei*, illumination 対照 *taishō*, contrast
焼	434 12 strokes	SHŌ; *ya(ku)*, to burn, to bake, to grill, to toast (v.t.), to burn with jealousy; *ya(keru)*, to be burned, to be roasted, to be jealous of 夕焼け *yūyake*, evening glow, sunset colors 焼失 *shōshitsu*, destruction by fire (火 13)

植 435 12 strokes	一 十 才 木 木一 木十 杙 植 植	SHOKU; *u(eru)*, to plant, to set up (type) 植物 *shokubutsu*, plant, vegetation 植民地 *shokuminchi*, colony 田植え *taue*, rice planting (目 25)
臣 436 7 strokes	丨 厂 厂 戸 戸 戸 臣	SHIN, JIN (retainer, subject) 大臣 *daijin*, cabinet minister 忠臣 *chūshin*, loyal retainer
信 437 9 strokes	丿 亻 亻 亻言 亻言 亻言 信 信 信	SHIN, sincerity, trust, faith; *shin-(zuru)*, to believe, to trust, to believe in 信用 *shin-yō*, trust, confidence, belief, credit 信号 *shingō*, signal 通信 *tsūshin*, communication
真 438 10 strokes	一 十 十 方 方 直 直 真 真	SHIN; *ma*, truth, reality 写真機 *shashinki*, camera 真夏 *manatsu*, midsummer
成 439 6 strokes	丿 厂 万 成 成 成	SEI, JŌ; *na(ru)*, to become, to be completed, to consist of, to come to, to succeed; to come, to go (honorific); *na(su)*, to do, to perform 成長 *seichō*, growth 完成 *kansei*, completion 賛成 *sansei*, agreement, approval

清	440 11 strokes	SEI; *kiyo(i)*, *kiyo(raka)*, pure, clear 清潔 *seiketsu*, cleanliness 清書 *seisho*, fair copy 血清 *kessei*, (blood) serum (氵 汽 60)
勢	441 13 strokes	SEI [ZEI]; *ikio(i)*, force, vigor, power, influence 勢力 *seiryoku*, power, influence 大勢 *taisei*, general trend; *ōzei*, large number of people 軍勢 *gunzei*, number of soldiers, troops (土 17)
静	442 14 strokes	SEI, JŌ; *shizu(ka)*, quiet, silent, peaceful; *shizu(maru)*, to become quiet; *shizu(meru)*, to make calm, to soothe 静止 *seishi*, stillness, standstill 静物 *seibutsu*, still life 安静 *ansei*, complete rest (青 36)
整	443 16 strokes	SEI; *totono(eru)*, to put in order, to get ready; *totono(u)*, to be ready 整理 *seiri*, adjustment, arrangement, reorganization 整備 *seibi*, adjustment, complete equipment, consolidation (口 27, 正 46)
席	444 10 strokes	SEKI, seat, place 出席 *shusseki*, attendance, presence 欠席 *kesseki*, absence 座席 *zaseki*, seat

積	445 16 strokes	SEKI, product (math.); *tsumo(ri)*, intention; *tsu(mu)*, to pile up, to load, to accumulate (v.t.); *tsumo-(ru)*, to be piled up 面積 *menseki*, area 積極的 *sekkyokuteki*, positive, active, progressive 積荷 *tsumini*, cargo, a load (貝 169, 禾 秋 89)
節	446 13 strokes	SETSU, paragraph, season, time; *fushi*, joint, knot, tune 節約 *setsuyaku*, economy, frugality 調節 *chōsetsu*, regulation, control 使節 *shisetsu*, delegate, envoy
線	447 15 strokes	SEN, line, track, wire, string 地平線 *chiheisen*, horizon (on land) 光線 *kōsen*, light, beam, ray 直線 *chokusen*, straight line (糸 83, 白 37)
戦	448 13 strokes	SEN; *tataka(i)*, fight, war, struggle; *tataka(u)*, to fight, to make war, to struggle, to compete in games 戦争 *sensō*, war 終戦 *shūsen*, end of a war 戦場 *senjō*, battlefield (単 671)
選	449 15 strokes	SEN; *era(bu)*, to choose, to select 選挙 *senkyo*, election 選手 *senshu*, player, champion 当選 *tōsen*, victory in an election (共 376)

然	丿 ク 夕 夕 夕 犬 犬 犬 然	ZEN, NEN (yes, but, however) 自然 *shizen*, nature 当然 *tōzen*, natural, just, as a matter of course 天然 *tennen*, nature (犬 66)
450 12 strokes		
争	丿 ク 勹 勹 勹 爭 爭	SŌ; *araso(i)*, quarrel, dispute, competition; *araso(u)*, to struggle, to dispute, to quarrel 競争 *kyōsō*, competition 言い争う *ii-arasou*, to quarrel 争奪戦 *sōdatsusen*, scramble, contest, challenge
451 6 strokes		
相	一 十 才 木 朴 相 相 相 相	SŌ, appearance, aspect, phase; SHŌ (minister of state); *ai*, each other, mutual 相談 *sōdan*, consultation, talk 相手 *aite*, companion, the other party 首相 *shushō*, prime minister
452 9 strokes		
速	一 丶 言 束 束 束 速 速 速	SOKU; *haya(i)*, speedy, quick 速度 *sokudo*, speed 速記 *sokki*, stenography, shorthand 速達 *sokutatsu*, express mail, special delivery (辶 27)
453 10 strokes		
息	丿 亻 冂 自 自 自 息 息 息	SOKU (son); *iki*, breath ため息 *tameiki*, sigh 休息 *kyūsoku*, rest 消息 *shōsoku*, news, letter, circumstances
454 10 strokes		

族 455 11 strokes	方 方 方 旂 旂 旂 旂 旂 族 族	ZOKU, family, tribe, clan 家族 *kazoku*, family, household 民族 *minzoku*, race, people, nation 水族館 *suizokukan*, aquarium (方 138)
続 456 13 strokes	糸 糸 糸 紅 紅 紅 結 結 結 続 続	ZOKU; *tsuzu(ki)*, continuation, sequel, range; *tsuzu(ku)*, to continue, to follow, to last (v.i.); *tsuzu(keru)*, to continue, to resume (v.t.) 続出 *zokushutsu*, successive occurrence 手続 *tetsuzuki*, procedure 相続 *sōzoku*, inheritance (糸 83)
卒 457 8 strokes	丶 亠 亠 亠 亠 亠 亠 卒	SOTSU, a private, common soldier; (to finish) 卒業 *sotsugyō*, graduation 卒業生 *sotsugyōsei*, graduate 兵卒 *heisotsu*, private (soldier)
孫 458 10 strokes	子 子 子 孫 孫 孫 孫 孫 孫 孫	SON; *mago*, grandchild 子孫 *shison*, descendants (糸 83)
他 459 5 strokes	亻 亻 亻 仁 仁 他	TA, other 他国 *takoku*, other countries 他人 *tanin*, other people, stranger その他 *sonota*, the others, the rest; and so forth

打 460 5 strokes	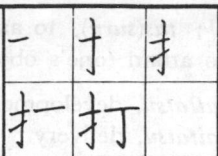	DA; *u(tsu)*, to strike, to beat 舌打ち *shita-uchi*, smacking one's lips, click of the tongue 打者 *dasha*, batter, hitter 三塁打 *sanrui-da*, three-base hit
対 461 7 strokes	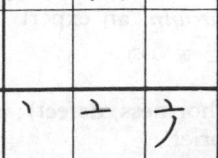	TAI, opposite, against; TSUI, pair, set 反対 *hantai*, opposition, opposite, objection, reverse 対面 *taimen*, interview, confrontation 二対一 *ni-tai-ichi*, (score of) 2 to 1
隊 462 12 strokes	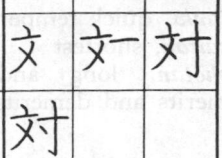	TAI, a party, a corps, band, unit 兵隊 *heitai*, soldier 楽隊 *gakutai*, band (musical) 隊長 *taichō*, captain, commander, leader (冢 家 53)
代 463 5 strokes	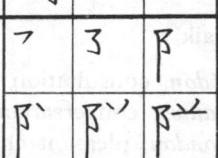	DAI, generation, price; *ka(wari)*, substitute, deputy, compensation, exchange; *ka(waru)*, to take the place of, to relieve; *yo*, generation, the age, the reign 時代 *jidai*, period, era, age 現代 *gendai*, the present age 代表 *daihyō*, representative
題 464 18 strokes	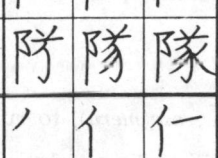	DAI, subject, topic, theme, title (of book, story, etc.) 問題 *mondai*, question, problem 話題 *wadai*, topic of conversation 宿題 *shukudai*, homework (日 11, 貝 169)

達	465 12 strokes	TATSU; *tas(suru)*, to arrive, to reach, to attain (one's object) 発達 *hattatsu*, development 配達 *haitatsu*, delivery 達人 *tatsujin*, an expert (土 17, 辶 近 195)
短	466 12 strokes	TAN (shortness, defect); *mijika(i)*, short, brief 短気 *tanki*, quick temper 最短 *saitan*, shortest 長短 *chōtan*, long and short, merits and demerits (口 27)
談	467 15 strokes	DAN, talk 相談 *sōdan*, consultation 談話 *danwa*, conversation, talk 歓談 *kandan*, pleasant chat (言 392)
治	468 8 strokes	CHI, JI; *osa(meru)*, to rule over 政治 *seiji*, politics, administration 自治 *jichi*, self-government 治療 *chiryō*, medical treatment
置	469 13 strokes	CHI; *o(ku)*, to put, to place 位置 *ichi*, position 置物 *okimono*, ornament (for a tokonoma) 物置 *mono-oki*, storeroom (目 25)

帳	470 11 strokes	CHŌ (curtain, register) 帳面 *chōmen*, notebook, account book 手帳 *techō*, memo book, note-book 日記帳 *nikkichō*, diary (長 116)
調	471 15 strokes	CHŌ; *shira(be)*, melody, inspection; *shira(beru)*, to investigate, to examine, to inspect 調子 *chōshi*, tune, key, rhythm, tone, way, condition 調査 *chōsa*, investigation, examination 調節 *chōsetsu*, adjustment (言 392, 口 27)
直	472 8 strokes	CHOKU, JIKI; *nao(su)*, to mend, to correct, to cure, to set right 直角 *chokkaku*, right angle 正直 *shōjiki*, honesty 素直 *sunao*, gentle, obedient
丁	473 2 strokes	TEI, "D" grade; CHŌ, Japanese linear unit (120 yds.), division of a ward or town, leaf of a book 横丁 *yokochō*, side street, alley-way 丁度 *chōdo*, exactly, just 丁寧 *teinei*, politeness
定	474 8 strokes	TEI, JŌ; *sada(meru)*, to fix, to decide, to establish 定員 *tei-in*, regular staff, full number of personnel 定期 *teiki*, fixed period or term, regularity; prefix for "regular" 予定 *yotei*, previous arrangement, program, schedule

底 475 8 strokes		TEI ; *soko* [*zoko*], bottom, depth 谷底 *tanizoko*, bottom of a ravine 海底 *kaitei*, bottom of the sea 徹底的 *tetteiteki*, thoroughgoing, out-and-out
停 476 11 strokes		TEI (to stop) 停止 *teishi*, stop, suspension 停電 *teiden*, electricity stoppage 停留所 *teiryūjo*, stopping place, streetcar (bus) stop
庭 477 10 strokes		TEI ; *niwa*, garden 庭園 *teien*, garden 校庭 *kōtei*, school playground 家庭 *katei*, home
的 478 8 strokes		TEKI (like, similar), suffix for forming adjectives from nouns; *mato*, mark, target 目的 *mokuteki*, purpose 世界的 *sekaiteki*, international, world-wide 社会的 *shakaiteki*, social
転 479 1 strokes		TEN (to turn round, to change, to fall, to tumble) 転校 *tenkō*, change of schools 転任 *tennin*, change of post 運転 *unten*, driving, working, operation (車 88)

徒 480 10 strokes		TO (companion) 生徒 *seito*, pupil, student 徒歩 *toho*, going on foot 徒競走 *tokyōsō*, running match (土 17)
努 481 7 strokes	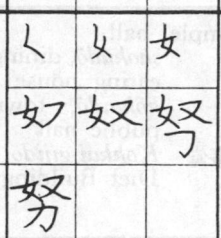	DO; *tsuto(meru)*, to make efforts 努力 *doryoku*, effort 努力家 *doryokuka*, hard worker
湯 482 12 strokes		TŌ; *yu*, hot water 湯気 *yuge*, steam 湯船 *yubune*, bathtub 熱湯 *nettō*, boiling water (日 11)
登 483 12 strokes		TŌ, TO; *nobo(ri)*, climbing (n.); *nobo(ru)*, to climb 登山 *tozan*, mountain climbing 登校 *tōkō*, attending school 木登り *ki-nobori*, tree climbing (口 27)
等 484 12 strokes	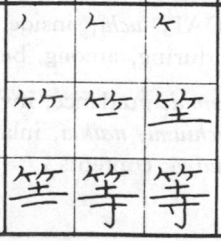	TŌ, class, quality; *hito(shii)*, like, equal 上等 *jōtō*, high-class, very good, superior 一等 *ittō*, first class, most, best 高等学校 *kōtōgakkō*, senior high「school (土 17)

燈	485 16 strokes	TŌ (light, lamp) 電燈 *dentō*, electric light 安全燈 *anzentō*, safety lamp 懐中電燈 *kaichūdentō*, flashlight, electric torch (火 13, 登 483)
堂	486 11 strokes	DŌ, temple, hall 食堂 *shokudō*, dining room, eating house 公会堂 *kōkaidō*, town hall, public hall 国会議事堂 *Kokkai-gijidō*, the Diet Building (口 27)
童	487 12 strokes	DŌ (child) 児童 *jidō*, child, boys and girls 童話 *dōwa*, nursery tale 童謡 *dōyō*, nursery song (里 332)
働	488 13 strokes	DŌ; *hatara(ki)*, work (n.); *hatara(ku)*, to work, to do (evil), to come into play 労働者 *rōdōsha*, laborer 働き手 *hatarakite*, bread winner, worker 働き者 *hatarakimono*, hard worker (重 245)
内	489 4 strokes	NAI, DAI; *uchi*, inside, home, within, during, among, between 案内 *annai*, guidance, invitation 内海 *uchiumi*, *naikai*, inland sea 内容 *naiyō*, contents

熱 490 15 strokes	土 夫 夫 埶 埶 埶 埶 埶 埶	NETSU, heat, fever, craze, zeal; *nes(suru)*, to heat, to become hot; *atsu(i)*, hot 熱病 *netsubyō*, fever 熱心 *nesshin*, zeal 熱帯 *nettai*, tropical zone (土 17)
農 491 13 strokes	冂 冊 曲 曲 農 農 農 農 農	NŌ, farming 農場 *nōjō*, farm 農業 *nōgyō*, agriculture 農家 *nōka*, farmhouse
反 492 4 strokes	一 厂 厂 反 	HAN, antithesis, anti-; TAN, unit of measure (for land and cloth) 反対 *hantai*, opposition, contrast 反省 *hansei*, self-examination 反射 *hansha*, reflection
飛 493 9 strokes	飞 飞 飞 飞 飛 飛 飛 飛 飛	HI; *to(bu)*, to fly 飛び込む *tobikomu*, to jump in, to dive into, to rush in 飛行機 *hikōki*, airplane 飛行場 *hikōjō*, airport
悲 494 12 strokes	丿 丿 丿 丿 非 非 非 非 悲	HI; *kana(shii)*, sad 悲劇 *higeki*, tragedy, tragic event 悲壮 *hisō*, pathetic 慈悲 *jihi*, mercy (心 95)

費 495 12 strokes	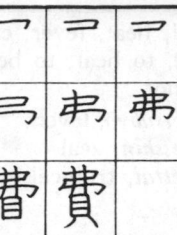	HI [PI]; *tsui(yasu)*, to spend 費用 *hiyō*, expense 旅費 *ryohi*, traveling expenses 出費 *shuppi*, expenditure (貝 169)
鼻 496 14 strokes	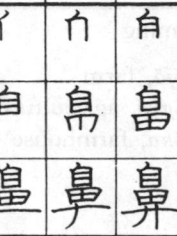	BI; *hana*, nose 鼻先 *hanasaki*, tip of one's nose, under one's very nose 鼻紙 *hanagami*, paper handkerchief 鼻血 *hanaji*, nosebleed (田 40, 自 229)
必 497 5 strokes	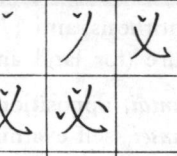	HITSU; *kanara(zu)*, without fail, by all means, invariably, necessarily 必要 *hitsuyō*, need 必死 *hisshi*, inevitable death, desperation 必勝 *hisshō*, sure victory
氷 498 5 strokes	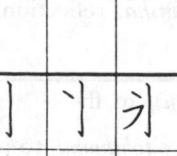	HYŌ; *kōri*, ice 氷すべり *kōrisuberi*, ice skating 氷山 *hyōzan*, iceberg 砕氷船 *saihyōsen*, icebreaker
秒 499 9 strokes	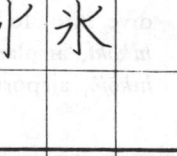	BYŌ, second (unit of time) 秒針 *byōshin*, second hand 一秒 *ichibyō*, one second 数秒 *sūbyō*, several seconds

不 500 4 strokes	一 ノ 不	FU, dis-, in-, un-, mal-, ill- 不自由 *fujiyū*, inconvenience, want 不平 *fuhei*, discontent, complaint 不幸 *fukō*, misfortune, unhappiness, death
夫 501 4 strokes	一 二 夫	FU [PU], (FŪ); *otto*, husband 工夫 *kōfu*, laborer, coolie 夫婦 *fūfu*, husband and wife 夫人 *fujin*, married lady, Mrs.
付 502 5 strokes	ノ 亻 付	FU; *tsu(ku)* [*zu(ku)*], to adhere, to stick (v.i.); *tsu(keru)*, to attach, to stick (v.t.) 付近 *fukin*, neighborhood 寄付 *kifu*, contribution 受付 *uketsuke*, acceptance, information office
府 503 8 strokes	丶 亠 广 府	FU, urban prefecture, center 政府 *seifu*, government 首府 *shufu*, capital 府県 *fuken*, prefectures
部 504 11 strokes	丶 亠 立 部	BU, department, copy, part 全部 *zembu*, all, whole 東部 *tōbu*, eastern part 部分 *bubun*, part (口 27)

服 505 8 strokes	丿 月 月 月 月 月 服 服	FUKU, dress, European clothes 洋服 *yōfuku*, European clothes 礼服 *reifuku*, full dress 制服 *seifuku*, uniform
福 506 13 strokes	丶 ㇇ 礻 礻 礻 礻 福 福 福	FUKU, good fortune 幸福 *kōfuku*, happiness 福の神 *fuku-no-kami*, God of Wealth 祝福 *shukufuku*, blessing (口 27, 田 40)
粉 507 10 strokes	丶 丷 ⺍ ⺍ 米 粉 粉 粉 粉	FUN; *kona*, *ko*, powder 火の粉 *hi-no-ko*, spark 小麦粉 *komugiko*, wheat flour 製粉 *seifun*, milling (flour)
別 508 7 strokes	丶 冂 口 冂 冂 別 別	BETSU, distinction, exception; different, particular; *waka*(*reru*), to part (from) 特別 *tokubetsu*, special 別問題 *betsumondai*, another question 別れ *wakare*, parting, separation
変 509 9 strokes	丶 亠 ナ 亠 亦 亦 亦 変 変	HEN, odd; disturbance, accident, change; *ka*(*waru*), to change, to be uncommon, to move (v.i.); *ka*(*eru*), to change, to reform 変化 *henka*, change, variety, conjugation 大変 *taihen*, serious, great, terrible

便 510 9 strokes		BEN, convenience, bodily waste; BIN, mail 便利 *benri*, convenience 便所 *benjo*, toilet 航空便 *kōkūbin*, air mail
包 511 5 strokes	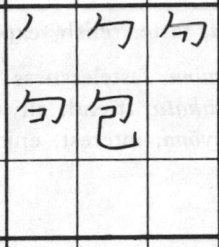	HŌ; *tsutsu(mu)*, to wrap, to cover 小包 *kozutsumi*, postal package 包み紙 *tsutsumigami*, wrapping paper 包囲 *hōi*, encirclement
放 512 8 strokes	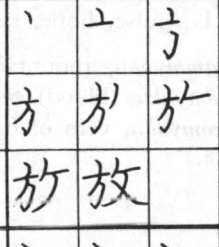	HŌ; *hana(su)*, to let go, to release; *hana(tsu)*, to set free, to send forth, to shoot 放送 *hōsō*, broadcasting 放課後 *hōkago*, after school 開放 *kaihō*, freedom, opening
法 513 8 strokes	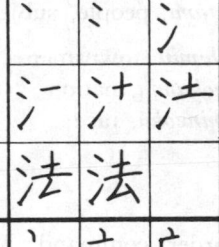	HŌ [PŌ], law, doctrine, reason, method 方法 *hōhō*, way, method 法律 *hōritsu*, law 文法 *bumpō*, grammar
望 514 11 strokes	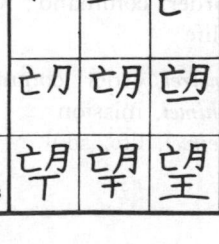	BŌ, MŌ; *nozo(mi)*, desire, wish; *nozo(mu)*, to desire, to expect, to see 失望 *shitsubō*, disappointment 希望 *kibō*, hope, wish 絶望 *zetsubō*, despair (月 12)

末 515 5 strokes	一 二 十 才 末	MATSU; *sue*, end, future, youngest child, trifle 末っ子 *suekko*, youngest child 月末 *getsumatsu*, end of the month 始末 *shimatsu*, management, circumstances
味 516 8 strokes	丶 口 口 口一 口二 口十 味 味	MI; *aji*, taste, relish, experience 無味 *mumi*, tastelessness 味方 *mikata*, friend, ally 興味 *kyōmi*, interest, enjoyment
脈 517 10 strokes	ノ 冂 月 月 月 月 脈 脈 脈	MYAKU, pulse, hope, range 山脈 *sammyaku*, mountain range 静脈 *jōmyaku*, (blood) vein 鉱脈 *kōmyaku*, vein of ore
民 518 5 strokes	乁 コ 尸 尸 民	MIN; *tami*, people, subjects 市民 *shimin*, townsman 国民 *kokumin*, nation 民族 *minzoku*, race
命 519 8 strokes	ノ 亼 亼 亼 亼 亼 命 命	MEI, order, command; MYŌ; *inochi*, life 命令 *meirei*, order, command 使命 *shimei*, mission 生命 *seimei*, life, soul

問 520 11 strokes	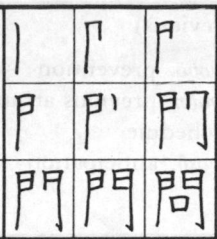	MON; *to(u)*, to ask, to question, to care, to accuse 問題 *mondai*, problem, issue, trouble 学問 *gakumon*, learning 疑問 *gimon*, doubt, question (口 27)
薬 521 16 strokes		YAKU; *kusuri*, medicine, chemicals 薬学 *yakugaku*, pharmacy (study) 火薬 *kayaku*, gunpowder 薬局 *yakkyoku*, pharmacy, pharmacist's office (木 15, 白 37)
油 522 8 strokes		YU; *abura*, oil 油絵 *abura-e*, oil painting 石油 *sekiyu*, petroleum 油田 *yuden*, oil field
有 523 6 strokes		YŪ, U; *a(ru)*, to exist, to have, to measure, to have experience, to happen, to consist of 有名 *yūmei*, fame, well-known 有益 *yūeki*, benefit, profit 有志 *yūshi*, volunteer
勇 524 9 strokes		YŪ; *isa(mashii)*, brave 勇気 *yūki*, courage 勇士 *yūshi*, brave man 勇敢 *yūkan*, bravery

予 525 4 strokes	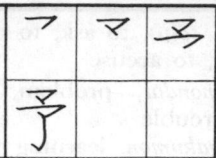	YO (previous) 予防 *yobō*, prevention 予定 *yotei*, previous arrangement, schedule 予想 *yosō*, anticipation
洋 526 9 strokes	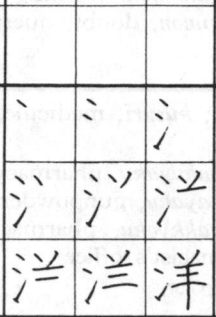	YŌ, ocean 西洋 *seiyō*, the West, the Occident 洋間 *yōma*, Western-style room 洋服 *yōfuku*, Western-style clothes
陽 527 12 strokes		YŌ (positive, male principle in nature) 太陽 *taiyō*, sun 太陽系 *taiyōkei*, solar system 陽気 *yōki*, season, weather, cheerfulness (日 11)
利 528 7 strokes		RI, advantage, profit, interest (on money) 利用 *riyō*, utilization 利益 *rieki*, gains, benefit 権利 *kenri*, a right, a claim
陸 529 11 strokes	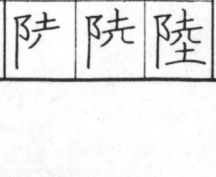	RIKU, land 大陸 *tairiku*, continent 上陸 *jōriku*, landing 着陸 *chakuriku*, landing (of an airplane)

良 530 7 strokes		RYŌ; *yo(i)*, good, well, fine, right, satisfactory 改良 *kairyō*, improvement 良心 *ryōshin*, conscience 最良 *sairyō*, the best, the ideal
料 531 10 strokes		RYŌ (charge, materials) 原料 *genryō*, raw material 料理 *ryōri*, cooking 料金 *ryōkin*, charge
緑 532 14 strokes		RYOKU, ROKU; *midori*, green 新緑 *shinryoku*, fresh verdure 緑地 *ryokuchi*, green tract of land 緑色 *midori-iro*, green (color) (糸 83)
輪 533 15 strokes		RIN; *wa*, ring, circle, wheel 三輪車 *sanrinsha*, tricycle, three-wheeled vehicle 車輪 *sharin*, wheel 首輪 *kubiwa*, collar (for a dog) (車 88)
類 534 18 strokes		RUI, a kind, a variety 種類 *shurui*, kind, sort 親類 *shinrui*, a relative 分類 *bunrui*, classification (米 135, 貝 169)

冷 535 7 strokes	冷	REI; *tsume(tai)*, cold; *hi(eru)*, to grow cold, feel chilly; *hi(yasu)*, to cool (v.t.) 冷水 *reisui*, cold water 冷気 *reiki*, cold air 冷蔵 *reizō*, cold storage, refrigeration
歴 536 14 strokes	歴	REKI (to pass, to travel about) 歴史 *rekishi*, history 経歴 *keireki*, background (of a person), career 履歴書 *rirekisho*, personal history (木 15)
列 537 6 strokes		RETSU, row, line 行列 *gyōretsu*, row, procession 列車 *ressha*, train 整列 *seiretsu*, standing in a row
連 538 10 strokes	連	REN, a ream (of paper), a group; *~ren*, suffix for "group"; *tsu(reru)*, to take along; *tsu(ranaru)*, to range; *~zure*, suffix for "companion" 連絡 *renraku*, connection, communication, contact 連盟 *remmei*, league (車 88)
練 539 14 strokes	練	REN; *ne(ru)*, to polish (one's style), to discipline (one's mind), to parade, to knead (a dough) 練習 *renshū*, practice 熟練 *jukuren*, skill, dexterity 訓練 *kunren*, drill, training (糸 83)

路	口 口 口 足 足 足 跡 跡 路	RO (road, route, path); ~*ji*, suffix denoting "way" 道路 *dōro*, road 線路 *senro*, railway track 航路 *kōro*, sea route (口 27)
540 13 strokes		
老	一 十 土 耂 耂 老	RŌ, old age; *o*(*i*), old age, the aged; *o*(*iru*), to grow old 老人 *rōjin*, old man 老木 *rōboku*, aged tree 養老院 *yōrōin*, asylum for the aged
541 6 strokes		
労	丶 丷 丷 冖 冖 労	RŌ, labor, service, trouble 苦労 *kurō*, toil, care 勤労 *kinrō*, labor 労働者 *rōdōsha*, laborer
542 7 strokes	労	
録	金 釒 釒 釒 舒 舒	ROKU (to copy, to write down) 記録 *kiroku*, record 新記録 *shinkiroku*, new record 録音 *rokuon*, (sound) recording, transcription
543 16 strokes	録 録 録	
圧	一 厂 厂 圧 圧	ATSU (pressure) 気圧 *kiatsu*, atmospheric pressure 圧力 *atsuryoku*, pressure 電圧 *den-atsu*, voltage
544 5 strokes		

易 545 8 strokes	丶 冂 日 日 月 易 易 易	I (easy); EKI, divination 容易 *yōi*, easy 貿易 *bōeki*, trade 易者 *ekisha*, fortuneteller
胃 546 9 strokes	丶 冂 冊 冊 田 胃 胃 胃 胃	I, stomach 胃袋 *ibukuro*, stomach 胃病 *ibyō*, stomach trouble 胃腸 *i-chō*, stomach and intestines
移 547 11 strokes	ノ 二 千 禾 禾 秂 移 移 移	I; *utsu(ru)*, to move (to a place, into a house), to change (v.i.), to sink into, to be infectious; *utsu(su)*, to remove (v.t.), to infect 移民 *imin*, immigration (emigration), immigrant 移り変わる *utsurikawaru*, to change, to shift
因 548 6 strokes	丨 冂 冃 冃 因 因	IN, cause; *yo(ru)*, to be due to, to be based on 原因 *gen-in*, cause 因果 *inga*, cause and effect, fate 因襲 *inshū*, long-established custom
栄 549 9 strokes	丶 ⺍ ⺍ノ ⺍ 宀 宀 栄 栄 栄	EI, honor; *saka(e)*, prosperity; *saka(eru)*, to prosper 光栄 *kōei*, honor 繁栄 *han-ei*, prosperity 栄養 *eiyō*, nutrition

永 550 5 strokes	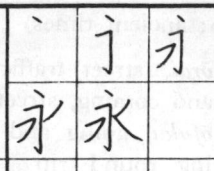	EI (long, eternal, perpetual) 永遠 *eien*, eternity 永眠 *eimin*, death 永住 *eijū*, permanent residence
衛 551 16 strokes	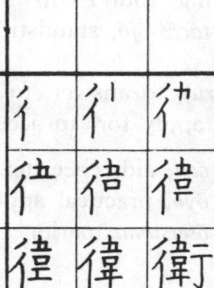	EI (to protect, to defend) 衛生 *eisei*, hygiene 防衛 *bōei*, defense 守衛 *shuei*, guard, watchman (行 73)
液 552 11 strokes		EKI, liquid, fluid, juice 液体 *ekitai*, liquid 血液 *ketsueki*, blood 消毒液 *shōdoku-eki*, antiseptic solution (氵 汽 60)
演 553 14 strokes		EN; *en*(*zuru*), to act, to perform a play, to create (a comic scene), to commit (a blunder) 演説 *enzetsu*, speech 演技 *engi*, acting 演奏 *ensō*, (musical) performance (氵 汽 60, 宀 空 65)
央 554 5 strokes	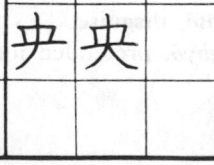	Ō (center, middle) 中央 *chūō*, center 中央線 *Chūō-sen*, the Chūō Line (electric railway in Tōkyō) 震央 *shin-ō*, the epicenter, the center of an earthquake

往 555 8 strokes	往 往 往 往 往 往 往 往	Ō (to go; ancient times) 往来 *ōrai*, (street) traffic, going and coming, street 往復 *ōfuku*, going and returning, round trip 立往生 *tachi-ōjō*, standstill
応 556 7 strokes	応 応 応 応 応 応 応	Ō, *ō(zuru)*, to answer, to comply with, to apply for, to accept 応援 *ōen*, aid, cheering 応用 *ōyō*, practical application 応接間 *ōsetsuma*, parlor
億 557 15 strokes	億 億 億 億 億 億 億 億	OKU, one hundred million 二十億年 *nijūoku-nen*, two billion years 数億円 *sūoku-en*, several hundred million yen (立 149, 日 早 104)
恩 558 10 strokes	恩 恩 恩 恩 恩 恩 恩 恩	ON, favor, kindness 恩人 *onjin*, benefactor 謝恩 *shaon*, expression of gratitude 恩返し *ongaeshi*, requital of another's favor (心 95)
仮 559 6 strokes	仮 仮 仮 仮 仮 仮	KA, KE; *kari*, temporary, false 仮定 *katei*, supposition 仮装 *kasō*, disguise 仮病 *kebyō*, pretended illness

果 560 8 strokes		KA (fruit, result); *hate*, end, result; *hata(su)*, to carry out, to realize, to fulfill 結果 *kekka*, result, effect 効果 *kōka*, effect 果実 *kajitsu*, fruit
河 561 8 strokes		KA [GA] (river) 河口 *kakō*, mouth of a river 銀河 *ginga*, Milky Way 運河 *unga*, canal
過 562 12 strokes		KA; *su(giru)*, to elapse, to pass, to exceed; *su(gosu)*, to pass (a day), to go to excess 通過 *tsūka*, passage 経過 *keika*, progress, lapse 過去 *kako*, past, past tense (辶 27, 辶 近 195)
価 563 8 strokes	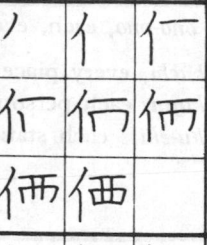	KA; *atai*, price, value 定価 *teika*, fixed price 価値 *kachi*, value 物価 *bukka*, prices of commodities
課 564 15 strokes		KA, section, lesson 課外 *kagai*, extra-curricular 課題 *kadai*, theme, homework 学課 *gakka*, lesson (言 392, 果 560)

賀	フ	カ	カロ	GA (congratulations) 年賀 *nenga*, New Year's greetings 年賀状 *nengajō*, New Year's card 祝賀 *shukuga*, celebration, congratulation (口 27)
	加	加	賀	
565 12 strokes	賀	賀	賀	
快	丶	忄	忄	KAI; *kokoroyo(i)*, pleasant, refreshing 快晴 *kaisei*, fine weather 愉快 *yukai*, pleasant 快活 *kaikatsu*, cheerful
	忄フ	忄ユ	快	
566 7 strokes	快			
解	𠂉	角	角	KAI (explanation); *to(ku)*, to solve, to untie, to dissolve 理解 *rikai*, understanding 解散 *kaisan*, breaking up, dissolution 分解 *bunkai*, analysis, decomposition (角 173)
	角フ	角刀	解	
567 13 strokes	解	解	解	
各	ノ	ク	夕	KAKU; *ono-ono*, each, every 各地 *kakuchi*, every place 各人 *kakujin*, each person 各駅 *kaku-eki*, each station
	冬	各	各	
568 6 strokes				
格	一	十	才	KAKU, status, case (in grammar) 性格 *seikaku*, personality, character 人格 *jinkaku*, character 価格 *kakaku*, price (各 568)
	木	杓	格	
569 10 strokes	格			

確 570 15 strokes	石 砂 砕 確	KAKU; *tashi(ka)*, sure, accurate, reliable; *tashi(kameru)*, to ascertain, to confirm 正確 *seikaku*, correctness 確実 *kakujitsu*, certainty 確定 *kakutei*, decision (石 44)
完 571 7 strokes	宀 完	KAN (end, completion) 完全 *kanzen*, perfection 完成 *kansei*, completion 完結 *kanketsu*, completion, finish, termination
漢 572 13 strokes	氵 漢	KAN (China); *~kan*, suffix for "man" 漢字 *kanji*, Chinese character 漢文 *kanbun*, Chinese composition 悪漢 *akkan*, villain, crook (氵 汽 60, 口 27)
管 573 14 strokes	竹 管	KAN (to control, to administer); *kuda*, tube, pipe 鉄管 *tekkan*, iron pipe (tube) 血管 *kekkan*, blood vessel 管理 *kanri*, administration, control, charge (官 364)
慣 574 14 strokes	忄 慣	KAN; *na(reru)*, to get accustomed (to), to become inured (to) 習慣 *shūkan*, habit, custom 慣用 *kan-yō*, common use, practice 見慣れる *minareru*, to get used to seeing, to be familiar (with) (貝 169)

希 575 7 strokes	希	KI (rare; desire) 希望 *kibō*, hope, desire 希望者 *kibōsha*, aspirant, applicant 希薄 *kihaku*, thin, weak, sparse
寄 576 11 strokes	寄	KI; *yo(ru)*, to approach, to drop in, to gather (v. i.); *yo(seru)*, to draw up (a chair), to push (a desk) aside 寄港 *kikō*, call at a port 寄付 *kifu*, contribution 寄与 *kiyo*, contribution, service (口 27)
規 577 11 strokes	規	KI (compass) 規律 *kiritsu*, order, discipline 規模 *kibo*, scale, scope 規準 *kijun*, standard (見 67)
紀 578 9 strokes	紀	KI (history, chronicle) 世紀 *seiki*, century, period 二十世紀 *nijisseiki*, twentieth century 紀元 *kigen*, era, epoch
技 579 7 strokes	技	GI (art, skill) 技師 *gishi*, engineer 競技 *kyōgi*, sporting events, contest 技術 *gijutsu*, art, technique

義 580 13 strokes	丶 ⺍ 羊 ⺍ 羊 羊 羊 羊 羊 義 義 義	GI, justice, morality, loyalty, relationship; prefix for "in-law," "artificial" 主義 *shugi*, principle, ~ism 講義 *kōgi*, lecture 義兄 *gikei*, elder brother-in-law (我 745)
議 581 20 strokes	言 言 言 言 言 言 言 言 言 議 議 議	GI (discussion) 会議 *kaigi*, conference 議論 *giron*, argument, discussion 議会 *gikai*, Diet (言 392, 義 580)
久 582 3 strokes	ノ ク 久	KYŪ, KU; *hisa*(*shii*), long (time), lasting; *hisa*(*shiku*), for a long time 永久 *eikyū*, permanence, eternity 久しぶり *hisashiburi*, after a long 「time 久遠 *kuon*, eternity
求 583 7 strokes	一 寸 寸 寸 寸 求 求	KYŪ; *moto*(*me*), request, demand; *moto*(*meru*), to request, to search for, to buy, to wish for 求人 *kyūjin*, offer of a job 請求 *seikyū*, demand 「ment 求職 *kyūshoku*, seeking employ-
救 584 11 strokes	一 寸 寸 求 求 求 求 求 救 救 救	KYŪ; *suku*(*i*), rescue, help; *suku*(*u*), to rescue, to help 救済 *kyūsai*, relief 救助 *kyūjo*, rescue 救急車 *kyūkyūsha*, ambulance (求 583)

給 585 12 strokes	糸 糸 糸 糸 糸 糸 糸 糸 糸 糸 糸 糸	KYŪ (to supply) 給料 *kyūryō*, pay, salary 供給 *kyōkyū*, supply 月給 *gekkyū*, monthly salary (合 77)
居 586 8 strokes	尸 尸 尸 尸 尸 尸 尸 尸	KYO (dwelling place); *i(ru)*, to be, to be present, to dwell 住居 *jūkyo*, dwelling 居眠り *inemuri*, napping, dozing (n.) 居間 *ima*, living room
許 587 11 strokes	言 言 言 言 言 言 言 言 言 言 言	KYO; *yuru(shi)*, permission, pardon, approval; *yuru(su)*, to permit, to forgive, to approve 許可 *kyoka*, permission, license, admission, approval 特許 *tokkyo*, patent, concession 免許 *menkyo*, license, certificate (口 27)
漁 588 14 strokes	氵 氵 氵 氵 氵 氵 氵 氵 氵 氵 氵 氵	GYO; RYŌ, fishing 漁船 *gyosen*, fishing boat 漁業 *gyogyō*, fishing industry 漁師 *ryōshi*, fisherman (氵 汽 60, 田 40)
興 589 16 strokes	臼 臼 臼 臼 臼 臼 臼 臼 臼 臼 臼 臼	KYŌ, interest; KŌ; *oko(ru)*, to prosper; *oko(su)*, to restore 興味 *kyōmi*, interest, appeal 興奮 *kōfun*, excitement 復興 *fukkō*, revival, reconstruction (同 295)

均 590 7 strokes	一 十 土 圴 均 均 均	KIN (level, equality) 平均 *heikin*, average, balance 均等 *kintō*, equality, identity
区 591 4 strokes	一 ㇇ 又 区	KU, ward, section 区別 *kubetsu*, distinction, classification 地区 *chiku*, area 区画 *kukaku*, boundary, block, division
句 592 5 strokes	ノ 勹 勹 句 句	KU, clause, phrase, verse, line 文句 *monku*, words, objection 語句 *goku*, words and phrases 句とう点 *kutōten*, punctuation marks
軍 593 9 strokes	冖 冖 冖 冖 冖 冖 冒 冒 軍	GUN, army, military authorities 軍備 *gumbi*, armaments 軍隊 *guntai*, troops, army 軍艦 *gunkan*, warship
群 594 13 strokes	⺕ 尹 君 君 君 君 君 群 群	GUN; *mu*(*re*), group, flock, herd; *mu*(*reru*), *mura*(*garu*), to throng (v. i.) 魚群 *gyogun*, school of fish 群島 *guntō*, group of islands 群衆 *gunshū*, crowd (of people) (君 198)

型	一 二 干	KEI; *kata* [*gata*], type, model, mold, conventionality
	开 刑 刑	模型 *mokei*, model 小型 *kogata*, small size 大型 *ō-gata*, large size
595 9 strokes	刑 刑 型	
経	幺 幺 幺	KEI, circles of longitude; KYŌ, the sutras, (law, reason, way, ordinary course of things); *he*(*ru*), to pass, to pass through
	糸 糸 糸	経費 *keihi*, expenditure 経由 *keiyu*, by way of, through 神経 *shinkei*, nerve
596 11 strokes	紀 経 経	(土 17)
欠	ノ 冂 ク	KETSU (lack, absence); *ka*(*keru*), to be broken off, to lack (v.i.); *ka*-(*ku*), to lack, to want (v.t.)
	欠	欠点 *ketten*, fault 欠席 *kesseki*, absence 欠乏 *ketsubō*, shortage
597 4 strokes		
件	ノ 亻 亻	KEN, matter
	仁 仁 件	事件 *jiken*, event, matter 用件 *yōken*, business 条件 *jōken*, condition, terms
598 6 strokes		
健	亻 亻 亻	KEN; *suko*(*yaka*), healthy, sound
	亻 亻 亻	強健 *kyōken*, robust 保健 *hoken*, (preservation of) health 健全 *kenzen*, healthy, sound
599 11 strokes	律 健 健	(亻 休 61)

験 600 18 strokes	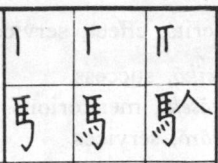	KEN (effect; to examine) 実験 *jikken*, experiment 経験 *keiken*, experience 試験 *shiken*, examination, experiment (馬 127, 僉 険 770)
限 601 9 strokes	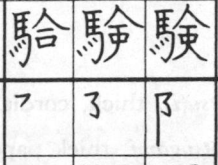	GEN; *kagi(ri)*, limit, end, as far as possible; *kagi(ru)*, to limit, to restrict 制限 *seigen*, limitation 期限 *kigen*, term 無限 *mugen*, infinity
現 602 11 strokes	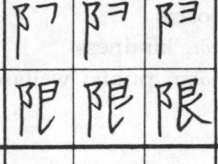	GEN (present, now); *ara(wareru)*, to show oneself, to come into sight, to be found (out); *ara(wasu)*, to manifest, to expose, to express 実現 *jitsugen*, realization 表現 *hyōgen*, expression 現代 *gendai*, present age (見 67)
個 603 10 strokes	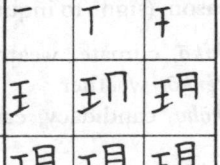	KO (individual), suffix for enumeration 個人 *kojin*, individual 個性 *kosei*, individual character, personality 数個 *sūko*, several (口 27)
護 604 20 strokes	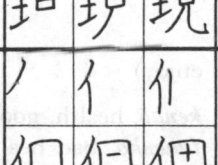	GO (to protect, to defend) 保護 *hogo*, protection 看護婦 *kangofu*, trained nurse 弁護士 *bengoshi*, lawyer (言 392, 隹 集 243)

功	一 丅 工	KŌ, merits, effect, service; KU
	工力 功	成功 *seikō*, success 功績 *kōseki*, meritorious deed 功労 *kōrō*, services
605 5 strokes		
厚	一 厂 厂	KŌ; *atsu(i)*, thick, cordial
	厂 厂 厚	厚紙 *atsugami*, thick paper, cardboard 厚意 *kōi*, kindness 厚生 *kōsei*, public welfare
606 9 strokes	厚 厚 厚	
候	亻 亻 亻	KŌ, season, (sign; to inquire after)
	亻 亻 亻	気候 *kikō*, climate, weather 天候 *tenkō*, weather 候補 *kōho*, candidacy, candidate
607 10 strokes	候 候 候	
康	丶 亠 广	KŌ (to enjoy)
	广 庀 庀	健康 *kenkō*, health, good health 不健康 *fukenkō*, bad health
608 11 strokes	庚 康 康	
講	言 言 讠	KŌ (investigation, lecture; to think out, to study, to explain)
	講 講 講	講演 *kōen*, lecture 講堂 *kōdō*, auditorium 講習 *kōshū*, short training course
609 17 strokes	講 講 講	(言 392)

鉱	610 13 strokes	KŌ (ore) 鉱山 *kōzan*, mine 鉱物 *kōbutsu*, mineral 鉄鉱 *tekkō*, iron ore (金 16)
査	611 9 strokes	SA (to examine, to investigate) 検査 *kensa*, inspection, examination 巡査 *junsa*, policeman 審査 *shinsa*, screening
際	612 14 strokes	SAI, occasion 実際 *jissai*, actual state, truth, reality 国際 *kokusai*, international 交際 *kōsai*, intercourse, acquaintance, association (祭 400)
在	613 6 strokes	ZAI, country, suburbs, (to exist) 存在 *sonzai*, existence, being 滞在 *taizai*, sojourn 現在 *genzai*, present time, present tense
殺	614 10 strokes	SATSU, SAI; *koro(su)*, to kill 殺人 *satsujin*, homicide, murder 殺風景 *sappūkei*, tasteless, dreary 自殺 *jisatsu*, suicide (又 収 631)

雑 615 14 strokes		ZATSU, rough; ZŌ (miscellaneous, rough) 複雑 *fukuzatsu*, complexity, complication 雑誌 *zasshi*, magazine 雑きん *zōkin*, floorcloth, mopping cloth (木 15)
参 616 8 strokes		SAN, three (used in legal papers); *mai(ru)*, to go, to come, to surrender, to be nonplussed, to visit for worship 参加 *sanka*, participation 参観 *sankan*, visit 参考書 *sankōsho*, reference book
蚕 617 10 strokes		SAN; *kaiko*, silkworm 養蚕 *yōsan*, sericulture 蚕室 *sanshitsu*, silkworm rearing room 養蚕地 *yōsanchi*, silkworm raising district (口 27)
酸 618 14 strokes		SAN, acid 酸素 *sanso*, oxygen 塩酸 *ensan*, hydrochloric acid 酸化 *sanka*, oxidization
賛 619 15 strokes		SAN (to praise, to assist, to agree) 賛成 *sansei*, approval, support 賛助 *sanjo*, support, help 協賛 *kyōsan*, cooperation (貝 169)

氏 620 4 strokes	一 ノ 氏	SHI, Mister (used as suffix); *uji*, family name, lineage 氏名 *shimei*, full name 氏族制度 *shizoku-seido*, the clan or the family system 諸氏 *shoshi*, Messrs., gentlemen
支 621 4 strokes	一 十 ㇇ 支	SHI (branch; to branch off, to support) 支配 *shihai*, rule, management 支払う *shiharau*, to pay 支店 *shiten*, a branch (store, office)
示 622 5 strokes	一 二 ㇇ 示 示	SHI, JI; *shime(su)*, to show, to point out 示唆 *shisa*, suggestion 掲示 *keiji*, notice 指示 *shiji*, instructions, indication
志 623 7 strokes	一 十 士 ㇇ 志 志 志	SHI; *kokorozashi*, will, intention, ambition, aim, kindness; *kokoroza(su)*, to intend, to aim at 意志 *ishi*, will 志望 *shibō*, desire 同志 *dōshi*, comrade
師 624 10 strokes	ノ 亻 阝 阝 阝 阝 師 師 師	SHI, teacher, expert; army 牧師 *bokushi*, pastor 教師 *kyōshi*, teacher 師団 *shidan*, division (army)

似 625 7 strokes	似	JI; *ni(ru)*, to resemble 類似 *ruiji*, similarity 似顔 *nigao*, portrait, likeness 不似合 *funiai*, unbecoming
辞 626 13 strokes	辞	JI, word, speech; *ji(suru)*, to resign, to take one's leave, to decline 辞書 *jisho*, dictionary 辞職 *jishoku*, resignation 祝辞 *shukuji*, congratulatory address (口 27, 立 149)
識 627 19 strokes	識	SHIKI (to know, to write down, to distinguish) 知識 *chishiki*, knowledge 標識 *hyōshiki*, mark 常識 *jōshiki*, common sense (言 392, 日 11)
質 628 15 strokes	質	SHITSU, quality, substance, (to inquire; simple and honest); SHICHI, pawn 質問 *shitsumon*, question 素質 *soshitsu*, makings, quality 質屋 *shichiya*, pawnshop (貝 169)
舎 629 8 strokes	舎	SHA (house, lodging) 校舎 *kōsha*, school building 牛舎 *gyūsha*, cowshed 宿舎 *shukusha*, lodging

謝 630 17 strokes	言 訁 訁 訓 謝 謝 謝 謝 謝	SHA; *sha*(*suru*), to apologize, to thank 感謝 *kansha*, thanks 謝絶 *shazetsu*, refusal 謝礼 *sharei*, remuneration, thanks (言 392, 身 255)
収 631 4 strokes	丨 ㇇ 收 收	SHŪ; *osa*(*meru*), to obtain, to pay (taxes), to accept, to store, to seize 収穫 *shūkaku*, harvest 収容 *shūyō*, admission, accommodation 収入 *shūnyū*, income
周 632 8 strokes	丿 冂 冂 冂 冂 周 周 周	SHŪ (circumference; to go round) 周囲 *shūi*, circumference, surroundings 周辺 *shūhen*, outskirts 一周 *isshū*, one round
修 633 10 strokes	丿 亻 亻 亻 亻 攸 攸 攸 修	SHŪ, SHU; *osa*(*meru*), to study, to finish, to practice 修理 *shūri*, repair 改修 *kaishū*, improvement, repair 修正 *shūsei*, amendment
宿 634 11 strokes	丶 丶 宀 宀 宿 宿 宿 宿 宿	SHUKU; *yado*, inn; *yado*(*ru*), to lodge at 宿屋 *yadoya*, inn 宿題 *shukudai*, homework 下宿 *geshuku*, boardinghouse (日 11)

祝 635 9 strokes	一 ラ 礻 礻 礻 礻口 礻口 礻口 祝	SHUKU; *iwa(i)*, celebration; *iwa-(u)*, to celebrate 祝賀 *shukuga*, celebration 祝福 *shukufuku*, blessing 祝日 *shukujitsu*, festival day
術 636 11 strokes	彳 彳 彳一 彳十 彳十 彳木 彳木 彳木二 術	JUTSU, art, artifice, means, magic 手術 *shujutsu*, surgical operation 技術 *gijutsu*, technique 美術 *bijutsu*, art (行 73)
準 637 13 strokes	氵 氵 氵 氵 氵 氵 准 準 準	JUN (water level; rule; to imitate); prefix denoting "semi-," "associate" 標準 *hyōjun*, standard 基準 *kijun*, standard 準急 *junkyū*, semi-express (氵 汽 60, 隹 集 243)
序 638 7 strokes	一 亠 广 广 广 序 序	JO, preface 順序 *junjo*, order, method 秩序 *chitsujo*, public order, discipline 序文 *jobun*, preface
承 639 8 strokes	了 了 子 子 子 承 承 承	SHŌ; *uketamawa(ru)*, to hear 承知 *shōchi*, consent, knowledge 承認 *shōnin*, approval 了承 *ryōshō*, acknowledgment

省	小 小 小 少 少 少	SHŌ, suffix for "government department"; SEI (to look); *habu-(ku)*, to omit, to cut down; *kaeri-(miru)*, to reflect upon (oneself) 省略 *shōryaku*, omission 外務省 *Gaimushō*, Ministry of Foreign Affairs (Japan) 反省 *hansei*, self-examination
640 9 strokes	省 省 省	
賞	小 小 小 尚 尚 尚	SHŌ, prize 賞品 *shōhin*, prize (thing) 賞金 *shōkin*, prize (money) 鑑賞 *kanshō*, appreciation
641 15 strokes	賞 賞 賞	(口 27, 貝 169)
常	小 小 小 尚 尚 尚	JŌ; *tsune*, usual, ordinary 非常に *hijō-ni*, very (much) 正常 *seijō*, normal 日常 *nichijō*, everyday
642 11 strokes	常 常 常	(口 27)
情	忄 忄 忄 忄一 忄十 忄キ	JŌ, feeling, sympathy; *nasa(ke)*, feeling, sympathy, love, mercy 愛情 *aijō*, affection 情け深い *nasakebukai*, compassionate 情勢 *jōsei*, state of things
643 11 strokes	忄主 情 情	(月 12)
織	糸 糸 糸 糸 糸 糸	SHOKU, SHIKI; *ori*, textile; *o(ru)*, to weave 織物 *orimono*, textile fabric 織機 *shokki*, weaving machine 組織 *soshiki*, organization
644 18 strokes	織 織 織	(糸 83, 日 11)

性 645 8 strokes		SEI, sex, nature; SHŌ, nature, temperament 性質 *seishitsu*, nature, property 習性 *shūsei*, habit 気性 *kishō*, temper
政 646 9 strokes		SEI, SHŌ; *matsurigoto*, government 政府 *seifu*, government 政治 *seiji*, administration, politics 政策 *seisaku*, policy
精 647 14 strokes		SEI, spirit, vitality, essence; SHŌ 精神 *seishin*, spirit, mind, soul 精巧 *seikō*, exquisite (workmanship) 精進 *shōjin*, diligence (米 135, 青 36)
製 648 14 strokes	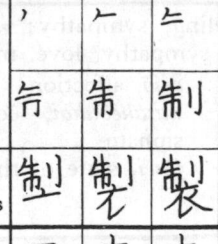	SEI (to manufacture), suffix for "make" or "manufacture" 製品 *seihin*, manufactured goods 銀製 *ginsei*, made of silver 米国製 *Beikokusei*, of American make (制 823, 衣 341)
責 649 11 strokes	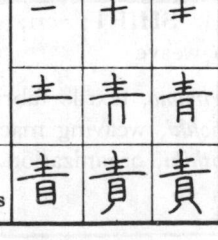	SEKI; *se*(*meru*), to blame, to urge, to torture 責任 *sekinin*, responsibility 責任者 *sekininsha*, person responsible 無責任 *musekinin*, irresponsibility (貝 169)

績	糸	SEKI (to spin; meritorious deed) 成績 *seiseki*, result, record 功績 *kōseki*, meritorious deeds 紡績 *bōseki*, spinning
650 17 strokes	績	(糸 83, 貝 169)
折	折	SETSU; *o(ru)*, to break, to fold, to bend 曲折 *kyokusetsu*, winding, complications 折合 *oriai*, mutual relations, compromise 折り目 *orime*, crease
651 7 strokes	折	
接	接	SETSU; *ses(suru)*, to come in contact with, to receive, to adjoin 直接 *chokusetsu*, directly 接待 *settai*, reception 接続 *setsuzoku*, junction (扌 折 651)
652 11 strokes	接	
設	設	SETSU; *mō(keru)*, to establish 設備 *setsubi*, equipment 設計 *sekkei*, plan, design (for construction) 建設 *kensetsu*, construction (言 392)
653 11 strokes	設	
説	説	SETSU, opinion, theory; ZEI; *to(ku)*, to explain, to persuade, to preach 説明 *setsumei*, explanation 伝説 *densetsu*, legend 社説 *shasetsu*, editorial (口 27)
654 14 strokes	説	

浅 655 9 strokes		SEN; *asa(i)*, shallow 浅見 *senken*, superficial view 浅薄 *sempaku*, superficial 遠浅 *tōasa*, shoaling beach, shallowness extending far from shore
銭 656 14 strokes		SEN, former unit of money (a hundredth part of a yen); *zeni*, money 金銭 *kinsen*, money こづかい銭 *kozukaisen*, pocket money (戔 浅 655)
祖 657 9 strokes		SO [ZO], ancestor, founder 祖国 *sokoku*, fatherland 祖母 *sobo*, grandmother 先祖 *senzo*, ancestor
素 658 10 strokes	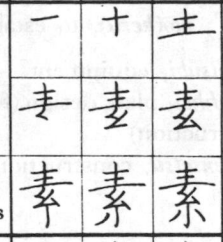	SO, SU (white, origin, source) 素ぼく *soboku*, simple 要素 *yōso*, element, important factor 素顔 *sugao*, unpainted face
倉 659 10 strokes		SŌ; *kura*, warehouse 倉庫 *sōko*, warehouse 船倉 *sensō*, hold (of a ship) 米倉 *komegura*, rice granary (口 27)

想 660 13 strokes	一 十 才 木 机 相 相 想 想	SŌ, idea, thought 想像 *sōzō*, imagination 理想 *risō*, ideal 予想 *yosō*, expectation (目 25, 心 95)
総 661 14 strokes	〈 幺 糸 糸 糸 糸 総 総 総	SŌ (whole, general) 総理大臣 *sōri-daijin*, prime minister 総員 *sōin*, entire staff, all hands, full force 総選挙 *sōsenkyo*, general election (糸 83, 心 95)
造 662 10 strokes	ノ 亠 ⺈ ⺈ 生 告 告 造 造	ZŌ; *tsuku(ri)*, structure, build (n.); *tsuku(ru)*, to make, to create, to build; ~*zuku(ri)*, made of ~ (suffix denoting type of structure) 木造 *mokuzō*, made of wood 人造 *jinzō*, artificial 石造り *ishizukuri*, built of stone (口 77)
象 663 12 strokes	ノ 冂 冂 冂 冂 冂 象 象 象	ZŌ, elephant; SHŌ (image) 対象 *taishō*, object 印象 *inshō*, impression 象げ *zōge*, ivory
像 664 14 strokes	ノ 亻 亻 亻 亻 亻 像 像 像	ZŌ, image, figure 銅像 *dōzō*, bronze statue 仏像 *butsuzō*, image of Buddha 現像 *genzō*, development (of a film)

665 14 strokes	増	ZŌ; *ma(su)*, to increase (v. i. & v. t.) 増加 *zōka*, increase 増強 *zōkyō*, reinforcement 増進 *zōshin*, promotion (田 40, 日 11)
666 9 strokes	則	SOKU (law; to act on) 法則 *hōsoku*, law 規則 *kisoku*, rule 原則 *gensoku*, principle
667 11 strokes	側	SOKU; *kawa* [*gawa*], side 内側 *uchigawa*, the inside 右側 *migigawa*, *usoku*, right side 側面 *sokumen*, the side
668 12 strokes	測	SOKU; *haka(ru)*, to fathom, to measure 観測 *kansoku*, observation 測量 *sokuryō*, surveying 測定 *sokutei*, measurement
669 10 strokes	帯	TAI; *obi*, girdle; *o(biru)*, to wear 地帯 *chitai*, zone 熱帯 *nettai*, torrid zone, tropics 帯封 *obifū*, half wrapper

貸 670 12 strokes	亻 亻 亻 代 代 代 貸 貸 貸	TAI ; *ka*(*shi*), loan ; *ka*(*su*), to lend, to loan, to hire out 貸家 *kashiya*, house for rent 貸ボート *kashibōto*, boat for hire 貸借 *taishaku*, borrowing and lending
単 671 9 strokes	丶 ⺍ ⺍ ⺍ 𠂆 𠂆 𠂆 𠂆 単	TAN (single) 単純 *tanjun*, simple 簡単 *kantan*, simple, easy 単価 *tanka*, unit price
団 672 6 strokes	丨 冂 冂 冂 冂 団	DAN, association ; *~dan*, suffix for "troupe" or "company" 団体 *dantai*, party, organization 楽団 *gakudan*, band (musical) 団結 *danketsu*, unity
築 673 16 strokes	𥫗 𥫗 𥫗 竹 竹 竹 筑 筑 築	CHIKU ; *kizu*(*ku*), to build 建築 *kenchiku*, building 築造 *chikuzō*, construction 新築 *shinchiku*, new building (竹 113, 木 15)
貯 674 12 strokes	冂 目 貝 貝 貝 貝 貯 貯 貯	CHO (to store, to save) 貯水池 *chosuichi*, reservoir 貯蔵 *chozō*, storage 貯金 *chokin*, savings (貝 169)

張 675 11 strokes	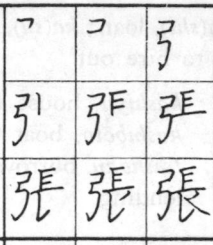	CHŌ; *ha(ri)* [*pa(ri)*, *ba(ri)*], tension, expansion; *ha(ru)*, to stretch, to spread, to cover 見張り *mihari*, lookout 引っ張る *hipparu*, to pull 主張 *shuchō*, insistence, opinion (長 116)
腸 676 13 strokes		CHŌ, the intestines 盲腸 *mōchō*, (vermiform) appendix 大腸 *daichō*, large intestine 腸カタル *chōkataru*, intestinal catarrh (月 12, 日 11)
低 677 7 strokes	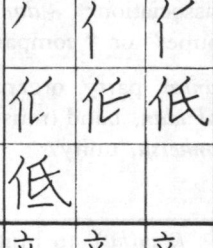	TEI; *hiku(i)*, low, short 低気圧 *tei-kiatsu*, low atmospheric pressure 低空 *teikū*, low altitude 低地 *teichi*, low ground
敵 678 15 strokes	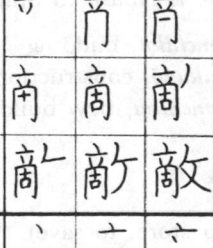	TEKI, enemy, opponent 強敵 *kyōteki*, formidable enemy 敵意 *teki-i*, hostile feeling 敵国 *tekikoku*, enemy country
適 679 14 strokes	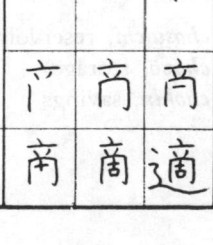	TEKI; *teki(suru)*, to be fit for 適当 *tekitō*, suitable, moderate 適任 *tekinin*, fitness 快適 *kaiteki*, agreeable (辶 近 195)

典	680 8 strokes	TEN (ceremony, celebration) 辞典 *jiten*, dictionary 古典 *koten*, classics 祭典 *saiten*, festival, rite
伝	681 6 strokes	DEN; *tsuta(eru)*, to report, to impart, to transmit; *tsuta(waru)*, to be reported (imparted, transmitted) 伝記 *denki*, biography 伝染病 *densembyō*, epidemic 宣伝 *senden*, propaganda
統	682 12 strokes	TŌ; *su(beru)*, to control 統計 *tōkei*, statistics 大統領 *daitōryō*, president (of a country) 伝統 *dentō*, tradition (糸 83)
銅	683 14 strokes	DŌ, copper 青銅 *seidō*, bronze 銅線 *dōsen*, copper wire 銅山 *dōzan*, copper mine (金 16, 口 27)
導	684 15 strokes	DŌ; *michibi(ki)*, guidance; *michibi(ku)*, to guide, to lead 指導 *shidō*, guidance 指導者 *shidōsha*, leader 補導 *hodō*, guidance (目 25, 辶 近 195)

特 685 10 strokes	牛 牛 牛 牛 牛 牛 牛 特 特	TOKU (special) 特別 *tokubetsu*, special, particular 特長 *tokuchō*, strong point 特急 *tokkyū*, limited express (土 17)
毒 686 8 strokes	一 十 ⺾ 主 毒 毒 毒 毒	DOKU, poison 気の毒 *ki-no-doku*, sorry, pitiful 毒草 *dokusō*, poisonous herb 中毒 *chūdoku*, poisoning
独 687 9 strokes	丿 犭 犭 犭 犭 犭 犭 独 独	DOKU (one person; Germany) 独立 *dokuritsu*, independence 独特 *dokutoku*, peculiar, unique 独唱 *dokushō*, vocal solo
任 688 6 strokes	丿 亻 亻 仁 任 任	NIN, duty; *maka(seru)*, to entrust, to leave (v. t.) 責任 *sekinin*, responsibility 転任 *tennin*, change of post 任務 *nimmu*, duty
念 689 8 strokes	丿 ⺅ 今 今 今 念 念 念	NEN, thought, feeling, desire 記念 *kinen*, commemoration 残念 *zannen*, regret, disappointment 念願 *nengan*, one's heart's desire

燃	690 16 strokes	NEN; *mo(eru)*, to burn (v. i.); *mo(yasu)*, to burn (v. t.) 燃料 *nenryō*, fuel 燃焼 *nenshō*, combustion 不燃性 *funensei*, incombustible (然 450)
能	691 10 strokes	NŌ, ability, the *Noh* 能力 *nōryoku*, ability, capacity, faculty 才能 *sainō*, talent 能率 *nōritsu*, efficiency
破	692 10 strokes	HA [PA]; *yabu(re)*, a tear (rent); *yabu(ru)*, to tear, to break (a promise) 破損 *hason*, breakdown 破産 *hasan*, bankruptcy 難破 *nampa*, shipwreck
敗	693 11 strokes	HAI [PAI]; *yabu(reru)*, to be defeated 敗戦 *haisen*, lost battle 腐敗 *fuhai*, putrefaction, corruption 失敗 *shippai*, failure (貝 169)
倍	694 10 strokes	BAI, two times, double; suffix denoting "times" 数倍 *sūbai*, several times 何倍 *nambai*, how many times? 倍率 *bairitsu*, magnifying power (口 27)

博	695 12 strokes	HAKU (learned; to spread; abundant) 博士 *hakushi*, doctor (degree) 博物館 *hakubutsukan*, museum 博覧会 *hakurankai*, exposition (専 830)
飯	696 12 strokes	HAN; *meshi*, boiled rice, a meal 朝飯 *asahan*, *asameshi*, breakfast 昼飯 *hirumeshi*, lunch 夕飯 *yūhan*, *yūmeshi*, supper (食 253)
比	697 4 strokes	HI, ratio, comparison; *kura*(*beru*), to compare 比較 *hikaku*, comparison 比率 *hiritsu*, ratio 比例 *hirei*, proportion
非	698 8 strokes	HI, fault, wrong; non-, un- 非常に *hijō-ni*, very 非常口 *hijōguchi*, emergency door 非難 *hinan*, censure
肥	699 8 strokes	HI; *ko*(*eru*), to grow fat; *ko*(*yasu*), to fertilize, to fatten, to enrich (oneself) 肥料 *hiryō*, manure, fertilizer たい肥 *taihi*, compost

備	700 12 strokes	BI; *sona(e)*, preparation(s); *sona-(eru)*, to furnish, to prepare; *sona-(waru)*, to be possessed of, to be furnished with 準備 *jumbi*, preparation(s) 守備 *shubi*, defense 予備 *yobi*, reserve (用 146)
筆	701 12 strokes	HITSU [PITSU]; *fude*, writing brush 万年筆 *mannenhitsu*, fountain pen 鉛筆 *empitsu*, pencil 筆者 *hissha*, writer
俵	702 10 strokes	HYŌ [BYŌ, PYŌ]; *tawara* [*da-wara*], straw bag 土俵 *dohyō*, sandbag; sumō (wrestling) ring 一俵 *ippyō*, one straw bag 炭俵 *sumidawara*, charcoal sack
票	703 11 strokes	HYŌ [PYŌ], vote 投票 *tōhyō*, voting 伝票 *dempyō*, chit 五十票 *gojippyō*, fifty votes (示 622)
標	704 15 strokes	HYŌ (mark, sign; to write down, to express) 標本 *hyōhon*, specimen 標語 *hyōgo*, motto 目標 *mokuhyō*, mark, object

貧		HIN, poverty; BIN; *mazu(shii)*, poor 貧弱 *hinjaku*, meager, poor 貧乏 *bimbō*, poverty 貧困 *hinkon*, poverty, lack (貝 169)
705 11 strokes		
布	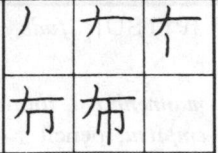	FU [PU]; *nuno*, cloth 毛布 *mōfu*, blanket 配布 *haifu*, distribution 綿布 *mempu*, cotton cloth
706 5 strokes		
婦		FU (woman, wife) 婦人 *fujin*, woman 主婦 *shufu*, housewife 夫婦 *fūfu*, husband and wife (女 32)
707 11 strokes		
武		BU, MU, military 武装 *busō*, arms, weapons 武器 *buki*, weapon 武力 *buryoku*, military power
708 8 strokes		
副		FUKU (vice-, sub-, secondary) 副詞 *fukushi*, adverb 副会長 *fukukaichō*, vice-president (of a society) 副業 *fukugyō*, side job (刂 27)
709 11 strokes		

復 710 12 strokes		FUKU (re-, again, repeat) 回復 *kaifuku*, recovery 復興 *fukkō*, revival, reconstruction 復活 *fukkatsu*, revival, resurrection (日 11)
仏 711 4 strokes	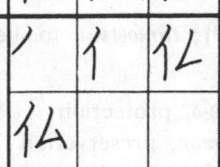	BUTSU; *hotoke*, Buddha 大仏 *daibutsu*, colossal statue of Buddha 仏像 *butsuzō*, image of Buddha 仏教 *bukkyō*, Buddhism
兵 712 7 strokes	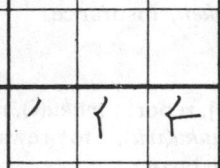	HEI, soldier 兵隊 *heitai*, soldier 兵器 *heiki*, arms 兵士 *heishi*, soldier
辺 713 5 strokes	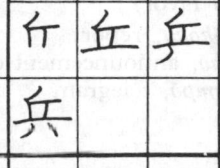	HEN [PEN], side, neighborhood 底辺 *teihen*, the base (geom.) 周辺 *shūhen*, outskirts 近辺 *kimpen*, neighborhood
編 714 15 strokes	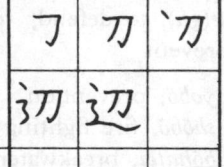	HEN; *a(mu)*, to knit, to edit 編集 *henshū*, editing 編集者 *henshūsha*, editor 編成 *hensei*, formation (糸 83)

弁 715 5 strokes	丶 ム 厶 弁 弁	BEN, speech 弁論 *benron*, debate 弁護人 *bengonin*, counsel 弁当 *bentō*, lunch
保 716 9 strokes	丿 亻 仁 仁 仁 但 保 保 保	HO [PO]; *tamo(tsu)*, to keep, to maintain 保護 *hogo*, protection 保存 *hozon*, preservation 保険 *hoken*, insurance
報 717 12 strokes	土 幸 幸 幸 幸 幸 報 報 報	HŌ [PŌ], report; *muku(i)*, retribution; *muku(iru)*, to reward, to return (a favor) 報告 *hōkoku*, report 時報 *jihō*, announcement of time 電報 *dempō*, telegram (土 17)
防 718 7 strokes	阝 阝 阝 阝 阝 防 防	BŌ; *fuse(gu)*, to defend, to keep off, to prevent 予防 *yobō*, prevention 消防 *shōbō*, fire fighting 防波堤 *bōhatei*, breakwater
貿 719 12 strokes	丶 ⺈ ⺈ ⺈ ⺈ 卯 貿 貿 貿	BŌ (to purchase, to exchange) 貿易商 *bōekishō*, trader 貿易会社 *bōekigaisha*, trading firm 貿易風 *bōekifū*, trade wind (目 25)

牧	720 8 strokes	BOKU; *maki* (pasture) 牧場 *bokujō*, *makiba*, stock farm 牧草 *bokusō*, grass 放牧 *hōboku*, grazing
満	721 12 strokes	MAN, fullness; *mi(chiru)*, to fill (v. i.), to rise (tide), to wax (moon); *man*~, prefix denoting "full" 満員 *man-in*, filled to capacity 満月 *mangetsu*, full moon 満七歳 *man-shichisai*, full seven years old (氵汽 60)
務	722 11 strokes	MU; *tsuto(me)*, duties 事務所 *jimusho*, office 勤務 *kimmu*, service, duty 義務 *gimu*, duty (予 525)
無	723 12 strokes	MU, BU; *na(shi)* (lit.), *na(i)*, to be non-existent, not to have, to be missing, to lack, to be deceased 無理 *muri*, unreasonable, compulsory, impossible, excessive 無線 *musen*, wireless (radio) 無事 *buji*, safe, peaceful, well
迷	724 9 strokes	MEI; *mayo(u)*, to be puzzled, to lose one's way, to go astray, to be tempted by; *mayo(wasu)*, to lead astray, to puzzle, to tempt 迷信 *meishin*, superstition 迷惑 *meiwaku*, trouble, annoyance

綿 725 14 strokes		MEN; *wata*, cotton 綿屋 *wataya*, cotton shop (dealer) 綿密 *memmitsu*, minute, careful (糸 83, 白 37)
約 726 9 strokes		YAKU (promise, abridgment); approximately, about (prefix) 約束 *yakusoku*, promise, appointment, regulations 予約 *yoyaku*, subscription, pre-engagement 約四十分 *yaku-yonjippun*, about forty minutes
輸 727 16 strokes		YU (to send) 輸出 *yushutsu*, export 輸血 *yuketsu*, blood transfusion 輸送 *yusō*, transportation (車 88)
余 728 7 strokes		YO, more (than), above; *ama(ri)*, the remainder, the balance; ~*ama-(ri)*, more than, over; *ama(ru)*, to remain, to be beyond (one's power); *ama(su)*, to leave over 余分 *yobun*, surplus 余暇 *yoka*, spare time 余地 *yochi*, room, scope
要 729 9 strokes	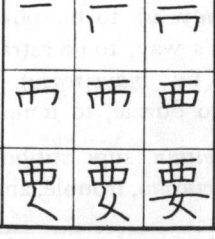	YŌ, the main point, necessity; *yō(suru)*, to require, to need 必要 *hitsuyō*, necessity, need 要求 *yōkyū*, request, demand 重要 *jūyō*, important

容 730 10 strokes		YŌ (figure; to admit) 形容詞 *keiyōshi*, adjective 内容 *naiyō*, content, substance 容積 *yōseki*, capacity, cubic measure (口 27)
養 731 15 strokes	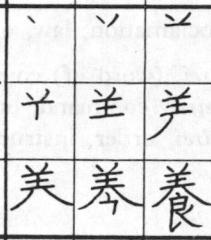	YŌ; *yashina(u)*, to bring up, to support, to recuperate, to cultivate 教養 *kyōyō*, culture 養成 *yōsei*, training 養殖 *yōshoku*, raising, culture (良 530)
浴 732 10 strokes		YOKU; *a(biru)*, to bathe oneself in (water, the sun) 水浴び *mizu-abi*, bathing 入浴 *nyūyoku*, taking a bath 日光浴 *nikkō-yoku*, sun bath (口 27)
留 733 10 strokes		RYŪ, RU; *to(meru)*, to fasten, to stop (v.t.) 停留所 *teiryūjo*, streetcar (bus) stop 留学 *ryūgaku*, studying abroad 留守 *rusu*, absence
量 734 12 strokes	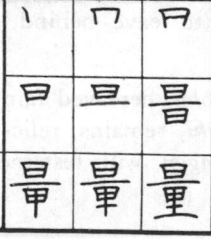	RYŌ, quantity, measure; *haka(ru)*, to weigh, to measure 雨量 *uryō*, rainfall 重量 *jūryō*, weight 分量 *bunryō*, quantity

領 735 14 strokes	令 令一 令丅 令丅 令百 領 領 領 領	RYŌ (chief point; to control) 要領 *yōryō*, the point, knack 領土 *ryōdo*, territory 領事 *ryōji*, consul (令 736, 貝 169)
令 736 5 strokes	ノ 人 亼 今 令	REI (proclamation, law, order) 号令 *gōrei*, (word of) command 命令 *meirei*, command, order 指令 *shirei*, order, instructions
例 737 8 strokes	ノ 亻 仁 仁 仁 例 例 例	REI, example 例外 *reigai*, exception 実例 *jitsurei*, (concrete) example 例年 *reinen*, ordinary year, every year
異 738 11 strokes	丶 冂 田 田 田 異 異 異	I; *koto*(*naru*), to be different, to be unusual 異常 *ijō*, unusual 異論 *iron*, different opinion, objection 異様 *iyō*, strange, odd, extraordinary (田 40)
遺 739 15 strokes	口 中 虫 貴 貴 貴 遺 遺 遺	I, YUI (to leave behind, to bequeath) 遺族 *izoku*, bereaved family 遺跡 *iseki*, remains, relics 遺言 *yuigon*, will, testament (口 27, 貝 169)

壱 740 7 strokes	一 十 士 十 壱 壱 壱	ICHI, one (used in writing checks and legal documents) 壱万円 *ichiman-en*, ten thousand yen 壱千弐百円 *issen-nihyaku-en*, one thousand two hundred yen
営 741 12 strokes	丶 丷 丷 丷 宀 営 営 営	EI; *itona(mi)*, occupation; *itona(mu)*, to run (a hotel), to perform (a religious service) 経営 *keiei*, management, operation 営業 *eigyō*, business, trade, operation (口 27)
益 742 10 strokes	丶 丶 ⺍ ⺍ 兴 兴 兴 益 益	EKI, benefit, profit; *eki(suru)*, to benefit 利益 *rieki*, gain, benefit 有益 *yūeki*, instructive, profitable 益虫 *ekichū*, useful insect
延 743 7 strokes	ノ 彳 彳 彳 正 延 延	EN; *no(biru)*, to be postponed, to be extended; *no(basu)*, to postpone, to extend; *no(be)*, total 延長 *enchō*, prolongation, extension 延着 *enchaku*, late arrival 延期 *enki*, postponement
可 744 5 strokes	一 丨 冂 可 可	KA, good, approval 可決 *kaketsu*, approval 可能 *kanō*, possibility 不可能 *fukanō*, impossibility

我	745 7 strokes	GA; *ware*, self, oneself, I 我々 *ware-ware*, we 無我 *muga*, selflessness, ecstasy 我流 *garyū*, one's own way, self-taught method
革	746 9 strokes	KAKU (leather; to reform) 革命 *kakumei*, revolution 革新 *kakushin*, innovation, reform 改革 *kaikaku*, reform
拡	747 8 strokes	KAKU (to extend, to unfold, to spread) 拡大 *kakudai*, magnification 拡張 *kakuchō*, extension, expansion 拡声機 *kakuseiki*, loud-speaker
額	748 18 strokes	GAKU, framed picture, amount (of money); *hitai*, forehead 金額 *kingaku*, amount of money 総額 *sōgaku*, sum total 多額 *tagaku*, large sum (客 184, 貝 169)
株	749 10 strokes	*kabu*, shares, stocks, speculation in shares, stub 切り株 *kirikabu*, stump 株式会社 *kabushiki-kaisha*, joint-stock corporation 株券 *kabuken*, share certificate

刊	一	二	干	KAN (publication, edition) 刊行 *kankō*, publication 週刊 *shūkan*, weekly publication 新刊 *shinkan*, new publication
	干丨	刊		
750 5 strokes				
幹	一	十	吉	KAN; *miki*, trunk (of a tree) 幹部 *kambu*, the executive, leading members 根幹 *konkan*, basis, root 幹線 *kansen*, trunk line (早 104)
	朝	朝	朝	
751 13 strokes	朝	朝	幹	
勧	ノ	亠	亠	KAN; *susu*(*meru*), to advise, to persuade, to encourage 勧業銀行 *kangyō-ginkō*, hypothec bank 勧告 *kankoku*, advice, counsel 勧誘 *kan-yū*, invitation, canvass (力 148)
	年	年	年	
752 13 strokes	年	雚	勧	
歓	亠	年	年	KAN (to rejoice) 歓迎 *kangei*, welcome 歓待 *kantai*, warm reception 歓談 *kandan*, pleasant talk
	雚	雚	雚	
753 15 strokes	歓	歓	歓	
眼	丨	冂	目	GAN; *manako*, eye 肉眼 *nikugan*, naked eye 近眼 *kingan*, near-sightedness 双眼鏡 *sōgankyō*, binoculars (目 25)
	目	目	目	
754 11 strokes	眼	眼	眼	

基	一	十	廿	KI; *motoi*, foundation, basis; *moto(zuku)*, to be based on
	甘	甘	甚	基本 *kihon*, foundation, basis, standard
755 11 strokes	其	其	基	基地 *kichi*, (air, etc.) base 基礎 *kiso*, foundation, basis
貴	口	中	虫	KI (noble, dear, precious)
	青	青	青	貴重 *kichō*, precious 貴金属 *kikinzoku*, precious metals 貴重品 *kichōhin*, valuables
756 12 strokes	貴	貴	貴	(貝 169, 冂 27)
疑	ノ	匕	匕 匕	GI; *utaga(i)*, doubt, suspicion; *utaga(u)*, to doubt, to suspect
	矢	矢	矢	疑問 *gimon*, question, doubt 質疑 *shitsugi*, question 疑惑 *giwaku*, suspicion, doubt
757 14 strokes	疑	疑	疑	(矢 112)
逆	丶	丶	屰	GYAKU, inverse, reverse; *gyaku(m)*, inversely, reversely; *saka(rau)*, to oppose, to go against
	屰	屰	屰	逆転 *gyakuten*, reversal, going backward 逆境 *gyakkyō*, adversity 反逆 *hangyaku*, treason
758 9 strokes	逆	逆	逆	
旧	丨	丨丨	丨冂	KYŪ (old)
	丨冂	丨日		旧式 *kyūshiki*, old-style 旧跡 *kyūseki*, place of historic interest 旧暦 *kyūreki*, lunar calendar
759 5 strokes				

供 760 8 strokes	丿 亻 亻一 亻十 亻亻 亻共 亻共 亻共	KYŌ, GU; *tomo*, attendant; *sona-(eru)*, to offer (to a god) 供給 *kyōkyū*, supply, provision 提供 *teikyō*, offer 供出 *kyōshutsu*, quota delivery
境 761 14 strokes	土 土立 土立 土竟 土竟 土竟 土竟 土竟 境	KYŌ, KEI; *sakai*, border, boundary, border line 境遇 *kyōgū*, circumstances, surroundings 国境 *kokkyō*, frontier 境内 *keidai*, precincts (土 17, 立 149)
勤 762 12 strokes	一 十 廿 廿 廿 廿 廿 勤 勤	KIN; *tsuto(me)*, duties, service; *tsuto(meru)*, to serve (in an office) 勤務 *kimmu*, service, duty 勤勉 *kimben*, diligence 出勤 *shukkin*, attendance (口 27)
禁 763 13 strokes	一 十 才 木 林 禁 禁 禁 禁	KIN; *kin~*, prefix for "forbidden" or "prohibited"; *kin(jiru)*, to forbid, to abstain from 禁止 *kinshi*, prohibition, ban 禁煙 *kin-en*, "No Smoking" 禁酒 *kinshu*, abstinence from alcoholic beverages
訓 764 10 strokes	丶 亠 言 言 言 言 訓 訓 訓	KUN (precept), Japanese rendering of a Chinese character (i.e., "kun" reading) 教訓 *kyōkun*, teachings, lesson 訓練 *kunren*, training, drill 訓辞 *kunji*, address of instructions

系 765 7 strokes	一 ⺈ 乡 幺 糸 系 系 系	KEI (system, family line) 系統 *keitō*, system, family line 系図 *keizu*, genealogical table 家系 *kakei*, family line
敬 766 12 strokes	一 艹 艹 艹 苟 苟 苟 苟 敬 敬 敬	KEI; *uyama(u)*, to respect 尊敬 *sonkei*, respect 敬語 *keigo*, honorific word 敬意 *kei-i*, respects (口 27)
潔 767 15 strokes	氵 氵 氵 氵 氵 氵 氵 氵 氵 氵 氵 氵 氵 氵 氵	KETSU; *isagiyo(i)*, manly, brave, pure 清潔 *seiketsu*, clean 潔白 *keppaku*, innocent, pure, upright 簡潔 *kanketsu*, concise (氵 汽 60, 糸 83)
券 768 8 strokes	丶 丶 ⺍ ⺍ 关 关 关 券 券	KEN, bond, ticket 定期券 *teikiken*, commutation ticket 旅券 *ryoken*, passport 入場券 *nyūjō-ken*, admission ticket, platform ticket
兼 769 10 strokes	丶 ⺍ 兰 兰 兰 兼 兼 兼 兼 兼	KEN, and, in addition, concurrently; *ka(neru)*, to combine, to serve in several capacities, to be unable to (suffix) 兼任 *kennin*, holding an additional post 兼備 *kembi*, combination 食べ兼ねる *tabekaneru*, to be unable to eat

険 770 11 strokes		KEN; *kewa(shii)*, steep, fierce 危険 *kiken*, danger 保険 *hoken*, insurance 冒険 *bōken*, adventure (口 27)
検 771 12 strokes		KEN (to examine) 探検 *tanken*, exploration 検診 *kenshin*, medical examination 検定 *kentei*, official approval (口 27)
絹 772 13 strokes		KEN; *kinu*, silk 絹糸 *kinu-ito*, silk thread 絹織物 *kinu-orimono*, silk fabrics 人絹 *jinken*, artificial silk, rayon (糸 83, 月 12)
憲 773 16 strokes		KEN (law, regulation) 憲法 *kempō*, constitution 憲兵 *kempei*, military police, shore patrol 憲章 *kenshō*, charter, constitution (心 95)
権 774 15 strokes		KEN (weight), authority, power; GON 人権 *jinken*, human rights 版権 *hanken*, copyright 政権 *seiken*, political power (木 15)

減 775 12 strokes	減	GEN; *he(ru)*, to decrease (v.i.), to wear out; *he(rasu)*, to decrease (v.t.) 加減 *kagen*, state of health, degree, adjustment, influence, addition and subtraction 減少 *genshō*, diminution, decrease 減退 *gentai*, decline, failing (口 27)
厳 776 17 strokes	厳	GEN, GON (severe, strict, austere) 厳禁 *genkin*, strict prohibition 厳格 *genkaku*, stern, austere 荘厳 *sōgon*, sublime, solemn (耳 26, 攵 故 778)
己 777 3 strokes	己	KO, KI (I, myself, oneself) 自己 *jiko*, one's self, self 利己主義 *rikoshugi*, egoism 知己 *chiki*, acquaintance, appreciative friend
故 778 9 strokes	故	KO (old, former times; reason) 事故 *jiko*, accident, hindrance 故郷 *kokyō*, one's native place 故障 *koshō*, mishap, trouble, accident, hindrance
誤 779 14 strokes	誤	GO; *ayama(ri)*, fault, mistake, error; *ayama(ru)*, to err, to mistake 誤解 *gokai*, misunderstanding 誤字 *goji*, wrong word 誤訳 *goyaku*, mistranslation

后 780 6 strokes	一 厂 厂 斤 后 后	KŌ [GŌ] (empress, queen) 皇后 *kōgō*, Empress (of Japan) 皇太后 *kōtaikō*, Empress Dowager (of Japan), Queen Mother (of England)
孝 781 7 strokes	一 十 土 耂 考 孝 孝	KŌ, filial duty 孝行 *kōkō*, filial piety 孝心 *kōshin*, filial affection 孝養 *kōyō*, discharge of filial duties
効 782 8 strokes	丶 亠 亠 六 交 交 交 効 効	KŌ, efficacy, effect 効果 *kōka*, effect, efficacy, result, sound effects 効力 *kōryoku*, effect, efficacy 有効 *yūkō*, valid, effective, efficacious
皇 783 9 strokes	丿 亻 白 白 白 皇 皇 皇 皇	KŌ, Ō (monarch, emperor) 皇太子 *kōtaishi*, Crown Prince (of Japan) 皇室 *kōshitsu*, Imperial Family (of Japan) 天皇 *tennō*, Emperor (of Japan)
耕 784 10 strokes	一 三 丰 耒 耒 耒一 耒二 耒十 耕	KŌ; *tagaya(su)*, to till 耕地 *kōchi*, arable (cultivated) land 耕作 *kōsaku*, cultivation 農耕 *nōkō*, farm labor

構	木	木一	木十	KŌ; *kama(e)* [*gama(e)*], structure, posture; *kama(eru)* [*gama(eru)*], to put oneself in a posture, to build 構成 *kōsei*, composition 構造 *kōzō*, structure, construction 心構え *kokorogamae*, mental attitude, preparation
	木廾	木丰	木丰	
785 14 strokes	構	構	構	
穀	士	士	士	KOKU (grain, cereals) 穀物 *kokumotsu*, grain, cereals 雑穀 *zakkoku*, minor cereals 穀類 *kokurui*, cereals, grain (士 410, 木 15)
	士	士	士	
786 14 strokes	穀	穀	穀	
混	丶	氵	氵	KON; *ma(zeru)*, to mix, to mingle; *ma(jiru)*, to be mixed, to be mingled; *kon(zuru)*, to mix, to confound 混乱 *konran*, confusion 混雑 *konzatsu*, congestion, confusion 混合 *kongō*, mixture
	氵口	氵日	氵日	
787 11 strokes	混	混	混	
再	一	一	冂	SAI, re- (prefix); *futata(bi)*, again 再建 *saiken*, reconstruction 再会 *saikai*, meeting again 再三 *saisan*, again and again
	冂	冂	再	
788 6 strokes				
災	巛	巛	巛	SAI; *wazawa(i)*, disaster, misfortune 災害 *saigai*, disaster, calamity 災難 *sainan*, misfortune, calamity 火災 *kasai*, fire, conflagration
	巛	巛	災	
789 7 strokes	災			

妻 790 8 strokes	一 ⺕ ⺕ ⺕ 事 妻 妻 妻	SAI, my wife; *tsuma* [*zuma*], wife 夫妻 *fusai*, husband and wife 妻子 *saishi*, wife and children 妻君 *saikun*, wife
採 791 11 strokes	一 扌 扌 扌 扌 扌 扌 採 採	SAI; *to*(*ru*), to gather (fruit, etc.), to employ (a person), to adopt (a measure) 採集 *saishū*, collection 採用 *saiyō*, employment, adoption 採掘 *saikutsu*, mining (木 15)
済 792 11 strokes	氵 氵 氵 氵 氵 氵 済 済 済	SAI [ZAI]; *su*(*mu*), to end, to be settled; *su*(*masu*), to finish, to pay back (a debt), to manage with (little money, etc.) 経済 *keizai*, economics, thrift 不経済 *fukeizai*, bad economy 返済 *hensai*, repayment (氵 水 60)
財 793 10 strokes	丨 冂 冂 目 貝 貝 貝 財 財	ZAI (treasure) 財産 *zaisan*, property, fortune 財政 *zaisei*, finance(s) 私財 *shizai*, private property
罪 794 13 strokes	丶 冂 罒 罒 罒 罒 罪 罪 罪	ZAI; *tsumi*, crime, sin 犯罪 *hanzai*, crime 罪悪 *zaiaku*, sin, crime 謝罪 *shazai*, apology

策	795 12 strokes	SAKU, policy, scheme, measure, plan 政策 *seisaku*, policy 策略 *sakuryaku*, stratagem 対策 *taisaku*, counterplan
至	796 6 strokes	SHI [JI]; *ita(ru)*, to reach, to go so far (as to), to come, to lead to, to be brought to 至急 *shikyū*, urgency 冬至 *tōji*, winter solstice
私	797 7 strokes	SHI; *watakushi*, I, personal (affairs), privacy 私用 *shiyō*, private use (business) 私物 *shibutsu*, private property 私有 *shiyū*, private ownership
視	798 11 strokes	SHI (to look at carefully) 視界 *shikai*, field of vision 視力 *shiryoku*, eyesight, vision 無視 *mushi*, disregard (目 25)
詞	799 12 strokes	SHI [JI] (speech, words) 歌詞 *kashi*, words (of a song) 名詞 *meishi*, noun 形容詞 *keiyōshi*, adjective (言 27)

資 800 13 strokes	丶 ン ン 次 次 次 資 資 資	SHI (wealth, help, nature) 資源 *shigen*, resources 資格 *shikaku*, capacity, qualification 物資 *busshi*, goods, materials (貝 169)
児 801 7 strokes	丨 冂 冂 旧 旧 旧 児	JI, NI (infant, child) 児童 *jidō*, child, boys and girls, juvenile 孤児 *koji*, orphan 小児まひ *shōni-mahi*, infantile paralysis
釈 802 11 strokes	ノ 丿 丿 釆 釆 釆 釈 釈 釈	SHAKU (to interpret, to explain) 解釈 *kaishaku*, interpretation, explanation 会釈 *eshaku*, bow, salutation 釈放 *shakuhō*, release (木 15)
授 803 11 strokes	一 扌 扌 扌 扌 扌 授 授 授	JU; *sazu(keru)*, to grant, to instruct; *sazu(karu)*, to be blessed with 授業 *jugyō*, lesson(s), teaching 教授 *kyōju*, teaching, professor 授賞 *jushō*, awarding a prize
需 804 14 strokes	冖 冖 雨 雨 雨 雨 需 需 需	JU (to request, to demand, to await) 需要 *juyō*, demand 需給 *jukyū*, supply and demand 必需品 *hitsujuhin*, a necessity (雨 42)

宗 805 8 strokes	SHŪ, SŌ (foundation, source, origin) 宗教 *shūkyō*, religion 宗派 *shūha*, sect 宗匠 *sōshō*, master (in an art), teacher	
衆 806 12 strokes	SHŪ (many) 衆議院 *Shūgi-in*, House of Representatives 観衆 *kanshū*, spectators 民衆 *minshū*, the masses (血 389)	
就 807 12 strokes	SHŪ, JU (to sit, to engage in, to be completed) 就学 *shūgaku*, entering school 就職 *shūshoku*, finding employment 成就 *jōju*, accomplishment, realization (口 27)	
従 808 10 strokes	JŪ; *shitaga(u)*, to obey, to comply with, to observe (rules), to yield to, to follow 服従 *fukujū*, obedience 従事 *jūji*, engaging in (business) 従業員 *jūgyōin*, employee	
述 809 8 strokes	JUTSU; *no(beru)*, to speak, to express, to state 著述 *chojutsu*, writing (of books), one's writings 口述 *kōjutsu*, oral statement 述語 *jutsugo*, predicate (gram.)	

純	810 10 strokes	JUN (purity, innocence) 単純 *tanjun*, simple 純粋 *junsui*, pure, genuine 純日本風 *jun-nihonfū*, purely Japanese style
処	811 5 strokes	SHO; *sho*(*suru*), to manage, to deal with, to sentence, to conduct oneself 処理 *shori*, management, transaction 処置 *shochi*, measure, treatment (medical) 処分 *shobun*, disposal, punishment
諸	812 15 strokes	SHO (many) 諸国 *shokoku*, various countries 諸君 *shokun*, gentlemen, you 諸島 *shotō*, group of islands (言 392)
除	813 10 strokes	JO, division (math.); *nozo*(*ku*), to take off, to remove, to exclude, to omit 除幕式 *jomakushiki*, unveiling ceremony 除名 *jomei*, dismissal from membership 駆除 *kujo*, extermination
招	814 8 strokes	SHŌ; *mane*(*ku*), to invite, to beckon 招待 *shōtai*, invitation 招待状 *shōtaijō*, invitation card

称	815 10 strokes	SHŌ (to praise); *shō*(*suru*), to call, to name, to pretend 名称 *meishō*, name, denomination 略称 *ryakushō*, abbreviation 称号 *shōgō*, title
証	816 12 strokes	SHŌ (evidence, testimony) 証明 *shōmei*, proof, certification 証人 *shōnin*, witness (law), surety 保証 *hoshō*, guarantee, security (口 27)
条	817 7 strokes	JŌ (clause in a law or treaty, logic, stripe) 条件 *jōken*, terms, conditions 条約 *jōyaku*, treaty 無条件 *mujōken*, unconditional
状	818 7 strokes	JŌ (state, condition, letter) 状態 *jōtai*, state (of things), condition 現状 *genjō*, existing state of affairs, present condition 礼状 *reijō*, letter of thanks
職	819 18 strokes	SHOKU, employment, duties 職業 *shokugyō*, occupation, business 内職 *naishoku*, side job 職場 *shokuba*, place of work (耳 26, 立 149, 日 11)

仁	820 4 strokes	JIN, perfect virtue, benevolence, humanity 仁徳 *jintoku*, benevolence 仁義 *jingi*, humanity and justice, humanity, duty, gamblers' moral code 仁愛 *jin-ai*, benevolence
推	821 11 strokes	SUI; *o(su)*, to infer, to guess, to recommend, to boost (a candidate) 推理 *suiri*, reasoning 推定 *suitei*, inference, presumption 推薦 *suisen*, recommendation
是	822 9 strokes	ZE (right, just) 是非 *zehi*, right and wrong, by all means 是認 *zenin*, approval 是正 *zesei*, correction, revision
制	823 8 strokes	SEI (law, rule); *sei(suru)*, to restrain, to control 制度 *seido*, system, institution 制服 *seifuku*, uniform 制限 *seigen*, restriction
聖	824 13 strokes	SEI (sage, saint) 聖人 *seijin*, sage, saint 聖書 *seisho*, the Bible 神聖 *shinsei*, sacred, holy (口 27)

誠	825 13 strokes	SEI; *makoto*, sincerity, truth 誠実 *seijitsu*, sincerity, faithfulness 誠意 *sei-i*, sincerity, good faith 至誠 *shisei*, sincerity, one's true heart (言 392)
税	826 12 strokes	ZEI, tax 税金 *zeikin*, tax 納税 *nōzei*, tax payment 税関 *zeikan*, custom house (木 15, 口 27)
舌	827 6 strokes	ZETSU; *shita*, tongue 舌打ち *shita-uchi*, click of the tongue, smacking one's lips 舌鼓 *shita-tsuzumi*, smacking of the lips
絶	828 12 strokes	ZETSU; *ta(eru)*, to cease, to become extinct 絶対 *zettai*, absoluteness 絶頂 *zetchō*, peak, zenith, summit 気絶 *kizetsu*, fainting (糸 83)
宣	829 9 strokes	SEN (to promulgate, to state) 宣言 *sengen*, declaration 宣伝 *senden*, propaganda 宣教師 *senkyōshi*, missionary

専 830 9 strokes	一 丶 冂 冂 冂 冂 冂 冂 冂	SEN (sole, exclusive) 専門 *semmon*, specialty 専用 *sen-yō*, exclusive use 専売 *sembai*, monopoly
善 831 12 strokes	丶 丶 羊 羊 羊 羊 羊 羊 羊	ZEN, good, goodness, virtue 親善 *shinzen*, amity, friendship 最善 *saizen*, the best 慈善 *jizen*, charity (口 27)
創 832 12 strokes	丿 人 人 今 今 今 今 倉 倉	SŌ (origin, beginning) 創立 *sōritsu*, establishment 創作 *sōsaku*, literary creation, original work 独創的 *dokusōteki*, original, creative (口 27)
蔵 833 15 strokes	一 十 艹 艹 艹 艹 艹 艹 艹	ZŌ; *kura*, warehouse; *zō(suru)*, to own, to have 冷蔵庫 *reizōko*, refrigerator 貯蔵 *chozō*, storage 蔵書 *zōsho*, one's library (臣 436)
俗 834 9 strokes	丿 亻 亻 亻 亻 亻 亻 俗 俗	ZOKU (customs, manners; vulgar) 風俗 *fūzoku*, manners, dress, popular morals 民俗 *minzoku*, folk customs 俗語 *zokugo*, colloquial language, slang

属 835 12 strokes	ZOKU, genus (biol.); *zoku(suru)*, to belong to 金属 *kinzoku*, metal 所属 *shozoku*, one's position 付属病院 *fuzoku-byōin*, attached hospital	
存 836 6 strokes	ZON, SON (to exist); *zon(zuru)*, to know, to think 保存 *hozon*, preservation 生存 *seizon*, existence, life, survival 存在 *sonzai*, existence, being	
損 837 13 strokes	SON, loss, disadvantage; *son(suru)*, to suffer a loss 損害 *songai*, loss, damage 損失 *sonshitsu*, loss 破損 *hason*, damage, breakdown (口 27, 貝 169)	
尊 838 12 strokes	SON [ZON]; *tatto(i)*, noble, valuable; *tatto(bu)*, to respect, to value 尊敬 *sonkei*, respect 尊重 *sonchō*, respect, deference 本尊 *honzon*, principal image, idol	
退 839 9 strokes	TAI; *shirizo(ku)*, to retreat, to withdraw, to retire (v.i.); *shirizo(keru)*, to drive back, to keep away, to refuse (v.t.) 退場 *taijō*, leaving, walk-out, exit 退治 *taiji*, stamping out, subjugation 後退 *kōtai*, retreat	

態	840 14 strokes	TAI [DAI] (appearance, state of affairs) 態度 *taido*, attitude 状態 *jōtai*, state (of things), condition 容態 *yōdai*, condition (of a patient) (心 95, 月 12)
断	841 11 strokes	DAN; *kotowa(ru)*, to decline, to refuse, to give notice, to ask leave; *ta(tsu)*, to sever, to give up (drinking), to exterminate 断食 *danjiki*, a fast 油断 *yudan*, negligence, carelessness, unpreparedness 判断 *handan*, judgment (米 135)
忠	842 8 strokes	CHŪ, loyalty, faithfulness 忠告 *chūkoku*, (friendly) advice 忠義 *chūgi*, loyalty 忠実 *chūjitsu*, faithful
著	843 11 strokes	CHO; *ichijiru(shii)*, remarkable, notable, conspicuous; *ara(wasu)*, to write (a book) 著書 *chosho*, book, work 著者 *chosha*, writer, author 著名 *chomei*, famous (日 11)
賃	844 13 strokes	CHIN (wages, rent) 賃金 *chingin*, wages 家賃 *yachin*, house rent 電車賃 *denshachin*, carfare (貝 169)

提	一 扌 扌	TEI (to carry in one's hand)
	扣 担 提	提出 *teishutsu*, presentation (of a thesis), filing (of an application)
845 12 strokes	提 提 提	提供 *teikyō*, offer, tender (law) 提案 *teian*, suggestion, proposition
程	ノ 二 千	TEI (degree, rule)
	禾 和 程	程度 *teido*, degree, standard, limit 日程 *nittei*, day's program, schedule
846 12 strokes	程 程 程	行程 *kōtei*, distance (口 27, 木 15)
展	㇇ コ 尸	TEN (to open, to exhibit)
	尸 屏 屈	展望車 *tembōsha*, observation car 発展 *hatten*, expansion, development, prosperity
847 10 strokes	展 展 展	展示会 *tenjikai*, exhibition
党	丨 丷 丷	TŌ, party, faction
	丷 丷 党	政党 *seitō*, political party 党派 *tōha*, party, faction, clique
848 10 strokes	党 党 党	
討	丶 二 三	TŌ; *u(tsu)*, to subjugate, to attack
	言 訁 討	検討 *kentō*, examination, investigation 討論 *tōron*, debate
849 10 strokes	討	討議 *tōgi*, discussion

得	850 11 strokes	TOKU, profit, benefit, advantage; *e(ru)*, to get, to obtain 得意 *tokui*, proud satisfaction; customer; one's forte 納得 *nattoku*, understanding, compliance 得点 *tokuten*, score (in a game) (日 11)
徳	851 14 strokes	TOKU, virtue, power of commanding love and respect 道徳 *dōtoku*, morality 徳望 *tokubō*, moral influence 人徳 *jintoku*, natural virtue (心 95, 彳 行 73)
届	852 8 strokes	*todo(ku)*, to reach; *todo(keru)*, to forward, to send, to report 欠席届 *kessekitodoke*, notice of one's absence 届け先 *todokesaki*, receiver's address 行き届く *yukitodoku*, to be attentive (to details), to be careful
難	853 18 strokes	NAN, disaster, difficulty; *kata(i)*, difficult, impossible 難破 *nampa*, shipwreck 非難 *hinan*, (adverse) criticism, censure 困難 *konnan*, difficulty, trouble, suffering (口 27, 隹 集 243)
弐	854 6 strokes	NI, two (used in legal documents) 弐千円 *nisen-en*, two thousand yen 拾弐円 *jūni-en*, twelve yen 弐百円 *nihyaku-en*, two hundred yen

認	855 14 strokes	NIN; *mito(meru)*, to see, to recognize; to approve of, to judge, to regard (as) 承認 *shōnin*, approval, consent, recognition 公認 *kōnin*, official recognition 認識 *ninshiki*, cognition (言 392, 心 95)
納	856 10 strokes	NŌ, NA, TŌ; *osa(meru)*, to put away, to pay, to supply, to dedicate, to obtain, to accept, to put back 納入 *nōnyū*, payment, delivery 納屋 *naya*, barn 出納 *suitō*, receipts and disbursements
派	857 9 strokes	HA [PA], group, party, school 左派 *saha*, left wing, radical 派遣 *haken*, dispatch
拝	858 8 strokes	HAI [PAI]; *oga(mu)*, to worship, to pray to 拝見 *haiken*, inspection, looking over (polite speech) 拝啓 *haikei*, Dear Sir, Dear Madam, etc. (salutation in a letter) 参拝 *sampai*, worship
犯	859 5 strokes	HAN [PAN]; *oka(su)*, to commit, to violate, to rape 犯罪 *hanzai*, crime 犯人 *hannin*, criminal 防犯 *bōhan*, crime prevention

判 860 7 strokes	、 ⺍ 半 判 判	HAN [BAN] (to decide); seal (for stamping); BAN, size 判断 *handan*, judgment, divination 裁判 *saiban*, justice, trial, judgment 大判 *ō-ban*, large size (paper, book)
版 861 8 strokes	丿 丿 片 片 片 版 版	HAN [PAN, BAN], plate, printing, edition 版画 *hanga*, woodblock print 版権 *hanken*, copyright 出版 *shuppan*, publication
否 862 7 strokes	一 ア 不 不 不 否 否	HI [PI]; *ina*, no 否定 *hitei*, denial 拒否 *kyohi*, refusal, rejection 安否 *ampi*, safety, well-being
評 863 12 strokes	、 亠 言 言 言 訂 訂 訂 評	HYŌ [PYŌ], criticism; *hyō*(*suru*), to criticize, to comment 評判 *hyōban*, reputation, popularity, rumor 評価 *hyōka*, appraisal, appreciation 批評 *hihyō*, criticism (言 392)
富 864 12 strokes	丶 宀 宀 宀 富 富 富 富	FU [PU], (FŪ); *tomi*, riches; *to*(*mu*), to be rich, to abound (in) 豊富 *hōfu*, abundance 富貴 *fuki*, *fūki*, *fukki*, rich and noble 富裕 *fuyū*, riches, wealth (口 27)

複 865 14 strokes		FUKU (to repeat); prefix for "double" 複雑 *fukuzatsu*, complication, complexity 複製 *fukusei*, reproduction 重複 *chōfuku*, *jūfuku*, duplication, repetition
奮 866 16 strokes		FUN; *furu(u)*, to rouse oneself 興奮 *kōfun*, excitement 奮闘 *funtō*, hard fighting, strenuous efforts 発奮 *happun*, being inspired, rousing oneself (大 22, 田 40)
陛 867 10 strokes		HEI (stairs of a palace) 陛下 *heika*, His (Her) Majesty, Your Majesty 天皇陛下 *tennō-heika*, His Majesty the Emperor (of Japan) 皇后陛下 *kōgō-heika*, Her Majesty the Empress (of Japan)
補 868 12 strokes		HO; *ogina(u)*, to supply, to compensate (for), to supplement 候補 *kōho*, candidacy, candidate 補助 *hojo*, assistance, supplement, subsidy 補給 *hokyū*, supply
墓 869 13 strokes		BO; *haka*, grave 墓地 *bochi*, graveyard 墓石 *boseki*, *haka-ishi*, gravestone 墓参 *bosan*, visit to a grave (日 早 104, 土 17)

豊	冂	丗	曲	HŌ; *yuta(ka)*, abundance 豊年 *hōnen*, year of abundance 豊作 *hōsaku*, good harvest (曲 381, 冂 27)
	曲	曲	豊	
870 13 strokes	豊	豊	豊	
暴	日	旦	昇	BŌ, BAKU (violent; to disclose) 暴力 *bōryoku*, violence, force 乱暴 *rambō*, violence, unreasonableness 暴露 *bakuro*, disclosure (日 早 104)
	昇	昇	昇	
871 15 strokes	暴	暴	暴	
未	一	二	丰	MI (yet, never, till now, un-) 未来 *mirai*, future 未開 *mikai*, uncivilized, uncultivated 未知 *michi*, unknown, strange
	未	未		
872 5 strokes				
盟	冂	日	明	MEI (to swear, to pledge) 連盟 *remmei*, league 同盟 *dōmei*, alliance 加盟 *kamei*, joining (an alliance), participation (明 141)
	明	明	明	
873 13 strokes	盟	盟	盟	
訳	亠	言	言	YAKU, translation; *wake*, reason, meaning, circumstances; *yaku(suru)*, to translate 翻訳 *hon-yaku*, translation 通訳 *tsūyaku*, interpretation, interpreter 言い訳 *iiwake*, excuse, apology (言 392)
	訳	訳	訳	
874 11 strokes	訳			

預 875 13 strokes		YO; *azu(karu)*, to keep, to take charge of, to refrain from, to receive; *azu(keru)*, to deposit, to put into the charge of 預金 *yokin*, money on deposit 預り物 *azukarimono*, item left in someone's charge 預り証 *azukarishō*, deposit receipt (貝 169)
欲 876 11 strokes	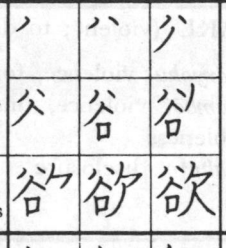	YOKU, avarice, desire; *hos(suru)* to desire, to wish 欲ばり *yokubari*, greedy person, miser 欲望 *yokubō*, desire 食欲 *shokuyoku*, appetite (口 27)
律 877 9 strokes	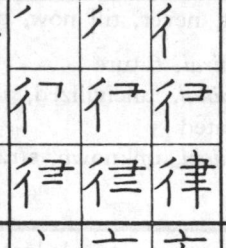	RITSU (law, degree) 法律 *hōritsu*, law 規律 *kiritsu*, order, discipline, regulations 旋律 *senritsu*, melody
率 878 11 strokes	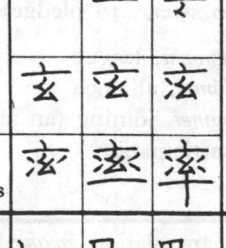	RITSU, rate; SOTSU; *hiki(iru)*, to lead, to command 能率 *nōritsu*, efficiency 出席率 *shussekiritsu*, percentage of attendance 統率 *tōsotsu*, command, leadership (幺 糸 83)
略 879 11 strokes		RYAKU, abbreviation, omission, outline; *ryaku(suru)*, to omit 計略 *keiryaku*, stratagem, plan, plot 省略 *shōryaku*, omission 略称 *ryakushō*, abbreviation (口 27)

臨 880 18 strokes	丨 厂 戸 臣 臣 臣 臨 臨 臨	RIN; *nozo(mu)*, to face, to meet, to be present at 臨終 *rinjū*, the hour of death 臨時 *rinji*, special, extra, temporary 臨席 *rinseki*, attendance (口 27, 臣 436)
論 881 15 strokes	言 訁 訁 訁 訁 訁 論 論 論	RON, argument, opinion, essay 結論 *ketsuron*, conclusion 討論 *tōron*, debate, discussion 理論 *riron*, theory (言 392)

The 1,850 GENERAL-USE CHARACTERS

1 STROKE

一	1 page 15	乙	OTSU, 2nd in a series, grade B; chic, witty; strange

2 STROKES

丁	473 page 109	入	125 page 40
七	7 page 16	八	8 page 16
九	9 page 16	刀	289 page 72
了	RYŌ (to come to an end, to understand)	力	148 page 44
二	2 page 15	十	10 page 17
人	30 page 21	又	*mata*, and, again, also

3 STROKES

丈	JŌ, old unit of length (3.316 yd.), length	千	101 page 35
三	3 page 15	及	KYŪ; *oyo(bi)*, and; *oyo(bu)*, to reach, to equal, to extend
上	20 page 19	口	27 page 20
下	21 page 19	土	17 page 18
丸	GAN, suffix denoting a pill; *maru(i)*, round, circular, globular	士	410 page 97
久	582 page 131	夕	98 page 34
亡	BŌ (to lose, to perish, to be non-existent, to flee); the late (prefix for "deceased")	大	22 page 19
凡	BON (generally, all, roughly, ordinary)	女	32 page 21
刃	JIN; *ha*, edge (of a knife, sword, etc.), blade	子	31 page 21
勺	SHAKU, old unit of capacity (0.152 gi.), old unit of area (0.355 sq.ft.)	寸	SUN, old unit of length (1.193 in.), measure

小	24 page 19	干	KAN; *ho(su)*, to dry, to air, to drain off (v.t.); *hi(ru)*, to dry (v.i.), to ebb
山	38 page 22	弓	KYŪ; *yumi*, bow, archery
川	39 page 22	才	217 page 58
工	71 page 29	与	YO; *ata(eru)*, to give, to award, to supply, to cause (damage), to assign (a task)
己	777 page 170	万	320 page 79
4 STROKES			
不	500 page 115	五	5 page 16
中	23 page 19	井	SEI, SHŌ; *i* (lit.), well (n.)
丹	TAN (cinnabar, red; elixir of life)	仁	820 page 179
乏	BŌ; *tobo(shii)*, scanty, short (of food, money)	今	81 page 31
互	GO; *taga(i)*, each other, one another, mutual	介	KAI (to come between, to aid); *kai-(shite)*, through the good offices of

仏	711 page 157	化	163 page 47
元	68 page 28	匹	HITSU (an equal); HIKI, suffix for counting small animals, rolls of cloth
内	489 page 112	区	591 page 133
公	210 page 57	升	SHŌ, old unit of capacity (3.81 pt.)
六	6 page 16	午	207 page 56
冗	JŌ (waste, uselessness, surplus)	友	145 page 44
凶	KYŌ (evil, calamity)	反	492 page 113
分	133 page 41	円	48 page 24
切	99 page 34	天	119 page 38
刈	*ka(ru)*, to mow, to reap, to prune, to shear, to cut (hair)	太	269 page 68
匁	*momme*, old unit of weight (2.117 dr.)	夫	501 page 115

孔	KŌ (hole; extremely; to pass)	文	134 page 41
少	93 page 33	斗	TO, old unit of capacity (19.04 qt.), one-*to* measure
尺	SHAKU, old measure of length (0.995 ft.), length	斤	KIN, old unit of weight (1.323 lb.)
幻	GEN; *maboroshi*, vision, phantom	方	138 page 42
弔	CHŌ; *tomura(i)*, funeral, condolence; *tomura(u)*, to condole, to mourn	日	11 page 17
引	156 page 46	月	12 page 17
心	95 page 34	木	15 page 18
戸	69 page 28	止	220 page 59
手	28 page 20	比	697 page 154
支	621 page 139	毛	142 page 43
收	631 page 141	氏	620 page 139

水	14 page 17	犬	66 page 28
火	13 page 17	王	49 page 24
父	131 page 41	欠	597 page 134
片	HEN, scrap, piece; *kata* (one of a pair, one side, the other one)	予	525 page 120
牛	62 page 27	双	SŌ (both, pair; to rival)

5 STROKES

且	*ka*(*tsu*), besides, moreover, at the same time	仕	221 page 59
世	263 page 67	他	459 page 106
丘	KYŪ; *oka*, hill	付	502 page 115
丙	HEI, 3rd class, the 3rd in a series, grade C	代	463 page 107
主	237 page 62	令	736 page 162

以	342 page 83	占	SEN; *urana(i)*, divination; *urana(u)*, to divine; *shi(meru)*, to occupy, to hold (a seat)
兄	199 page 54	去	189 page 52
冊	SATSU, suffix for counting books and magazines	古	70 page 29
冬	120 page 39	句	592 page 133
出	90 page 33	召	SHŌ; *me(su)*, honorific for "to wear," "to summon"
刊	750 page 165	可	744 page 163
功	605 page 136	史	411 page 97
加	356 page 86	右	19 page 18
包	511 page 117	司	412 page 97
北	139 page 42	囚	SHŪ (to capture; captivity, slavery, prisoner)
半	129 page 40	四	4 page 15

圧	544 page 123	布	706 page 156
外	56 page 26	平	315 page 78
央	554 page 125	幼	YŌ; *osana(i)*, infant, childish
失	418 page 98	広	211 page 57
奴	DO (manservant, fellow, guy)	庁	CHŌ (government office, board)
写	419 page 98	必	497 page 114
尼	NI; *ama*, nun	打	460 page 107
左	18 page 18	払	FUTSU; *hara(u)*, to pay, to clear away, to lop off (branches), to dispose of
巧	KŌ; *taku(mi)*, skill	斥	SEKI (to drive away, to keep away, to refuse)
巨	KYO (many, much, huge, gigantic)	未	872 page 189
市	222 page 59	末	515 page 118

本	45 page 24	生	34 page 21
札	SATSU, bill, paper money; *fuda*, card, label, tag, ticket, charm	用	146 page 44
正	46 page 24	田	40 page 23
母	137 page 42	由	325 page 80
民	518 page 118	甲	KŌ, grade A, the former; back (of the hand); shell (of a tortoise); KAN
氷	498 page 114	申	254 page 65
永	550 page 125	白	37 page 22
犯	859 page 186	皮	307 page 76
玄	GEN (dark, black, abstruse; heaven; quiet)	目	25 page 20
玉	64 page 27	矛	MU (halberd)
甘	KAN; *ama(i)*, sweet, indulgent, flattering, over-optimistic, easy to deal with	矢	*ya*, arrow

石	44 page 23	旧	759 page 166
示	622 page 139	処	811 page 177
礼	337 page 82	号	215 page 58
穴	KETSU; *ana*, hole, burrow, cave; deficit; unexpected win	弁	715 page 158
立	149 page 44	込	*ko*(*mu*), to be crowded; *ko*(*meru*), to load (a gun), to include; to concentrate (on)
台	272 page 69	辺	713 page 157

6 STROKES

交	212 page 57	任	688 page 152
仰	GYŌ, KŌ; *ao*(*gu*), to look up at (to), to ask for; *ō*(*se*), another's word or instructions	企	KI; *kuwada*(*te*), attempt, plan, intrigue; *kuwada*(*teru*), to attempt, to plan
仲	CHŪ; *naka*, relations (between persons), terms	伏	FUKU; *fu*(*seru*), to turn over (v.t.), to cover, to conceal, to lay (an ambush)
件	598 page 134	伐	BATSU (to attack, to fell; to boast)

休	61 page 27	刑	KEI, punishment, penalty
仮	559 page 126	列	537 page 122
伝	681 page 151	劣	RETSU; *oto(ru)*, to be inferior
充	JŪ (to fill); *a(teru)*, to allot, to appropriate	匠	SHŌ (carpenter, artisan)
兆	CHŌ, trillion (U.S.), billion (Eng.); sign, symptom, portent	印	348 page 84
先	33 page 21	危	KI; *ayau(i)*, dangerous, unsafe, doubtful, unsteady
光	72 page 29	叫	KYŌ; *sake(bu)*, to exclaim, to shout, to cry for
全	267 page 68	各	568 page 128
両	336 page 82	合	77 page 30
共	376 page 90	吉	KICHI, good luck, good omen
再	788 page 172	同	295 page 74

名	140 page 43	壮	SŌ (powerful, influential, brave)
后	780 page 171	多	108 page 36
吏	RI (an official)	好	KŌ; *kono(mu)*, *su(ku)*, to like, to love, to take delight in
吐	TO; *ha(ku)*, to vomit, to spew, to emit, to confess, to express	如	JO, NYO (as if, looking like; to equal, to reach)
向	213 page 57	妃	HI (empress, married princess)
吸	KYŪ; *su(u)*, to sip, to breathe in, to suck, to absorb, to smoke (tobacco)	字	86 page 32
回	168 page 48	存	836 page 182
因	548 page 124	宅	TAKU, home, our home, my husband
団	672 page 149	宇	U (eaves, house, sky)
在	613 page 137	守	421 page 99
地	111 page 37	安	153 page 45

寺	228 page 60	旬	JUN (period of ten days)
州	424 page 99	曲	381 page 91
巡	JUN; *megu(ru)*, to go one's rounds, to patrol, to travel about	会	54 page 25
帆	HAN; *ho*, sail, canvas	有	523 page 119
年	126 page 40	朱	SHU, cinnabar, vermilion
式	417 page 98	机	KI; *tsukue*, desk
忙	BŌ; *isoga(shii)*, busy	朽	KYŪ; *ku(chiru)*, to rot, to perish, to remain in obscurity
成	439 page 102	次	227 page 60
扱	*atsuka(u)*, to deal with, to receive, to manage, to deal in, to work (manipulate)	死	223 page 59
旨	SHI; *mune*, purport, effect, principle, command	毎	318 page 78
早	104 page 35	気	59 page 26

汗	KAN; *ase*, sweat	糸	83 page 31
汚	O; *kega(su)*, to bring disgrace upon, to soil; *kega(reru)*, to be dishonored, to get dirty	羊	YŌ; *hitsuji*, sheep, lamb, ewe, ram
江	KŌ; *e* (inlet, bay)	羽	U; *ha*, *hane*, wing, feather
池	110 page 37	老	541 page 123
灰	KAI; *hai*, ashes	考	74 page 29
争	451 page 105	耳	26 page 20
当	290 page 73	肉	297 page 74
百	130 page 41	自	229 page 60
尽	JIN; *tsu(kusu)*, to render service to; to exhaust, to use up	至	796 page 174
竹	113 page 37	舌	827 page 180
米	135 page 42	舟	SHŪ; *fune*, boat, ship

色	94 page 33	行	73 page 29
芋	*imo*, taro, Irish potato, sweet potato, etc.	衣	341 page 83
芝	*shiba*, turf, grass	西	96 page 34
虫	114 page 37	弐	854 page 185
血	389 page 92	迅	JIN (swift, quick, fast)

7 STROKES

乱	RAN, civil war, riot; *mida*(*reru*), to be disordered; *mida*(*su*), to throw into disorder	伺	SHI; *ukaga*(*u*), to visit, to ask, to hear
亜	A, sub~, near~ (used as prefix)	似	625 page 140
伯	HAKU (a count, a chief, elder brother)	但	*tada*(*shi*), but, provided (that)
伴	HAN, BAN; *tomo*(*nau*), to accompany, to take with	位	344 page 83
伸	SHIN; *no*(*biru*), to extend, to grow; to collapse (v.i.); *no*(*basu*), to lengthen, to stretch	低	677 page 150

住	244 page 63	判	860 page 187
佐	SA (to help)	別	508 page 116
何	51 page 25	利	528 page 120
作	82 page 31	助	248 page 64
体	270 page 69	努	481 page 111
来	147 page 44	労	542 page 123
克	KOKU (to be able to do, to conquer)	励	REI; *hage(mu)*, to strive, to make an effort
児	801 page 175	却	KYAKU (to reject, to withdraw)
兵	712 page 157	卵	RAN; *tamago*, egg, spawn, hen's egg; (in) embryo
冷	535 page 122	即	SOKU (at once; namely, nothing but, accession)
初	428 page 100	君	198 page 54

吟	GIN; *gin(zuru)*, to recite (a poem)	均	590 page 133
否	862 page 187	坊	BŌ, sonny, boy, priest, priest's lodge
含	GAN; *fuku(mu)*, to contain, to include, to keep in one's mouth, to harbor, to cherish	坑	KŌ (hole, mine pit, cave)
呈	TEI; *tei(suru)*, to offer (congratulations), to present (a tragic sight)	壱	740 page 163
呉	GO (ancient province of China)	寿	JU; *kotobuki*, congratulations; longevity
吹	SUI; *fu(ku)*, to blow, to breathe out, to play (a wind instrument), to talk big	妊	NIN (to conceive, to become pregnant)
告	398 page 94	妙	MYŌ, strange, mysterious; clever, admirable
困	KON; *koma(ru)*, to be troubled, to be perplexed, to be badly off	妥	DA (peaceful, calm)
囲	343 page 83	妨	BŌ; *samata(geru)*, to obstruct, to disturb, to prevent
図	261 page 67	孝	781 page 171
坂	304 page 75	完	571 page 129

対	461 page 107	形	200 page 55
尾	BI, suffix for counting fish; *o*, tail, ridge, trail (of a shooting star)	役	324 page 79
尿	NYŌ, urine	忌	KI; *i(mu)*, to abhor, to detest, to avoid, to taboo
局	194 page 53	忍	NIN; *shino(bu)*, to bear (pain), to endure; to conceal oneself
岐	KI (fork of a road)	志	623 page 139
希	575 page 130	忘	BŌ; *wasu(reru)*, to forget, to fail to notice, to leave behind
床	SHŌ; *toko*, bed, alcove; *yuka*, floor	快	566 page 128
序	638 page 142	応	556 page 126
延	743 page 163	我	745 page 164
廷	TEI (public office)	戒	KAI; *imashi(meru)*, to admonish, to warn; *imashi(me)*, admonition, warning, lesson
弟	282 page 71	扶	FU (to help)

批	HI (to criticize; to strike)	更	KŌ (to change, to renew, to reform); *sara-(ni)*, anew, again, still more, (not) at all
技	579 page 130	材	403 page 95
抄	SHŌ (to excerpt; extract, excerpt)	村	107 page 36
抑	YOKU (to restrain, to hold down, to stop)	束	SOKU, suffix for counting bundles; *ta-ba*, bundle, bunch
投	291 page 73	条	817 page 178
抗	KŌ (to resist, to confront)	求	583 page 131
折	651 page 145	決	202 page 55
抜	BATSU; *nu(ku)*, to pull out, to outstrip, to omit, to remove, to capture	汽	60 page 27
択	TAKU (to choose, to select, to sort out)	沈	CHIN; *shizu(mu)*, to sink, to feel depressed
改	359 page 86	没	BOTSU, rejection (of a manuscript); *bos-(suru)*, to sink, to set (sun), to die
攻	KŌ; *se(meru)*, to attack, to assault; *se-(me)*, attack	沖	*oki*, offing, open sea

沢	TAKU; *sawa*, marsh, swamp	声	97 page 34
災	789 page 172	肖	SHŌ (to resemble, to pattern after, to copy after)
状	818 page 178	肝	KAN (vital point); *kimo*, the liver; pluck, mind
狂	KYŌ, ~addict; *kuru-(i)*, disorder, warp; *kuru(u)*, to go mad, to get out of order	臣	436 page 102
男	109 page 36	良	530 page 121
町	115 page 38	花	43 page 23
社	234 page 61	芳	HŌ; *kumba(shii)*, fragrant
秀	SHŪ, excellent; (to surpass, to excel)	芽	358 page 86
私	797 page 174	芸	388 page 92
究	185 page 52	見	67 page 28
系	765 page 168	角	173 page 49

言	392 page 93	迎	GEI; *muka(eru)*, to meet, to welcome, to invite; *muka(e)*, meeting, greeter
谷	78 page 30	近	195 page 54
豆	TŌ, ZU; *mame*, peas, beans; *mame*~, baby ~, midget~ (prefix for "miniature")	返	316 page 78
貝	169 page 48	邦	HŌ (country, land)
売	301 page 75	邪	JA, wrong, injustice, evil
赤	35 page 22	医	345 page 84
走	105 page 36	里	332 page 81
足	29 page 20	防	718 page 158
身	255 page 66	余	728 page 160
車	88 page 32	麦	128 page 40
辛	SHIN (bitter, hard, severe); *kara(i)*, pungent, spicy, hot, salty		

8 STROKES

乳	NYŪ; *chichi*, *chi*, milk, breasts	侮	BU; *anado(ru)*, to look down upon, to hold in contempt
事	230 page 61	併	HEI (to amalgamate, to combine)
享	KYŌ (to receive, to enjoy)	価	563 page 127
京	63 page 27	免	MEN; *manuka(reru)*, to escape, to avoid, to be exempt; *men(zuru)*, to dismiss, to excuse
佳	KA, good, beautiful	具	383 page 91
使	224 page 59	典	680 page 151
例	737 page 162	到	TŌ (to reach, to go or come to)
侍	JI (samurai); *ji(suru)*, to attend on	制	823 page 179
供	760 page 167	刷	405 page 96
依	I, E (to depend on)	券	768 page 168

刺	SHI (name card; thorn, splinter); *sa-(su)*, to sting, to pierce, to stab	受	240 page 63
刻	KOKU; *kiza(mu)*, to cut fine, to hash, to chop, to carve (an image)	周	632 page 141
効	782 page 171	味	516 page 118
劾	GAI (to investigate thoroughly)	呼	KO; *yo(bu)*, to call, to send for, to invite, to attract, to bring about, to name
卒	457 page 106	命	519 page 118
卓	TAKU (to excel, to surpass); table, desk	和	338 page 82
協	377 page 90	固	393 page 93
卸	*oro(su)*, to sell wholesale; *oroshi*, wholesale	国	79 page 30
参	616 page 138	坪	*tsubo*, old unit of area (3.952 sq. yd.)
叔	SHUKU (younger brother of one's parent)	垂	SUI (to hang, to dangle, to droop)
取	238 page 62	夜	144 page 43

奇	KI (unusual, rare, surpassing, strange, mysterious)	宗	805 page 176
奉	HŌ; *tatematsu(ru)*, to offer, to revere; *hō-(zuru)*, to believe in, to present, to obey	官	364 page 87
奔	HON (to run)	宙	CHŪ (heaven, sky, space)
妹	319 page 78	定	474 page 109
妻	790 page 173	宜	GI (all right, good, just, proper, natural)
姉	413 page 97	実	233 page 61
始	225 page 60	宝	HŌ; *takara*, treasure, riches
姓	SEI, surname, family name; SHŌ	居	586 page 132
委	346 page 84	届	852 page 185
季	369 page 88	屈	KUTSU; *kus(suru)*, to yield to, to be daunted, to bend
学	57 page 26	岩	178 page 50

岸	177 page 50	忠	842 page 183
岳	GAKU; *take* (lit.), peak, mountain	念	689 page 152
幸	395 page 94	怖	FU (to fear, to be afraid)
底	475 page 110	性	645 page 144
店	284 page 71	怪	KAI, mystery, apparition; *aya(shii)*, suspicious; *aya(shimu)*, to doubt, to suspect
府	503 page 115	房	BŌ (chamber, house; bunch, cluster, tuft)
弦	GEN, *tsuru*, string (for musical instruments), bowstring, chord	所	246 page 64
彼	HI; *kare*, he; *ka(no)*, that	承	639 page 142
往	555 page 126	抱	HŌ; *da(ku)*, to hold in one's arms, to hug, to sit (on eggs)
征	SEI (to subjugate)	抵	TEI (to touch, to go against)
径	KEI (path, lane, method; diameter; immediately)	押	Ō; *o(su)*, to push, to press; *o(shi)*, influence, audacity; *osa(eru)*, to repress

抽	CHŪ (to draw out, to pull)	放	512 page 117
拍	HAKU, HYŌ (to clap; musical time, beat)	昇	SHŌ (to rise, to go up)
拒	KYO; *koba(mu)*, to refuse, to decline, to resist, to deny	明	141 page 43
拓	TAKU (clearing, reclamation; production of copies by rubbing)	易	545 page 124
拘	KŌ (to catch, to affect, to adhere to)	昔	SEKI, SHAKU; *mukashi*, ancient times, bygone days; long ago, formerly
拙	SETSU (clumsy, unskillful, inexpert)	服	505 page 116
招	814 page 177	杯	HAI, suffix for counting cuptuls, glassfuls, etc.; *sakazuki*, saké cup
拝	858 page 186	東	121 page 39
担	TAN (to carry on the shoulder; to deceive; to be superstitious)	松	SHŌ; *matsu*, pine, pine tree
拠	KYO, KO (to depend on, to be based on, to hold; foundation, ground, authority)	板	305 page 76
拡	747 page 164	析	SEKI (to divide, to tear, to break)

林	150 page 45	沸	FUTSU; *wa(ku)*, to boil, to seethe, to ferment (v.i.)
枚	MAI, suffix for counting thin or flat things	油	522 page 119
果	560 page 127	治	468 page 108
枝	SHI; *eda*, branch, bough, twig	沼	SHŌ; *numa*, swamp, marsh, bog
枢	SŪ (pivot, vital point, center)	沿	EN; *so(u)*, to go (be) along, to be on (beside)
欧	Ō (Europe)	況	KYŌ (state of things; still more)
殴	Ō (to beat, to strike)	泊	HAKU; *to(maru)*, to stay overnight, to stop over; *to(meru)*, to lodge (v.t.)
歩	136 page 42	泌	HITSU (to ooze out)
武	708 page 156	法	513 page 117
毒	686 page 152	波	298 page 74
河	561 page 127	泣	KYŪ; *na(ku)*, to cry, to weep, to blubber

注	277 page 70	直	472 page 109
泳	352 page 85	知	112 page 37
炊	SUI (to cook, to boil)	祈	KI; *ino(ru)*, to pray, to invoke, to wish; *ino(ri)*, prayer, wish
炎	EN (to burn); *hono-o*, flame, blaze	祉	SHI (blessing, happiness)
炉	RO, fireplace, hearth, smelting furnace	空	65 page 28
版	861 page 187	突	TOTSU (sudden); *tsu(ku)*, to pierce, to thrust, to strike, to attack
牧	720 page 159	並	HEI; *nami*, ordinary; *nara(beru)*, to place in order; *nara(bu)*, to line up; *nara(bini)*, and
物	313 page 77	者	235 page 62
画	167 page 48	肥	699 page 154
的	478 page 110	肩	KEN; *kata*, shoulder
盲	MŌ; *mekura*, blindness, blind person; ignorance	肪	BŌ (fat, grease, tallow)

肯	KŌ (to consent, to agree; daringly, boldly)	迭	TETSU (to change places with; by turns)
育	347 page 84	述	809 page 176
舎	629 page 140	邸	TEI (mansion, residence)
苗	BYŌ; *nae*, seedling, sapling	金	16 page 18
若	JAKU; *waka(i)*, young, younger, immature, low (number); *mo(shikuwa)*, or	長	116 page 38
苦	197 page 54	門	143 page 43
英	353 page 85	阻	SO (steep; to separate, to obstruct)
茂	MO; *shige(ru)*, to grow thick, to grow rank	附	FU (to stick to, to adhere to)
茎	KEI; *kuki*, stalk, stem	雨	42 page 23
表	309 page 76	青	36 page 22
迫	HAKU; *sema(ru)*, to press, to urge, to draw near	非	698 page 154

9 STROKES

乗	251 page 65	冒	BŌ; *oka(su)*, to brave, to defy, to attack, to damage, to profane
侯	KŌ (feudal lord; marquis)	冠	KAN; *kammuri*, crown
侵	SHIN; *oka(su)*, to invade, to violate	則	666 page 148
係	385 page 92	削	SAKU; *kezu(ru)*, to shave (wood), to sharpen, to delete, to curtail
便	510 page 117	前	102 page 35
促	SOKU; *unaga(su)*, to urge	勅	CHOKU (Imperial edict)
俊	SHUN (to be excellent, to surpass, to be high)	勇	524 page 119
俗	834 page 181	卑	HI; *iya(shii)*, base, vulgar, low-lived; *iya(shimeru)*, to despise
保	716 page 158	南	124 page 39
信	437 page 102	巻	KAN, volume, reel (used as suffix); *maki*, volume, roll; *ma(ku)*, to roll, to wind (v.t.)

厘	RIN, old unit of money (0.001 yen); old unit of length (about 0.0119 in.)	姿	SHI; *sugata*, figure, shape, appearance, aspect, condition
厚	606 page 136	威	I (majestic, solemn; to threaten)
咲	*sa(ku)*, to bloom, to blossom	孤	KO (orphan; solitary, alone)
哀	AI; *awa(re)*, pathos, misery, pity; *awa(remu)*, to feel pity for	客	184 page 51
品	311 page 77	宣	829 page 180
単	671 page 149	室	232 page 61
型	595 page 134	封	FŪ, seal; *fū(zuru)*, to prevent, to enclose, to blockade, to seal; HŌ, fief
城	JŌ; *shiro*, castle	専	830 page 181
奏	SŌ; *sō(suru)*, to play (music, a musical instrument); to report to the Throne	屋	161 page 47
契	KEI; *chigi(ru)*, to pledge, to promise	峠	*tōge*, mountain pass, ridge, peak, crisis
姻	IN (to get married)	峡	KYŌ (gorge, ravine)

帝	TEI (emperor, sovereign, Mikado)	怠	TAI; *okota(ru)*, to neglect, to be idle
帥	SUI (to command an army)	急	186 page 52
幽	YŪ (faint, profound, quiet)	恒	KŌ (always, eternal)
度	288 page 72	恨	KON; *ura(mi)*, spite, grudge; *ura(mu)*, to bear a grudge against, to regret
建	391 page 93	悔	KAI; *ku(iru)*, to regret; *kuya(mi)*, condolence; *kuya(mu)*, to mourn, to repent
弧	KO, arc	括	KATSU (to fasten, to bind, to tie up)
待	271 page 69	拷	GŌ (to beat, to strike)
律	877 page 190	拾	425 page 100
後	208 page 56	持	231 page 61
怒	DO; *ika(ru)* (lit.), to get angry	指	226 page 60
思	84 page 31	政	646 page 144

故	778 page 170	架	KA; *ka(suru)*, to build, to span (a river with a bridge, etc.)
叙	jO (preface); *jo(suru)*, to describe; to confer (a rank) upon	柄	HEI; *e*, handle; *gara*, pattern, design, build, character, nature
施	SHI, SE; *hodoko(su)*, to give in charity; to perform, to administer	某	BŌ, a certain person, Mr. So-and-so; one, a, a certain~ (used as prefix)
星	264 page 67	染	SEN; *so(meru)*, to dye; *so(maru)*, to be dyed, to be imbued
映	EI; *utsu(ru)*, to be reflected, to match (v.i.); *utsu(su)*, to project on a screen, to reflect	柔	JŪ, NYŪ; *yawa(rakai)*, soft, tender, mild, mellow
春	91 page 33	査	611 page 137
昨	404 page 95	柱	278 page 70
昭	249 page 64	柳	RYŪ; *yanagi*, willow tree
是	822 page 179	栄	549 page 124
昼	279 page 70	段	DAN, degree, step, grade, platform
枯	KO; *ka(reru)*, to wither, to mature (v.i.); *ka(rasu)*, to blight	泉	SEN; *izumi*, spring, fountain

洋	526 page 120	狩	SHU; *ka(ri)*, hunting, gathering, (maple-, etc.) viewing; *ka(ru)*, to hunt
洗	SEN; *ara(u)*, to wash; to inquire into (a person's past)	狭	KYŌ; *sema(i)*, narrow, small
津	*tsu*, harbor, ferry	独	687 page 152
活	174 page 49	珍	CHIN; *mezura(shii)*, rare, novel, unusual
派	857 page 186	界	170 page 49
海	55 page 26	畑	302 page 75
浄	JŌ (pure, innocent)	疫	EKI (epidemic)
浅	655 page 146	発	303 page 75
炭	274 page 69	皆	KAI; *mina*, all, everything, everyone
為	I (to do, to make, to think; benefit, reason, cause, purpose)	皇	783 page 171
牲	SEI (sacrifice, victim)	盆	BON, tray; the Bon festival (Buddhist celebration held in Japan in mid-July)

県	203 page 55	秋	89 page 32
相	452 page 105	科	164 page 47
盾	JUN (shield)	秒	499 page 114
省	640 page 143	窃	SETSU (to steal, to rob)
看	KAN (to watch, to pay a visit of inquiry, to see from afar)	糾	KYŪ (to investigate, to examine; to twist, to twine around)
砂	SHA, SA; *suna*, sand	紀	578 page 130
研	204 page 55	約	726 page 160
砕	SAI; *kuda*(*ku*), to break into pieces, to smash; to explain in simple words	紅	KŌ, KU; *kurenai*, crimson; *beni*, rouge, lipstick; crimson
祖	657 page 146	級	187 page 52
祝	635 page 142	美	308 page 76
神	257 page 66	耐	TAI; *ta*(*eru*), to endure, to bear, to stand (v.t.)

肺	HAI, lung	虐	GYAKU (to treat harshly, to spoil)
胃	546 page 124	要	729 page 160
背	HAI (to disobey, to rebel); *se*, the back (of a body, a chair, etc.), stature, ridge	訂	TEI (to correct, to establish)
胎	TAI (to conceive; womb, fetus)	計	201 page 55
胞	HŌ (placenta)	変	509 page 116
胆	TAN (liver; spirit, courage)	貞	TEI (right, just, chaste)
臭	SHŪ (smell, stink); *kusa(i)*, ill-smelling, suspicious; ~*kusa(i)*, smelling of ~	負	312 page 77
茶	275 page 70	赴	FU (to go)
草	106 page 36	軌	KI (space between two wheels, print of a wheel)
荒	KŌ; *ara(i)*, violent, rude, wild; *a(reru)*, to become rough, to be dilapidated	軍	593 page 133
荘	SŌ (majestic, solemn; villa)	迷	724 page 159

追	280 page 71	面	322 page 79
退	839 page 182	革	746 page 164
送	268 page 68	音	50 page 25
逃	TŌ; *ni(geru)*, to run away, to flee	風	132 page 41
逆	758 page 166	飛	493 page 113
郊	KŌ (suburbs, the country)	食	253 page 65
郎	RŌ (man, male—used as suffix in men's given names)	首	239 page 62
重	245 page 64	香	KŌ, incense; *ka* (lit.), perfume, fragrance
限	601 page 135	点	285 page 72
10 STROKES			
修	633 page 141	俳	HAI (fun, play, humor; actor, actress)

俵	702 page 155	兼	769 page 168
倉	659 page 146	准	JUN (rule; to imitate, to approve)
個	603 page 135	凍	TŌ; *kō(ru)*, to freeze (v.i.); *kogo(eru)*, to be benumbed with cold
倍	694 page 153	剖	BŌ (to divide, to distinguish)
倒	TŌ; *tao(reru)*, to fall, to break down, to go to ruin; *tao(su)*, to fell, to overthrow	剛	GŌ (inflexible, stubborn, stiff, hard)
候	607 page 136	剤	ZAI (medicine, drug)
借	420 page 99	剣	KEN, *tsurugi*, sword
倣	HŌ (to model after, to imitate)	勉	317 page 78
値	CHI; *ne*, price; *atai*, price, value	匿	TOKU (to give refuge to, to conceal, to hide, to keep secret)
倫	RIN (principles, duty, rules)	原	205 page 56
倹	KEN (frugal, modest, humble)	員	349 page 84

哲	TETSU (wise, sagacious)	宰	SAI (to administer, to manage, to take charge of; chief, head)
唆	SA (to tempt, to instigate)	害	362 page 87
唐	TŌ, Tang (an ancient Chinese dynasty); China (old name used in Japan)	宴	EN, feast, banquet
埋	MAI; *u(meru)*, to bury, to fill up; *u(maru)*, to be buried, to be filled up	家	53 page 25
夏	52 page 25	容	730 page 161
姫	*hime*, princess, young lady of birth; also used as prefix for "small" or "dainty"	射	SHA; *i(ru)*, to shoot (an arrow, a bird), to strike (one's eyes)
娘	*musume*, girl, daughter	将	SHŌ (commander; to command; to be about to)
娯	GO (to enjoy, to take pleasure in)	展	847 page 184
娠	SHIN (to conceive, to become pregnant)	峰	HŌ; *mine*, peak, back (of a sword)
孫	458 page 106	島	292 page 73
宮	374 page 89	差	399 page 94

師	624 page 139	恥	CHI; *haji*, shame, disgrace, humiliation; *ha(jiru)* to be ashamed of
席	444 page 103	恩	558 page 126
帯	669 page 148	恭	KYŌ (respectful, reverent)
座	ZA, seat, gathering, (stand, theater, constellation)	息	454 page 105
庫	206 page 56	悦	ETSU (to be glad, to rejoice)
庭	477 page 110	悟	GO; *sato(ru)*, to be spiritually awakened, to perceive, to comprehend
弱	236 page 62	恵	KEI, E; *megu(mi)*, grace, blessing; *megu(mu)*, to give in charity
徐	JO (slowly, gently)	悩	NŌ; *naya(mi)*, affliction, trouble, pain; *naya(mu)*, to be troubled with
徒	480 page 111	恋	REN; *koi*, love; *koi(shii)*, dear, beloved
従	808 page 176	扇	SEN; *ōgi*, folding fan
恐	KYŌ; *oso(re)*, fear, anxiety; *oso(reru)*, to fear; *oso(roshii)*, fearful, fierce, awful	振	SHIN; *fu(ru)*, to wave (v.t.), to shake (v.t.), to wield; to discard, to jilt

捕	HO; *tora(eru)*, to catch, to take hold of	校	75 page 30
捜	SŌ; *saga(su)*, to hunt for, to search for	株	749 page 164
挙	375 page 90	核	KAKU, nucleus, kernel, core, stone (of a fruit)
敏	BIN (clever, quick)	根	216 page 58
料	531 page 121	格	569 page 128
旅	335 page 82	栽	SAI (to plant)
既	KI; *sude(ni)*, already, previously	桃	TŌ; *momo*, peach
時	87 page 32	案	340 page 83
書	92 page 33	桑	SŌ; *kuwa*, mulberry
朕	CHIN, We, Our (formerly used by the Emperor of Japan in Imperial rescripts)	梅	BAI; *ume*, plum, plum tree
朗	RŌ; *hoga(raka)*, fine, cheerful, clear, sonorous	桜	Ō; *sakura*, cherry tree

帰	182 page 51	浸	SHIN; *hita(su)*, to soak, to wet
殉	JUN; *jun(zuru)*, to follow even to death, to sacrifice oneself	消	429 page 100
殊	SHU (especially; to be different)	涙	RUI; *namida*, tear (from the eye)
残	409 page 96	浜	HIN; *hama*, beach, shore
殺	614 page 137	烈	RETSU (valiant, violent, brave, strong)
泰	TAI (peaceful; great, extravagant, extremely)	特	685 page 152
流	334 page 81	珠	SHU (pearl)
浦	HO; *ura*, inlet, beach	班	HAN, squad (mil.), group
浪	RŌ (billow; to wander about)	畔	HAN (vicinity; footpath between rice fields, edge)
浮	FU; *u(ku)*, to float, to be gay, to be left over; *u(kabu)*, to float, to come to mind	留	733 page 161
浴	732 page 161	畜	CHIKU (to raise cattle, to cultivate)

畝	*se*, old unit for measuring land (3.92 sq. rd.)	祥	SHŌ (good fortune, omen)
疲	HI; *tsuka(re)*, fatigue; *tsuka(reru)*, to get tired, to become fatigued	租	SO (tribute)
疾	SHITSU (sickness; to fall ill; quick, swift)	秩	CHITSU (order, er, rank)
病	310 page 77	称	815 page 178
症	SHŌ (nature of a disease)	笑	SHŌ; *wara(i)*, laughter; *wara(u)*, to laugh, to smile, to chuckle
益	742 page 163	粉	507 page 116
真	438 page 102	粋	SUI, essence, elegance; delicate, smart, stylish
眠	MIN; *nemu(ri)*, sleep; *nemu(ru)*, to sleep	紋	MON, family insignia, crest, figures (in cloth)
砲	HŌ, gun, cannon	納	856 page 186
破	692 page 153	純	810 page 177
秘	HI (to keep secret; secretly)	紙	85 page 32

紛	FUN; *magi(reru)*, to be obscure, to be diverted, to be confused	脅	KYŌ; *obiya(kasu)*, to threaten, to menace, to intimidate
素	658 page 146	脈	517 page 118
紡	BŌ; *tsumu(gu)*, to spin (thread)	致	CHI (to do, to bring about; taste, appearance)
索	SAKU (cable, rope; to seek for, to search for)	航	396 page 94
翁	Ō, old man, honorific title for an old man	般	HAN (generally; to carry, to turn; to enjoy)
耕	784 page 171	荷	165 page 48
耗	MŌ (to decrease, to spend)	華	KA (flower, blossom; gay, gaudy, colorful, showy)
胴	DŌ, trunk (of the body), body armor	蚊	*ka*, mosquito
胸	KYŌ; *mune*, breast, chest, heart, mind	蚕	617 page 138
能	691 page 153	衰	SUI; *otoro(eru)*, to become weak, to decline
脂	SHI (fat, grease, tallow)	衷	CHŪ (heart, sincerity)

被	HI; *kōmu(ru)*, to suffer (damage, etc.), to receive (a favor, etc.)	逐	CHIKU (to chase, to pursue)
討	849 page 184	途	TO (way, road)
訓	764 page 167	通	281 page 71
託	TAKU (to entrust to a person, to make a pretext of)	速	453 page 105
記	180 page 51	造	662 page 147
財	793 page 173	連	538 page 122
貢	KŌ (tribute)	逓	TEI (alternately, by turns; to convey)
起	181 page 51	郡	384 page 91
軒	KEN, suffix for counting houses; *noki*, eaves	配	299 page 74
辱	JOKU (to put to shame, to disgrace)	酒	422 page 99
透	TŌ (to penetrate); *su(ku)*, to be transparent, to leave a gap, to be thin	針	SHIN; *hari*, needle, hook, sting (of a bee, etc.), hand (of a clock)

降	KŌ; *fu(ru)*, to fall (rain, snow); *o(riru)*, to get off, to come down, to alight	飢	KI; *u(e)*, hunger, starvation; *u(eru)*, to be hungry, to starve
陛	867 page 188	馬	127 page 40
院	350 page 85	骨	KOTSU; *hone*, bone, frame
陣	JIN, camp, position (mil.), battle array	高	76 page 30
除	813 page 177	鬼	KI; *oni*, ogre, fiend, demon
陷	KAN; *ochii(ru)*, to fall into, to yield, to cave in, to fall (to surrender to a siege)	党	848 page 184
隻	SEKI, suffix for counting ships		

11 STROKES

乾	KAN (to dry, to be thirsty)	健	599 page 134
偏	HEN (to be one-sided, to be partial)	側	667 page 148
停	476 page 110	偶	GŪ (even number; by chance, accidentally)

偽	GI; *itsuwa(ru)*, to tell a lie, to pretend, to deceive	域	IKI (boundary, border, end, limits)
剰	JŌ (surplus; moreover)	執	SHITSU, SHŪ; *to-(ru)*, to do (business, etc.), to manage, to take, to grasp
副	709 page 156	培	BAI (to cultivate)
動	296 page 74	基	755 page 166
勘	KAN, perception, intuition	堂	486 page 112
務	722 page 159	婆	BA (old woman, old mother)
唯	YUI (merely, only, alone)	婚	KON (marriage)
唱	430 page 101	婦	707 page 156
商	431 page 101	宿	634 page 141
問	520 page 119	寂	JAKU; *sabi(shii)*, lonesome, lonely, solitary
啓	KEI (to enlighten, to open)	寄	576 page 130

密	MITSU, dense, secret, (close, minute)	強	192 page 53
尉	I (military rank)	彩	SAI (coloration; to color)
崇	SŪ (lofty, noble; to respect, to worship)	彫	CHŌ; *ho*(*ru*), to carve, to engrave
崩	HŌ (to crumble, to collapse, to change for the worse, to be destroyed)	得	850 page 185
巣	SŌ; *su*, nest, lair, den, cobweb, beehive	御	GYO, GO; *on*, honorific prefix; *gyo*(*suru*), to drive (a horse)
帳	470 page 109	患	KAN (sickness, anxiety, trouble)
常	642 page 143	悼	TŌ (to mourn over, to lament, to feel pity for)
庶	SHO (various, all, many)	情	643 page 143
康	608 page 136	惜	SEKI; *o*(*shii*), regrettable; precious; wasteful; *o*(*shimu*), to begrudge, to regret
庸	YŌ (moderate, ordinary, mediocre)	悪	152 page 45
張	675 page 150	惨	SAN (cruel, horrible, appalling)

捨	SHA; *su(teru)*, to throw away, to abandon	措	SO (to put aside, to except, to dispose of; to place)
掃	SŌ; *ha(ku)*, to sweep	描	BYŌ; *ega(ku)*, to picture, to describe
授	803 page 175	掲	KEI; *kaka(geru)*, to put up, to hoist, to carry
排	HAI (to reject; to display, to push open)	教	191 page 53
掘	KUTSU; *ho(ru)*, to dig, to dig up	救	584 page 131
掛	*ka(keru)*, to hang (v.t.), to sit on (a chair, etc.), to cover with	敗	693 page 153
採	791 page 173	斜	SHA; *nana(me)*, slanting, oblique
探	TAN; *sagu(ru)*, to spy into, to search, to feel after, to fathom	断	841 page 183
接	652 page 145	旋	SEN (to rotate, to return)
控	KŌ; *hika(eru)*, to write down; to refrain from, to be moderate in, to wait	族	455 page 106
推	821 page 179	望	514 page 117

械	360 page 87	渴	KATSU, thirst; (to be thirsty, to dry up)
欲	876 page 190	渋	JŪ; *shibu*, astringent juice; *shibu(i)*, astringent, tasteful, refined, sober, glum
渉	SHŌ (to wade, to cross over, to walk about; to be related to)	済	792 page 173
液	552 page 125	猛	MŌ (strong, valiant, brave, fierce, wild)
涼	RYŌ (lit.), coolness; *suzu(shii)*, cool	猟	RYŌ, hunting, shooting
淑	SHUKU (graceful, gentle)	率	878 page 190
淡	TAN; *awa(i)*, light (color, taste, etc.), transitory (love, joy, etc.)	現	602 page 135
深	258 page 66	球	188 page 52
混	787 page 172	理	333 page 81
清	440 page 103	産	408 page 96
添	TEN; *so(eru)*, to annex (to), to add (to), to garnish (cooking)	略	879 page 190

異	738 page 162	符	FU (tally, mark, sign, good omen, charm, talisman)
盛	SEI, JŌ (prosperous); *saka(ri)*, prime, heyday; *mo(ru)*, to dish up, to heap up	第	273 page 69
盗	TŌ; *nusu(mu)*, to steal, to rob	粒	RYŪ; *tsubu*, grain, drop
眼	754 page 165	粗	SO (rough, loose, coarse, humble)
票	703 page 155	粘	NEN; *neba(ru)*, to be sticky; to persevere
祭	400 page 95	紫	SHI; *murasaki*, purple, violet
移	547 page 124	累	RUI, trouble, involvement; (to pile up, to trouble; to be acquainted with)
窒	CHITSU (to block up, to obstruct; nitrogen)	細	218 page 58
窓	SŌ; *mado*, window	紳	SHIN (ceremonial sash; man of high birth)
章	432 page 101	紹	SHŌ (to introduce a person; to succeed to)
笛	TEKI; *fue*, flute	紺	KON, dark blue

終	241 page 63	菊	KIKU, chrysanthemum
組	103 page 35	菌	KIN, germ, fungus
経	596 page 134	菓	KA (fruit, nut, berry)
翌	YOKU (the next~, the following~; used before "day," "morning," "year," etc.)	菜	401 page 95
習	426 page 100	著	843 page 183
粛	SHUKU (to be respectful, to be modest, to admonish, to be severe)	虚	KYO, KO (empty, vain)
脚	KYAKU (leg, lower part, position), suffix for counting legged furniture	術	636 page 142
脱	DATSU (to omit, to escape); *nu(gu)*, to take off (shoes, coat, etc.)	袋	TAI; *fukuro*, bag, sack, pouch
脳	NŌ, brain, brains	規	577 page 130
舶	HAKU (ocean-going ship)	視	798 page 174
船	266 page 68	訟	SHŌ (to sue, to go to law)

訪	HŌ; *otozu(reru)*, to visit, to call on (at)	軟	NAN (soft, weak, feeble)
設	653 page 145	転	479 page 110
許	587 page 132	逮	TAI (to catch, to arrest, to overtake, to pursue)
訳	874 page 189	週	242 page 63
豚	TON; *buta*, pig	進	259 page 66
貧	705 page 156	逸	ITSU (to excel, to be lost, to be rash, to run off, to enjoy oneself)
貨	357 page 86	部	504 page 115
販	HAN (to sell, to deal in)	郭	KAKU (enclosure, red-light district)
貫	KAN, old unit of weight (8.27 lb.); *tsuranu(ku)*, to pierce, to carry out, to attain	郵	YŪ (collection and delivery of goods, letters, etc.; post town)
責	649 page 144	都	287 page 72
赦	SHA (to forgive, to pardon)	郷	KYŌ, GŌ (the country, village, one's native place)

酔	SUI; *yo(u)*, to get drunk, to become sick (sea, car, air), to be in ecstasy	険	770 page 169
釈	802 page 175	雪	100 page 35
野	323 page 79	頂	CHŌ (to receive); *itadaki*, summit, top
閉	HEI; *to(jiru)*, to shut, to close	魚	190 page 53
陪	BAI (to attend upon; attendant)	鳥	117 page 38
陰	IN, gloom, negative, the female principle (yin); *kage*, shadow, shade, back	麻	MA; *asa*, hemp, flax
陳	CHIN (to state, to display; to be old)	黄	214 page 57
陵	RYŌ; *misasagi*, Imperial mausoleum	黒	80 page 31
陶	TŌ (pottery, porcelain)	斎	SAI (religious purification; a room)
陸	529 page 120	隆	RYŪ (high, prosperous, flourishing)

12 STROKES

偉	I; *era(i)*, great, admirable	喚	KAN (to call, to cry, to summon)
傍	BŌ (side, neighborhood)	喜	370 page 89
備	700 page 155	喪	SŌ (to lose, to ruin); *mo*, mourning
割	KATSU; *wa(ru)*, to divide, to separate, to split, to dilute; *wari*, rate, percentage	喫	KITSU (to eat, to drink)
創	832 page 181	圏	KEN, sphere, range
勝	250 page 65	堅	KEN; *kata(i)*, hard, tough, tight, firm, solid, strict, sound
募	BO; *tsuno(ru)*, to collect, to raise (troops, etc.); to grow intense	堤	TEI; *tsutsumi*, bank (of a river, etc.)
勤	762 page 167	堪	KAN; *ta(eru)*, to endure, to bear, to withstand, to resist
博	695 page 154	報	717 page 158
善	831 page 181	場	252 page 65

堕	DA (to fall, to get into, to let fall, to lose)	属	835 page 182
塔	TŌ, tower, pagoda, steeple	帽	BŌ (headgear, head-dress)
塁	RUI, base (in base-ball), fort	幅	FUKU, scroll, suffix for counting scrolls; *haba*, width, difference in price
奥	OKU, interior, depths, heart; Ō (interior)	幾	KI; *iku*~, how many?, how much?, some (used as prefix)
婿	SEI; *muko*, son-in-law, bridegroom	廊	RŌ (corridor, passage)
媒	BAI (intermediation, matchmaking, intermediary, go-between)	廃	HAI (to go out of use or fashion, to be abolished, to decline)
富	864 page 187	弾	DAN (bullet, ball; to investigate; to play on a musical instrument)
寒	175 page 50	復	710 page 157
尊	838 page 182	循	JUN (to obey, to observe, to follow; to revolve)
尋	JIN; *tazu(neru)*, to ask, to look for	悲	494 page 113
就	807 page 176	惑	WAKU; *mado(u)*, to be puzzled, to go astray, to be captivated by

惰	DA (to be idle, to neglect)	敢	KAN (daringly, boldly)
愉	YU (to rejoice, to enjoy oneself)	散	407 page 96
慌	KŌ (busy, bustling; to be flurried, to lose one's presence of mind)	敬	766 page 168
掌	SHŌ (palm of the hand; to control, to preside over)	晩	BAN (late), evening, night
提	845 page 184	普	FU (wide, universal, general)
揚	YO; *a(geru)*, to raise, to send up, to hoist; to fry	景	386 page 92
換	KAN; *ka(eru)*, to exchange, to change (v. t.); *ka(waru)*, to change (v. i.)	晴	265 page 68
握	AKU; *nigi(ru)*, to grasp, to clasp, to hold, to seize	晶	SHŌ (bright; crystal)
援	EN (to help, to rescue, to pull)	暑	247 page 64
揮	KI (to wield, to display, to command)	暁	GYŌ; *akatsuki*, dawn, daybreak
揺	YŌ; *yu(reru)*, to shake (v. i.), to swing, to flicker	替	TAI; *ka(eru)*, to exchange, to substitute, to convert

最	402 page 95	款	KAN (sincerity, goodwill; article in a legal document)
朝	118 page 38	殖	SHOKU (to increase, to grow up, to plant)
期	183 page 51	減	775 page 170
棋	KI (chessman, Japanese chess)	渡	TO; *wata(ru)*, to go over, to be imported, to change hands, to migrate
棒	BŌ, stick, club	測	668 page 148
森	41 page 23	港	397 page 94
棺	KAN, casket, coffin	湖	394 page 93
植	435 page 102	湯	482 page 111
極	382 page 91	温	162 page 47
検	771 page 169	滋	JI (nourishing; to flourish, to be luxuriant)
欺	GI; *azamu(ku)*, to deceive, to cheat	満	721 page 159

湿	SHITSU; *shime(ru)*, to become damp, to moisten	畳	JŌ, suffix for counting mats; *tatami*, mat
湾	WAN, bay, gulf	疎	SO (to be estranged; to know little of; to be sparse)
無	723 page 159	痘	TŌ (smallpox)
焦	SHŌ (to pine for); *ko(geru)*, to scorch, to burn (v. i.); *ko(gasu)*, to burn (v. t.)	痛	TSŪ; *ita(mi)*, pain; *ita(mu)*, to feel pain, to ache
然	450 page 105	痢	RI (diarrhoea)
煮	SHA; *ni(ru)*, to cook (v. t.)	登	483 page 111
焼	434 page 101	短	466 page 108
営	741 page 163	硝	SHŌ (niter, gunpowder)
猶	YŪ (to hesitate; moreover, even, still; as if)	硫	RYŪ (sulfur)
琴	KIN; *koto*, Japanese harp	硬	KŌ (hard, tough, stiff, firm)
番	306 page 76	税	826 page 180

程	846 page 184	絞	KŌ; *shibo(ru)*, to wring, to squeeze, to extort, to scold; *shi-(meru)*, to strangle
童	487 page 112	絡	RAKU (to twine around, to surround)
筆	701 page 155	給	585 page 132
等	484 page 111	統	682 page 151
筋	KIN; *suji*, sinew, plot (of a story), source, logic, lineage, stripe, line, vein	絵	172 page 49
筒	TŌ; *tsutsu*, pipe, tube	着	276 page 70
答	293 page 73	脹	CHŌ (to swell)
策	795 page 174	腕	WAN; *ude*, arm, talent, ability
粧	SHŌ (to paint and powder, to embellish)	落	330 page 81
結	390 page 93	葉	327 page 80
絶	828 page 180	葬	SŌ; *hōmu(ru)*, to bury, to consign to oblivion, to shelve

蛮	BAN (barbarian)	詐	SA (to tell a lie, to pretend, to deceive)
衆	806 page 176	詔	SHŌ; *mikotonori*, Imperial edict
街	GAI, street, avenue (used as suffix)	評	863 page 187
裁	SAI (to judge, to decide); *ta(tsu)*, to cut (cloth, etc.)	詞	799 page 174
裂	RETSU; *sa(ku)*, to tear, to rend (v. t.); *sa(keru)*, to tear, to rend (v. i.)	詠	EI, poem, ode, recitation of poetry
裕	YŪ (abundant, broad-minded, at ease)	証	816 page 178
補	868 page 188	象	663 page 147
装	SŌ, SHŌ; *yoso-o(i)*, dress, decoration; *yoso-o(u)*, to dress, to adorn, to pretend	貯	674 page 149
覚	363 page 87	貴	756 page 166
訴	SO; *utta(e)*, lawsuit, appeal, complaint; *utta(eru)*, to sue, to resort to, to appeal	買	300 page 75
診	SHIN (to examine, to diagnose)	貸	670 page 149

費	495 page 114	運	157 page 46
貿	719 page 158	遍	HEN (wide, universal)
賀	565 page 128	過	562 page 127
超	CHŌ, super- (used as prefix); (to exceed, to surpass, to jump over, to go over)	道	122 page 39
越	ETSU; *ko(eru)*, to go over, to exceed; *ko-(su)*, to cross, to exceed, to move (to)	達	465 page 108
距	KYO (to separate, to be distant, to reach)	遲	CHI (late, slow); *oku-(reru)*, to be late
軸	JIKU, axis, axle, scroll picture, holder, stalk	酢	SAKU; *su*, vinegar
軽	387 page 92	量	734 page 161
遂	SUI (at last); *to(geru)*, to accomplish, to attain	鈍	DON; *nibu(i)*, dull, slow, blunt, dim
遇	GŪ (to treat, to deal with, to meet with, to come across)	開	171 page 49
遊	326 page 80	閑	KAN (quiet, tranquil; leisure, time to spare)

間	58 page 26	雇	KO; *yato(u)*, to hire, to employ
陽	527 page 120	雲	47 page 24
隊	462 page 107	項	KŌ, clause, paragraph, item
階	361 page 87	順	427 page 100
隨	ZUI (to follow, to accompany; freely; as one pleases)	飲	351 page 85
雄	YŪ (strong, valiant, brave, surpassing); *osu*, *o*, male animal	飯	696 page 154
雅	GA (elegant, graceful)	歯	414 page 97
集	243 page 63		
13 STROKES			
傑	KETSU (to excel, to surpass; man of great caliber)	債	SAI (debt, loan)
催	SAI; *moyo-o(shi)*, meeting, auspices; *moyo-o(su)*, to hold (a meeting), to feel	傷	SHŌ (to hurt, to spoil, to worry); *kizu*, wound, injury

傾	KEI; *katamu(ki)*, inclination; *katamu(ku)* (v. i.), *katamu(keru)* (v. t.), to incline	墓	869 page 188
働	488 page 112	夢	MU; *yume*, dream, vision, transiency
僧	SŌ, Buddhist priest, bonze	奬	SHŌ (to encourage, to promote)
勢	441 page 103	嫁	KA; *yome*, daughter-in-law, young wife, bride
勧	752 page 165	寝	SHIN; *ne(ru)*, to go to bed, to sleep, to lie down
嗣	SHI (to succeed to, to inherit; heir, successor)	寛	KAN (generous, easy)
嘆	TAN; *nage(ku)*, to bewail, to deplore, to sigh	幕	BAKU; MAKU, curtain, screen, hangings; act (of a play, opera, etc.)
園	159 page 46	幹	751 page 165
塊	KAI (clod, lump)	廉	REN (noble, lofty, pure; cheap)
塑	SO (earthen figure)	微	BI (slight, little, faint, dim)
塗	TO; *nu(ru)*, to paint, to plaster, to coat, to lacquer, to smear	想	660 page 147

愁	SHŪ (grief, sorrow, distress)	携	KEI; *tazusa(eru)*, to carry in one's hand, to take with one
意	155 page 46	搾	SAKU (to squeeze, to compress)
愚	GU; *oro(ka)*, foolish, stupid, silly	摂	SETSU (to take, to cultivate, to act in place of)
愛	339 page 82	数	262 page 67
感	176 page 50	新	256 page 66
慎	SHIN; *tsutsushi(mu)*, to be discreet, to refrain from	暇	KA; *hima*, time, leisure, dismissal
慈	JI (to love, to cherish, to pity)	暖	DAN; *atata(kai)*, warm, cordial
慨	GAI (to deplore, to lament)	暗	154 page 45
戦	448 page 104	棄	KI (to throw away, to abandon, to reject)
損	837 page 182	業	380 page 91
搬	HAN (to carry, to transport, to remove)	楽	331 page 81

楼	RŌ (lit.), stately mansion with two or more stories, watchtower	煙	EN; *kemuri*, smoke
歳	SAI, ~ years old (used as suffix); SEI (year, age, time)	照	433 page 101
殿	TEN, DEN; *~dono*, Mr., Mrs., etc. (used in formal letters); *tono*, lord, my lord	煩	HAN, trouble, worry; *wazura*(*washii*), complicated, troublesome
源	GEN; *minamoto*, origin, source	献	KEN, KON (to dedicate, to offer, to present)
準	637 page 142	痴	CHI (foolish, stupid)
溶	YŌ; *to*(*keru*), to melt, to dissolve (v. i.); *to*-(*kasu*), to melt (v. t.)	盟	873 page 189
滅	METSU; *horo*(*biru*), to go to ruin, to die out; *horo*(*bosu*), to ruin, to destroy	睡	SUI (to sleep, to doze)
滑	KATSU (smooth, even; to slide)	督	TOKU (to control, to supervise, to urge)
滞	TAI; *todokō*(*ru*), to stagnate, to fall into arrears, to be left undone	碁	GO, the Japanese game of *go*
漢	572 page 129	禁	763 page 167
滝	*taki*, waterfall, cataract, cascade	禍	KA (misfortune, disaster, evil)

福	506 page 116	義	580 page 131
禅	ZEN, Dhyāna, the Zen sect of Buddhism, religious meditation	聖	824 page 179
稚	CHI (infant, young, childish, raw)	腰	YŌ; *koshi*, waist, loins
節	446 page 104	腸	676 page 150
絹	772 page 169	腹	FUKU; *hara*, belly, abdomen, guts; heart, mind
継	KEI; *tsu(gi)* a patch; *tsu(gu)*, to inherit, to succeed to, to come into (property, etc.)	艇	TEI (boat)
続	456 page 106	蒸	JŌ; *mu(su)*, to steam, to foment, to be sultry or sweltering
罪	794 page 173	蓄	CHIKU (to store, to save)
置	469 page 108	虜	RYO (captive, prisoner of war)
署	SHO, station (police, fire, etc.), suffix for "government office"	虞	*osore*, anxiety, apprehension
群	594 page 133	裏	RI; *ura*, reverse side, back, opposite, second half (baseball)

裸	RA; *hadaka*, nakedness, nude	誉	YO; *homa(re)*, honor, credit, glory, reputation
解	567 page 128	豊	870 page 189
触	SHOKU; *fu(reru)*, to touch, to mention; to conflict with; to proclaim	賃	844 page 183
試	416 page 98	賄	WAI (wealth, bribe; to cater for)
詩	415 page 98	資	800 page 175
詰	KITSU (to call to account); *tsu(meru)*, to cram, to put close to, to shorten	賊	ZOKU, thief, robber, burglar
話	151 page 45	跡	SEKI; *ato*, mark, trace, trail, wake, ruins
該	GAI, that, the very, the ~ in question (used as prefix)	路	540 page 123
詳	SHŌ; *kuwa(shii)*, detailed, minute; well-informed	跳	CHŌ (to jump, to leap, to flee)
誇	KO; *hoko(ri)*, pride; *hoko(ru)*, to be proud of, to boast of	践	SEN (to step on, to go, to carry out)
誠	825 page 180	較	KAKU (to compare)

載	SAI; *no(seru)*, to load, to place (on); to put on record, to publish	鉱	610 page 137
辞	626 page 140	隔	KAKU; *heda(teru)*, to separate, to screen, to estrange; *heda(taru)*, to be distant from
農	491 page 113	雌	SHI; *mesu*, *me*, female (animal, bird; *me* is also used in the case of plants)
違	I; *chiga(u)*, to differ from, to be wrong	零	REI, zero, (to fall, to rain; fragment)
遠	160 page 47	雷	RAI; *kaminari*, thunder, thunderbolt
遣	KEN (to send, to dispatch, to bestow)	電	286 page 72
酬	SHŪ (to reward, to recompense, to return, to repay)	預	875 page 190
酪	RAKU (dairy products)	頒	HAN (to distribute, to divide)
鈴	REI; RIN, *suzu*, small bell	飼	SHI; *ka(u)*, to raise, to rear, to keep (animals)
鉛	EN; *namari*, lead (metal)	飽	HŌ; *a(ki)*, weariness, tiresomeness; *a(kiru)*, to grow tired of, to become weary of
鉄	283 page 71	飾	SHOKU; *kaza(ru)*, to ornament, to embellish, to exhibit, to affect

塩	354 page 85	鼓	KO; *tsuzumi*, hand drum
	14 STROKES		
像	664 page 147	寧	NEI (quiet, peaceful, easy; kind; rather)
僚	RYŌ (an official; friend, colleague)	層	SŌ, stratum, layer; (to be piled up)
境	761 page 167	彰	SHŌ (manifest, clear; to elucidate)
増	665 page 148	徴	CHŌ (symptom, sign; effect, proof; to summon)
墨	BOKU; *sumi*, India ink, ink stick	徳	851 page 185
奪	DATSU; *uba(u)*, to take by force, to rob, to captivate	態	840 page 183
嫡	CHAKU (heir, legitimate child)	慕	BO; *shita(u)*, to yearn for, to adore, to follow
察	406 page 96	慢	MAN (to be idle, to neglect; to despise, to be haughty, to be selfish)
寡	KA (few, little, small, scanty; alone; widow)	慣	574 page 129

憎	ZŌ; *niku(mu)*, to hate, to detest	滴	TEKI (drop of liquid, trickle; to drip); suffix for counting drops of liquid
摘	TEKI (to disclose, to reveal, to point out); *tsu(mu)*, to pick, to pluck	漁	588 page 132
旗	371 page 89	漂	HYŌ (to wander about; to bleach); *tadayo(u)*, to drift, to float
暮	BO; *ku(re)*, year end; *ku(reru)*, to grow dark, to end; *ku(rasu)*, to live, to make a living	漆	SHITSU; *urushi*, lacquer
暦	REKI; *koyomi*, calendar, almanac	漏	RŌ; *mo(ru)*, to leak; *mo(reru)*, to leak, to get out (secret, etc.), to be omitted
構	785 page 172	演	553 page 125
概	GAI (roughly, generally, as a rule)	漫	MAN (in spite of oneself, involuntarily, self-willfulness; vast, wide, lax)
模	MO, BO (model, mold; to model after)	漸	ZEN (gradually; to advance gradually; at last)
様	328 page 80	獄	GOKU, prison, jail
歌	166 page 48	疑	757 page 166
歴	536 page 122	碑	HI, monument, tombstone

磁	JI (magnet, compass; porcelain)	綱	KŌ (basic principles); *tsuna*, rope, cable; last hope (of life, etc.)
種	423 page 99	網	MŌ; *ami*, net, netting
稻	TŌ; *ine*, rice plant	綿	725 page 160
穀	786 page 172	緒	SHO, beginning, (lineage; clue); *o*, cord, string (of a musical instrument)
端	TAN (right, correct, just); *hashi*, end, tip, edge, border	練	539 page 122
箇	KA (used as auxiliary in counting)	総	661 page 147
算	219 page 58	罰	BATSU, penalty, punishment; *bas-(suru)*, to punish, to penalize
管	573 page 129	聞	314 page 77
精	647 page 144	腐	FU; *kusa(ru)*, to go bad, to rot; to be dejected, to lose heart
緑	532 page 121	膜	MAKU, membrane
維	I (to keep; to fasten; fundamental principles)	製	648 page 144

複	865 page 188	踊	YŌ; *odo(ri)*, dance; *odo(ru)*, to dance, to jump
誌	SHI (record; to write down)	適	679 page 150
認	855 page 186	遭	SŌ (to encounter, to come across)
誓	SEI; *chika(i)*, oath, vow; *chika(u)*, to swear, to take a vow	酵	KŌ (yeast, ferment, saké lees)
誕	TAN (to be born; to give birth to)	酷	KOKU, severity, cruelty, harshness
誘	YŪ; *saso(i)*, invitation, temptation; *saso(u)*, to invite, to induce, to allure	酸	618 page 138
語	209 page 56	銀	196 page 54
誤	779 page 170	銃	JŪ, gun, rifle
説	654 page 145	銅	683 page 151
読	123 page 39	銑	SEN (pig iron)
豪	GŌ (to excel, to stand pre-eminent; strong, vigorous)	銘	MEI, signature, inscription, appellation, motto, (to inscribe)

銭	656 page 146	静	442 page 103
閣	KAKU (mansion, palace, tower; government office)	領	735 page 162
閥	BATSU, clique, faction, clan	駆	KU (to drive a vehicle, to chase); *ka*(*keru*), to run, to gallop
関	365 page 88	駅	158 page 46
際	612 page 137	髪	HATSU; *kami*, hair, hairdo
障	SHŌ (to hinder, to interfere with)	魂	KON; *tamashii*, soul, spirit, ghost
隠	IN; *kaku*(*reru*), to hide (v.i.), to disappear; *kaku*(*su*), to hide (v.t.), to conceal	鳴	321 page 79
雑	615 page 138	鼻	496 page 114
需	804 page 175		
	15 STROKES		
儀	GI, rule, ceremony, affair, matter	億	557 page 126

劇	GEKI, drama, play, (intense, violent, severe, hard)	幣	HEI (pendant paper strips in a Shinto shrine; riches, offering, money)
勲	KUN (meritorious deed, distinguished service)	弊	HEI, evil, abuse, vice; our (used as prefix denoting modesty)
器	372 page 89	影	EI; *kage*, shadow, reflection, image, phantom, light)
噴	FUN (to emit, to belch, to send forth)	徹	TETSU (to pierce, to penetrate)
嘱	SHOKU (to entrust, to request)	慮	RYO (to consider, to deliberate, to plan, to be anxious)
墜	TSUI (to fall, to drop)	慰	I; *nagusa(me)*, comfort; *nagusa(mi)*, pastime; *nagusa(meru)*, to comfort, to console
墳	FUN (mound, tumulus, hillock, tomb)	慶	KEI (congratulation, happiness; to rejoice)
審	SHIN (detailed, full, clear, evident, obvious)	憂	YŪ; *ure(i)*, grief, anxiety, affliction; *ure(eru)*, to fear, to lament, to be worried
寮	RYŌ, boarding house, dormitory	憤	FUN; *ikidō(ru)*, to be indignant, to resent
導	684 page 151	戯	GI (fun, play, flirtation); *tawamu(reru)*, to joke, to play, to flirt with
履	RI (footwear; to walk; to do, to experience)	摩	MA (to rub, to grind, to wear away); *ma(suru)* (lit.), to nearly touch; to scrape

撤	TETSU; *tes(suru)*, to remove, to get rid of, to withdraw (an army, etc.)	歓	753 page 165
撮	SATSU (to pinch, to pick, to gather; to take a photograph)	潔	767 page 168
撲	BOKU (to strike, to beat)	潜	SEN (to dive into water; secretly); *hiso-(mu)*, to conceal oneself, to lurk
撃	GEKI; *u(tsu)*, to fire (a gun, etc.), to attack, to strike, to fight	潤	JUN; *uruo(i)*, moisture; profit; charm; *uruo(su)* (v. t.), to moisten; to profit
敵	678 page 150	潮	CHŌ; *shio*, tide, sea water; opportunity
敷	FU; *shi(ku)*, to spread, to pave, to sit on (a cushion), to lay (a railway)	澄	CHŌ; *su(mu)*, to become clear or serene (moon, stream, sky, mind, etc.)
暫	ZAN (for a little while, for some time)	熟	JUKU (carefully, attentively); *juku(suru)*, to grow ripe, to mature
暴	871 page 189	熱	490 page 113
標	704 page 155	監	KAN (to watch over, to keep control over, to supervise; prison, jail)
横	355 page 86	盤	BAN, board (for chess, etc.), (shallow basin, phonograph record, plate)
権	774 page 169	確	570 page 129

稿	KŌ, draft, rough copy, manuscript	緩	KAN (slow, easy, slack, lenient)
穂	SUI; *ho*, ear (of wheat, etc.), head	罷	HI (to pause, to intermit, to dismiss, to release, to get tired)
窮	KYŪ; *kiwa(meru)*, to carry to extremes; *kiwa(maru)*, to end, to reach the extreme	膚	FU; *hada*, skin (of the body)
窯	YŌ (kiln for baking tiles, ceramics, etc.)	舗	HO (store; to pave)
箱	*hako*, box, case	舞	BU; *mai*, dancing, dance; *ma(u)*, to dance
範	HAN, example, model	蔵	833 page 181
緊	KIN (to shrink, to become tight, to contract; severe, strict, hard, solid)	衝	SHŌ, important position, focus; (to attack, to strike against; to brave)
線	447 page 104	課	564 page 127
締	TEI; *shi(maru)*, to be shut, to be tight; *shi(meru)*, to tie, to tighten, to shut (v.t.)	調	471 page 109
縁	EN, relation, ties, blood relation; fate; veranda, porch; *fuchi*, edge, verge	談	467 page 108
編	714 page 157	請	SEI, SHIN; *ko(u)*, to beg, to ask, to request; *u(keru)*, to receive, to undertake

論	881 page 191	趣	SHU; *omomuki*, taste, elegance, grace, air, appearance, purport, effect
諸	812 page 177	踏	TŌ; *fu(mu)*, to step on, to tread on
諾	DAKU, consent, assent	輝	KI; *kagaya(ku)*, to shine, to be radiant
謁	ETSU, (Imperial) audience; audience with persons of high rank	輩	HAI (fellows, companions)
賓	HIN (guest)	輪	533 page 121
賜	SHI; *tama(waru)*, to deign to give, to grant, to award	遵	JUN (to obey, to observe, to abide by)
賞	641 page 143	遷	SEN (to move from one location to another, to transfer)
賠	BAI (to make up for, to compensate for)	選	449 page 104
賦	FU (lit.), ode, poetical prose; tribute, levy, allotment	遺	739 page 162
質	628 page 140	鋭	EI; *surudo(i)*, sharp, pointed, biting, acute, keen, smart
賛	619 page 138	鋳	CHŪ; *i(ru)*, to cast (metal), to found

閲	ETSU (lit.), inspection, examination; (to examine, to inspect, to peruse, to elapse)	餓	GA (to be hungry, to starve)
震	SHIN; *furu(u)*, *furu(eru)*, to shake (v. i.), to tremble; *furu(waseru)*, to shake (v. t.)	駐	CHŪ (to stop, to stay)
霊	REI, soul, spirit, ghost	魅	MI; *mi(suru)* (lit.), to fascinate, to enchant, to bewitch
養	731 page 161	黙	MOKU; *dama(ru)*, to become silent, to close one's lips

16 STROKES

儒	JU (Confucianism, Confucianist, scholar; cowardice, tenderness)	奮	866 page 188
凝	GYŌ; *ko(ri)*, stiffness; *ko(ru)*, to be absorbed in, to elaborate, to grow stiff	嬢	JŌ, Miss (used as suffix), (girl, unmarried lady, daughter)
墾	KON (to cultivate, to farm, to reclaim)	憩	KEI (to take a rest)
壁	HEKI; *kabe*, wall	憲	773 page 169
壇	DAN, platform, dais, raised floor	憶	OKU (to remember, to keep in mind, to think)
壞	KAI (to collapse, to be destroyed; to break, to destroy)	憾	KAN (to regret, to be sorry for)

懐	KAI (one's pocket; to think, to long for)	燃	690 page 153
擁	YŌ; *yō(suru)*, to protect, to embrace, to hold	燈	485 page 112
操	SŌ (to handle, to manage, to manipulate); *misao*, chastity, virtue, constancy	獲	KAKU; *e(ru)*, to get, to obtain, to gain
整	443 page 103	獣	JŪ; *kemono*, beast, brute
曇	DON; *kumo(ri)*, cloudy weather, blur; *kumo(ru)*, to become cloudy, to become dim	積	445 page 104
樹	JU (living tree, vegetation; to stand, to plant)	穏	ON; *oda(yaka)*, calm, quiet, peaceful, mild
橋	193 page 53	築	673 page 149
機	373 page 89	篤	TOKU (genuine, sincere, hearty, cordial)
激	GEKI; *geki(suru)*, to be excited or enraged; *hage(shii)*, violent, intense, passionate	糖	TŌ (sugar)
濁	DAKU; *nigo(ri)*, turbidity; voiced sound; *nigo(ru)*, to become muddy or cloudy	緯	I (parallels of latitude; cross-threads)
濃	NŌ; *ko(i)*, dark, deep, thick, heavy, strong	縛	BAKU; *shiba(ru)*, to bind, to tie, to arrest

縫	HŌ; *nu(u)*, to sew, to stitch	衛	551 page 125
縱	JŪ; *tate*, vertical direction, length, height	衡	KŌ (scale beam; to measure, to weigh)
繁	HAN (thick, many, much, thriving; troublesome, busy, mixed)	親	260 page 67
膨	BŌ (to swell, to expand)	諭	YU (to admonish)
興	589 page 132	諮	SHI (to consult, to ask counsel of)
薄	HAKU; *usu(i)*, thin, light, pale, weak, small (profit, etc.)	謀	BŌ (plan, device, stratagem, plot)
薦	SEN (to recommend)	謡	YŌ; *utai*, chanting of a *Noh* drama text
薪	SHIN (firewood)	賢	KEN; *kashiko(i)*, wise, intelligent, tactful, smart, shrewd
薫	KUN, (fragrance; to be fragrant)	頼	RAI; *tano(mi)*, request, recourse; *tano-(mu)*, to ask, to entrust with, to rely on
藥	521 page 119	輸	727 page 160
融	YŪ (to melt; to circulate, to ventilate)	避	HI; *sa(keru)*, to avoid, to keep away from, to shirk

還	KAN (to return, to come back)	錬	REN (to temper or forge metal; to train, to cultivate, to polish, to drill morally)
鋼	KŌ, steel	隣	RIN; *tonari*, next-door house; next to, neighboring
録	543 page 123	隷	REI (servant, follower)
錘	SUI (weight for scales, sinker for fishing line); *tsumu*, spindle	頭	294 page 73
錠	JŌ, lock, padlock; tablet (medical) (used as suffix for counting tablets)	館	366 page 88
錯	SAKU (to be mixed together, to make a mistake)		

17 STROKES

償	SHŌ; *tsuguna(i)*, indemnity, atonement; *tsuguna(u)*, to make up for, to atone for	懇	KON (kind, cordial, in love with, intimate)
優	YŪ, excellent; *yasa-(shii)*, gentle, tender, kind, affectionate, graceful	擦	SATSU (to rub, to scrub, to scratch)
嚇	KAKU (to threaten, to menace)	擬	GI; *gi(suru)*, to point or aim (an object) at; to imitate; to compare
厳	776 page 170	燥	SŌ (to dry)

爵	SHAKU (peerage, title and court rank)	謄	TŌ (to take a copy of, to transcribe)
犠	GI (sacrifice, victim)	謙	KEN (to humble oneself, to condescend)
環	KAN (ring, link; to surround)	講	609 page 136
療	RYŌ (to cure, to heal)	謝	630 page 141
礁	SHŌ (submerged rock, unknown reef)	謹	KIN (to restrain oneself, to be respectful)
縮	SHUKU; *chiji(mu)* (v.i.), *chiji(meru)* (v.t.), to shrink, to contract, to draw in	購	KŌ (to purchase, to buy)
績	650 page 145	轄	KATSU (control, management)
繊	SEN (thin, slender, fine, small)	醜	SHŪ; *miniku(i)*, ugly, unseemly, ignoble
翼	YOKU (to aid, to assist); *tsubasa*, wing	鍛	TAN; *kita(eru)*, to forge; to train, to cultivate (morally)
聴	CHŌ (to listen to, to comply with)	霜	SŌ; *shimo*, frost
覧	RAN (to see, to look at)	鮮	SEN (Korea; fresh, newly produced, vivid, bright, splendid; few, little)

齢	REI (age, years)		
18 STROKES			
懲	CHŌ; *ko(rasu)*, to punish, to discipline, to chasten	織	644 page 143
曜	329 page 80	繕	ZEN; *tsukuro(u)*, to patch up, to mend, to trim, to smooth over
濫	RAN (at random, wantonly; excessive; to overflow, to float)	繭	KEN; *mayu*, silkworm cocoon
癖	HEKI; *kuse*, habit, peculiar way, friz (of hair), weakness	職	819 page 178
瞬	SHUN (a short time; to wink, to twinkle, to flicker)	臨	880 page 191
礎	SO; *ishizue*, foundation, cornerstone	藩	HAN, Japanese feudal clan or domain
穫	KAKU (to reap, to harvest)	覆	FUKU (to upset, to overturn, to cover, to wrap, to hide, to shelter)
簡	KAN, simplicity, brevity, conciseness; (letter, book)	覧	367 page 88
糧	RYŌ (food, provisions)	贈	ZŌ; *oku(ru)*, to present as a gift

鎖	SA (hasp; to shut, to close); *kusari*, chain	類	534 page 121
鎮	CHIN (to calm, to quiet, to tranquilize; to suppress)	顕	KEN (bright, clear, distinguished, manifest; to show, to manifest)
離	RI; *hana(reru)* (v.i.), *hana(su)* (v.t.), to separate, to part, to divide, to keep apart	翻	HON; *hirugae(ru)*, to flutter; *hirugae(su)*, to wave (v.t.); to change (one's mind)
難	853 page 185	騎	KI, suffix for counting horsemen; (cavalry, saddle horse; to ride, to mount)
題	464 page 107	騒	SŌ; *sawa(gi)*, noise, disturbance; *sawa(gu)*, to make a noise, to make a disturbance
額	748 page 164	験	600 page 135
顔	179 page 50	闘	TŌ (to fight)

19 STROKES

瀬	*se*, shallows, rapids	簿	BO (notebook)
爆	BAKU (to burst, to explode)	繰	*ku(ru)*, to reel (thread, etc.), to gin (cotton), to turn over (pages, etc.)
璽	JI (Imperial seal)	臓	ZŌ (entrails)

識	627 page 140	願	368 page 88
譜	FU, music, musical score; family record, genealogy	髓	ZUI, marrow, pith
警	KEI (to warn, to caution, to guard against; smart, agile)	鯨	GEI; *kujira*, whale
鏡	378 page 90	鶏	KEI; *niwatori*, chicken
霧	MU; *kiri*, mist, fog, spray	麗	REI; *uruwa*(*shii*), fine, lovely, beautiful, elegant, graceful
韻	IN, rhyme, (echo, taste, elegance)		

20 STROKES

懸	KEN, KE (to hang, to suspend; to offer a reward; to be anxious; to depend on)	議	581 page 131
欄	RAN, column (of a newspaper, etc.); railing	護	604 page 135
競	379 page 90	譲	JŌ; *yuzu*(*ru*), to hand over, to concede to, to yield to, to reserve
籍	SEKI, census register, membership	醸	JŌ (to brew)

鐘	SHŌ; *kane*, bell	騰	TŌ (to rise, to ascend, to leap)
響	KYŌ; *hibi(ki)*, sound, echo, vibration; *hibi-(ku)*, to echo, to vibrate, to affect		
21 STROKES			
艦	KAN (warship)	顧	KO; *kaeri(miru)*, to look back, to reflect upon oneself, to think of, to heed
躍	YAKU (to leap, to jump, to rise, to go up)	魔	MA, devil, demon, evil spirit
露	RO (to expose, to lay bare; to be exposed, to come to light); *tsuyu*, dew		
22 STROKES			
驚	KYŌ; *odoro(ki)*, surprise; *odoro(ku)*, to be surprised or frightened, to marvel (at)		
23 STROKES			
襲	SHŪ; *oso(u)*, to attack; to succeed to; to make a surprise visit	鑑	KAN (model, pattern, example)

PROPOSED CHANGES
in the List of General-Use Characters

Characters to Be Added

厄	YAKU, misfortune, calamity, ill luck 4 strokes	亭	TEI, restaurant, arbor, cottage; suffix used in stage names 9 strokes
汁	JŪ; *shiru*, soup; sap, gravy, juice 5 strokes	挑	CHŌ (to challenge, to make advances to) 9 strokes
朴	BOKU (simple and honest, unsophisticated) 6 strokes	洪	KŌ (flood; great) 9 strokes
戻	*modo(su)*, to return (v.t.), to vomit; *modo-(ru)*, to return (v.i.) 7 strokes	俸	HŌ (stipend, salary, rations) 10 strokes
杉	*sugi*, Japanese cedar, cryptomeria 7 strokes	宵	SHŌ; *yoi*, early evening 10 strokes
尚	SHŌ (to respect, to hope, to desire; still, indeed; old) 8 strokes	桟	SAN, frame (of a *shōji*, etc.), crosspiece, cleat, bolt 10 strokes
披	HI (to open) 8 strokes	酌	SHAKU, serving *sake*, helping (a person) to *sake* 10 strokes
泥	DEI; *doro*, mud, mire 8 strokes	竜	RYŪ, dragon 10 strokes
斉	SEI (in good order, equal, the same; to arrange, to manage) 8 strokes	偵	TEI (to inquire secretly into, to spy on) 11 strokes

堀	*hori*, moat 11 strokes	釣	*tsuri*, angling, fishing with a rod and line; change (money) 11 strokes
据	*su*(*eru*), to set, to lay, to place 11 strokes	渦	KA; *uzu*, whirlpool, eddy, vortex 12 strokes
殻	KAKU; *kara*, shell, valve, husk, nut-shell, cast-off skin 11 strokes	僕	BOKU (servant), I, me (used by men) 14 strokes
涯	GAI (end, extremity, limits, water's edge) 11 strokes	壌	JŌ (earth, soil) 16 strokes
渓	KEI (ravine, gorge, valley) 11 strokes	矯	KYŌ (to correct, to make straight, to redress) 17 strokes

Additional Readings and Simplified Writings

個	10 strokes page 135 (603)	個	KO KA (additional reading)
燈	16 strokes page 112 (485)	灯	TŌ; *hi* (additional reading) 6 strokes simplified writing

Characters to Be Dropped

又	2 strokes page 192	朕	10 strokes page 232
丹	4 strokes page 194	逋	10 strokes page 236
且	5 strokes page 197	堪	12 strokes page 246
奴	5 strokes page 199	脹	12 strokes page 251
迅	6 strokes page 206	煩	13 strokes page 257
但	7 strokes page 206	虞	13 strokes page 258
劾	8 strokes page 214	頒	13 strokes page 260
附	8 strokes page 220	寡	14 strokes page 261
唐	10 strokes page 230	箇	14 strokes page 263
悦	10 strokes page 231	罷	15 strokes page 268

謁	15 strokes page 269	嚇	17 strokes page 273
遵	15 strokes page 269	爵	17 strokes page 274
鍊	16 strokes page 273	濫	18 strokes page 275
隸	16 strokes page 273	璽	19 strokes page 276

SYLLABARY

Katakana and Hiragana

ア *a*	㇇ア	あ *a*	㇂ㇳああ
イ *i*	ノイ	い *i*	いい
ウ *u*	丶宀ウ	う *u*	丶う
エ *e*	一工エ	え *e*	丶うえ
オ *o*	一十オ	お *o*	一ㇷおお
カ *ka*	力カ	か *ka*	㇇かか
キ *ki*	一二キ	き *ki*	一二きき
ク *ku*	ノ ク	く *ku*	く
ケ *ke*	ノ 𠂉 ケ	け *ke*	いけ

コ *ko*	フコ	こ *ko*	こ
サ *sa*	一十サ	さ *sa*	一さ さ
シ *shi*	シシシ	し *shi*	し
ス *su*	フス	す *su*	一す す
セ *se*	フセ	せ *se*	一十せ
ソ *so*	ソ	そ *so*	そそ
タ *ta*	ノクタ	た *ta*	一十たた
チ *chi*	ノ二チ	ち *chi*	一ち
ツ *tsu*	ツツツ	つ *tsu*	つ
テ *te*	一二テ	て *te*	一て
ト *to*	丨ト	と *to*	いと

ナ *na*	一ナ	な *na*	一ナナな
ニ *ni*	一ニ	に *ni*	しにに
ヌ *nu*	フヌ	ぬ *nu*	しめぬ
ネ *ne*	丶ラネネ	ね *ne*	しれね
ノ *no*	ノ	の *no*	ノの
ハ *ha*	ノハ	は *ha*	しには
ヒ *hi*	一ヒ	ひ *hi*	てひ
フ *fu*	フ	ふ *fu*	丶ふふふ
ヘ *he*	ヘ	へ *he*	へ
ホ *ho*	一十オホ	ほ *ho*	しにほ
マ *ma*	フマ	ま *ma*	一二ま

ミ *mi*	ミミ	み *mi*	みみ
ム *mu*	ムム	む *mu*	むむ
メ *me*	メ	め *me*	め
モ *mo*	モ	も *mo*	も
ヤ *ya*	ヤ	や *ya*	や
ユ *yu*	ユ	ゆ *yu*	ゆ
ヨ *yo*	ヨ	よ *yo*	よ
ラ *ra*	ラ	ら *ra*	ら
リ *ri*	リ	り *ri*	り
ル *ru*	ル	る *ru*	る
レ *re*	レ	れ *re*	れ

ロ *ro*	ロ	ろ *ro*	ろ
ワ *wa*	ワ	わ *wa*	わ
ヲ *o*	ヲ	を *o*	を
ン *n*	ン	ん *n*	ん

Sound Changes and Kana Combinations

ガ	ga	ギ	gi	グ	gu	ゲ	ge	ゴ	go
ザ	za	ジ	ji	ズ	zu	ゼ	ze	ゾ	zo
ダ	da	ヂ	ji	ヅ	zu	デ	de	ド	do
バ	ba	ビ	bi	ブ	bu	ベ	be	ボ	bo
パ	pa	ピ	pi	プ	pu	ペ	pe	ポ	po
キャ	kya	キュ	kyu	キョ	kyo	シャ	sha	シュ	shu
ショ	sho	チャ	cha	チュ	chu	チョ	cho	ニャ	nya
ニュ	nyu	ニョ	nyo	ヒャ	hya	ヒュ	hyu	ヒョ	hyo
ミャ	mya	ミュ	myu	ミョ	myo	リャ	rya	リュ	ryu
リョ	ryo	ギャ	gya	ギュ	gyu	ギョ	gyo	ジャ	ja
ジュ	ju	ジョ	jo	ビャ	bya	ビュ	byu	ビョ	byo
ピャ	pya	ピュ	pyu	ピョ	pyo				

INDEX OF READINGS

THIS INDEX contains an alphabetical listing of all Japanese readings given in the body of the book. *On* readings are in small capitals and *kun* readings in italics. Main reference numerals indicate pages. Such page references are followed by : (1) an *a* or a *b*, indicating that a given character is to be found in the left- or right-hand column, or (2) a numeral in parentheses, indicating the number of the character as used in the listing of the 881 essential characters. When readings include *okurigana* these are not indicated by parentheses, since they can be found under the individual characters. In most cases where different *okurigana* are added to the same root pronunciation of a character, all readings appear under one entry.

— A —

A 亜 206a
abiru 浴 161(732)
abura 油 119(522)
agaru, ageru 上 19(20)
ageru 揚 248a
AI, *aisuru* 愛 82(339)
AI 哀 222a
ai 相 105(452)
aida 間 26(58)
aji 味 118(516)
aka, akai 赤 22(35)
akarui 明 43(141)
akatsuki 暁 248b
akeru 明 43(141)
aki 秋 32(89)
aki, akiru 飽 260b
akinau 商 101(431)
akiraka 明 43(141)
AKU 悪 45(152)
AKU 握 248a
ama 尼 199a
amai 甘 200a
amari, amaru, amasu 余 160(728)
ame 雨 23(42)
ame 天 38(119)
ami 網 263b
amu 編 157(714)
AN 行 29(73)
AN 安 45(153)
AN 暗 45(154)
AN, *anjiru* 案 83(340)
ana 穴 201a
anadoru 侮 213b
ane 姉 97(413)
ani 兄 54(199)
ao, aoi 青 22(36)
aogu 仰 201a
arai 荒 227a
arasoi, arasou 争 105(451)
aratamaru, aratameru 改 86(359)
aratani 新 66(256)
arau 洗 225a
arawareru, arawasu 現 135(602)
arawasu 表 76(309)
arawasu 著 183(843)
areru 荒 227a
aru 有 119 (523)
aruku 歩 42(136)
asa 朝 38(118)
asa 麻 245b
asai 浅 146(655)
ase 汗 205a
ashi 足 20(29)
asobu 遊 80(326)
ataeru 与 194b
atai 価 127(563)
atai 値 229a
atama 頭 73(294)
atarashii 新 66(256)
ataru, ateru 当 73(290)
atatakai 暖 256b
ateru 充 202a

ato 跡 259b
ATSU 圧 123(544)
atsui 暑 64(247)
atsui 熱 113(490)
atsui 厚 136(606)
atsukau 扱 204a
atsumaru, atsumeru 集 63(243)
au 会 25(54)
au 合 30(77)
awai 淡 241a
aware, awaremu 哀 222a
ayamari, ayamaru 誤 170(779)
ayashii, ayashimu 怪 216b
ayaui 危 202b
ayumu 歩 42(136)
aza 字 32(86)
azamuku 欺 249a
azukaru, azukeru 預 190(875)

— B —

BA 馬 40(127)
BA 婆 238b
ba 場 65(252)
BAI 買 75(300)
BAI 売 75(301)
BAI 倍 153(694)
BAI 梅 232b
BAI 培 238b
BAI 陪 245a
BAI 媒 247a
BAI 賠 269a
bakasu, bakeru 化 47(163)
BAKU 麦 40(128)
BAKU 暴 189(871)
BAKU 幕 255b
BAKU 縛 271b
BAKU 爆 276a
BAN 番 76 (306)
BAN 万 79 (320)
BAN 判 187(860)
BAN 伴 206a
BAN 晩 248b
BAN 蛮 252a
BAN 盤 267b
BATSU 伐 201b
BATSU 抜 210a
BATSU, *bassuru* 罰 263b
BATSU 閥 265a
BEI 米 42(135)
BEN 勉 78(317)
BEN 便 117(510)
BEN 弁 158(715)
beni 紅 226b
BETSU 別 116(508)
BI 美 76(308)
BI 鼻 114(496)
BI 備 155(700)
BI 尾 209a
BI 微 255b
BIN 便 117(510)
BIN 貧 156(705)
BIN 敏 232a
BO 母 42(137)
BO 墓 188(869)
BO 募 246a
BO 慕 261b
BO 暮 262a
BO 模 262a
BO 簿 276b
BŌ 望 117(514)
BŌ 防 158(718)
BŌ 貿 158(719)
BŌ 暴 189(871)
BŌ 亡 193a
BŌ 乏 194a
BŌ 忙 204a
BŌ 坊 208b
BŌ 妨 208b
BŌ 忘 209b
BŌ 房 216b
BŌ 肪 219b
BŌ 冒 221b
BŌ 某 224b
BŌ 剖 229b
BŌ 紡 235a
BŌ 傍 246a
BŌ 帽 247b
BŌ 棒 249a
BŌ 膨 272a
BŌ 謀 272b
BOKU 木 18(15)
BOKU 牧 159(720)
BOKU 墨 261a
BOKU 撲 267a
BOKU 朴 279a
BOKU 僕 280b
BON 凡 193a
BON 盆 225b
BOTSU, *bossuru* 没 210b
BU 分 41(133)
BU 歩 42(136)
BU 部 115(504)
BU 武 156(708)
BU 無 159(723)
BU 侮 213b
BU 舞 268b
BUN 分 41(133)
BUN 文 41(134)
BUN 聞 77(314)
buta 豚 244a
BUTSU 物 77(313)
BUTSU 仏 157(711)
BYAKU 白 22(37)
BYŌ 病 77(310)
BYŌ 平 78(315)
BYŌ 秒 114(499)
BYŌ 苗 220a
BYŌ 描 240b

— C —

CHA 茶 70(275)
CHAKU 着 70(276)
CHAKU 嫡 261a
CHI 池 37(110)
CHI 地 37(111)
CHI 知 37(112)
CHI 治 108(468)
CHI 置 108(469)
CHI 値 229a
CHI 恥 231b
CHI 致 235b
CHI 遅 253b
CHI 痴 257b
CHI 稚 258a

chi 千 35(101)
chi 血 92(389)
chi, chichi 乳 213a
chichi 父 41(131)
chigau 違 260a
chigiru 契 222a
chiisai 小 19(24)
chijimeru, chijimu 縮 274a
chikai 近 54(195)
chikai, chikau 誓 264a
chikara 力 44(148)
CHIKU 竹 37(113)
CHIKU 築 149(673)
CHIKU 畜 233b
CHIKU 逐 236b
CHIKU 蓄 258b
CHIN 賃 183(844)
CHIN 沈 210b
CHIN 珍 225b
CHIN 朕 232a, 281b
CHIN 陳 245a
CHIN 鎮 276a
chirasu, chiru 散 96(407)
CHITSU 秩 234b
CHITSU 窒 242a
CHO 貯 149(674)
CHO 著 183(843)
CHŌ 町 38(115)
CHŌ 長 38(116)
CHŌ 鳥 38(117)
CHŌ 朝 38(118)
CHŌ 重 64(245)
CHŌ 帳 109(470)
CHŌ 調 109(471)
CHŌ 丁 109(473)
CHŌ 張 150(675)
CHŌ 腸 150(676)
CHŌ 弔 196a
CHŌ 庁 199b
CHŌ 兆 202a
CHŌ 彫 239b
CHŌ 頂 245b
CHŌ 脹 251b, 281b
CHŌ 超 253a
CHŌ 跳 259b
CHŌ 徴 261b
CHŌ 潮 267b
CHŌ 澄 267b
CHŌ 聴 274a
CHŌ 懲 275a
CHŌ 挑 279b
CHOKU 直 109(472)
CHOKU 勅 221b
CHŪ 中 19(23)
CHŪ 虫 37(114)
CHŪ 注 70(277)
CHŪ 柱 70(278)
CHŪ 昼 70(279)
CHŪ 忠 183(842)
CHŪ 仲 201a
CHŪ 宙 215b
CHŪ 抽 217a
CHŪ 衷 235b
CHŪ 鋳 269b
CHŪ 駐 270b

—D—

DA 打 107(460)
DA 妥 208b
DA 堕 247a
DA 惰 248a
DAI 大 19(22)
DAI 台 69(272)
DAI 第 69(273)
DAI 弟 71(282)
DAI 代 107(463)
DAI 題 107(464)
DAI 内 112(489)
DAKU 諾 269a
DAKU 濁 271a
daku 抱 216b
damaru 黙 270b
DAN 男 36(109)
DAN 談 108(467)
DAN 団 149(672)
DAN 断 183(841)
DAN 段 224b
DAN 弾 247b
DAN 暖 256b
DAN 壇 270a
dasu 出 33(90)
~date 建 93(391)
DATSU 脱 243a
DATSU 奪 261a
DEI 泥 279a
DEN 田 23(40)
DEN 電 72(286)
DEN 伝 151(681)
DEN 殿 257a
deru 出 33(90)
DO 土 18(17)
DO 度 72(288)
DO 努 111(481)
DO 奴 199a, 281a
DO 怒 223a
DŌ 道 39(122)
DŌ 同 74(295)
DŌ 動 74(296)
DŌ 堂 112(486)
DŌ 童 112(487)
DŌ 働 112(488)
DŌ 銅 151(683)
DŌ 導 151(684)
DŌ 胴 235a
DOKU 読 39(123)
DOKU 毒 152(686)
DOKU 独 152(687)
DON 鈍 253b
DON 曇 271a
~dono 殿 257a
doro 泥 279a

—E—

E 会 25(54)
E 絵 49(172)
E 依 213a
E 恵 231b
e 江 205a
e 柄 224b
eda 枝 218a
egaku 描 240b
EI 泳 85(352)
EI 英 85(353)
EI 栄 124(549)
EI 永 125(550)
EI 衛 125(551)
EI 営 163(741)
EI 映 224a

EI 詠 252b
EI 影 266b
EI 鋭 269b
EKI 駅 46(158)
EKI 役 79(324)
EKI 易 124(545)
EKI 液 125(552)
EKI, *ekisuru* 益 163(742)
EKI 疫 225b
EN 円 24(48)
EN 園 46(159)
EN 遠 47(160)
EN 塩 85(354)
EN, *enzuru* 演 125(553)
EN 延 163(743)
EN 沿 218b
EN 炎 219a
EN 宴 230b
EN 援 248a
EN 煙 257b
EN 鉛 260a
EN 縁 268a
erabu 選 104(449)
erai 偉 246a
eru 得 185(850)
eru 獲 271b
ETSU 悦 231b, 281a
ETSU 越 253a
ETSU 謁 269a, 282a
ETSU 閲 270a

— F —

FU 父 41(131)
FU 負 77(312)
FU 不 115(500)
FU 夫 115(501)
FU 付 115(502)
FU 府 115(503)
FU 布 156(706)
FU 婦 156(707)
FU 富 187(864)
FU 扶 209b
FU 怖 216b
FU 附 220b, 281a
FU 赴 227b
FU 浮 233a
FU 符 242b
FU 普 248b
FU 腐 263b
FU 敷 267a
FU 膚 268b
FU 賦 269a
FU 譜 277a
FŪ 風 41(132)
FŪ 夫 115(501)
FŪ 富 187(864)
FŪ, *fūzuru* 封 222b
fuchi 縁 268a
fuda 札 200a
fude 筆 155(701)
fue 笛 242a
fukai, fukasa 深 66(258)
FUKU 服 116(505)
FUKU 福 116(506)
FUKU 副 156(709)
FUKU 復 157(710)
FUKU 複 188(865)
FUKU 伏 201b
FUKU 幅 247b
FUKU 腹 258b
FUKU 覆 275b
fuku 吹 208a
fukumu 含 208a
fukuro 袋 243b
fumu 踏 269b
FUN 分 41(133)
FUN 粉 116(507)
FUN 奮 188(866)
FUN 紛 235a
FUN 噴 266a
FUN 墳 266a
FUN 憤 266b
fune, funa 船 68(266)
fune 舟 205b
fureru 触 259a
furu 振 231b
furu 降 237a
furuoru, furuu, furuwaseru 震 270a
furui 古 29(70)
furuu 奮 188(866)
fusegu 防 158(718)
fuseru 伏 201b
fushi 節 104(446)
futatabi 再 172(788)
futatsu 二 15(2)
futoi, futoru 太 68(269)
FUTSU 払 199b
FUTSU 沸 218b
fuyu 冬 39(120)

— G —

GA 画 48(167)
GA 芽 86(358)
GA 賀 128(565)
GA 我 164(745)
GA 雅 254a
GA 餓 270b
GAI 外 26(56)
GAI 害 87(362)
GAI 劾 214a, 281a
GAI 街 252a
GAI 慨 256a
GAI 該 259a
GAI 概 262a
GAI 涯 280a
GAKU 学 26(57)
GAKU 楽 81(331)
GAKU 額 164(748)
GAKU 岳 216a
GAN 元 28(68)
GAN 岸 50(177)
GAN 岩 50(178)
GAN 顔 50(179)
GAN 願 88(368)
GAN 眼 165(754)
GAN 丸 193a
GAN 含 208a
gara 柄 224b
~gata 形 55(200)
GATSU 月 17(12)
GE 下 19(21)
GE 外 26(56)
GEI 芸 92(388)
GEI 迎 212b
GEI 鯨 277b
GEKI 劇 266a
GEKI 撃 267a

GEKI, *gekisuru* 激 271a
GEN 元 28(68)
GEN 原 56(205)
GEN 言 93(392)
GEN 限 135(601)
GEN 現 135(602)
GEN 減 170(775)
GEN 厳 170(776)
GEN 幻 196a
GEN 玄 200a
GEN 弦 216a
GEN 源 257a
GETSU 月 17(12)
GI 技 130(579)
GI 義 131(580)
GI 議 131(581)
GI 疑 166(757)
GI 宜 215b
GI 偽 238a
GI 欺 249a
GI 儀 265a
GI 戯 266b
GI, *gisuru* 擬 273b
GI 犠 274a
GIN 銀 54(196)
GIN, *ginzuru* 吟 208a
GO 五 16(5)
GO 期 51(183)
GO 午 56(207)
GO 後 56(208)
GO 語 56(209)
GO 護 135(604)
GO 誤 170(779)
GO 互 194a
GO 呉 208a
GO 娯 230a
GO 悟 231b
GO 御 239b
GO 碁 257b
GŌ 合 30(77)
GŌ 強 53(192)
GŌ 号 58(215)
GŌ 業 91(380)
GŌ 拷 223b
GŌ 剛 229b
GŌ 郷 244b
GŌ 豪 264a
GOKU 極 91(382)
GOKU 獄 262b
GON 言 93(392)
GON 権 169(774)
GON 厳 170(776)
GU 具 91(383)
GU 供 167(760)
GU 愚 256a
GŪ 宮 89(374)
GŪ 偶 237b
GŪ 遇 253a
GUN 郡 91(384)
GUN 軍 133(593)
GUN 群 133(594)
GYAKU, *gyakuni* 逆 166(758)
GYAKU 虐 227b
GYO 魚 53(190)
GYO 漁 132(588)
GYO, *gyosuru* 御 239b
GYŌ 行 29(73)
GYŌ 形 55(200)
GYŌ 業 91(380)
GYŌ 仰 201a
GYŌ 暁 248b
GYŌ 凝 270a
GYOKU 玉 27(64)
GYŪ 牛 27(62)

—H—

HA 波 74(298)
HA 破 153(692)
HA 派 186(857)
ha 葉 80(327)
ha 歯 97(414)
ha 刃 193a
ha 羽 205b
haba 幅 247b
habuku 省 143(640)
HACHI 八 16(8)
hada 膚 268b
hadaka 裸 259a
hagemu 励 207b
hageshii 激 271a
haha 母 42(137)
HAI 配 74(299)
HAI 敗 153(693)
HAI 拝 186(858)
HAI 杯 217b
HAI 肺 227a
HAI 背 227a
HAI 俳 228b
HAI 排 240a
HAI 廃 247b
HAI 輩 269b
hai 灰 205a
haji, *hajiru* 恥 231b
hajimaru, *hajimeru* 始 60(225)
hajime 初 100(428)
haka 墓 188(869)
hakaru 計 55(201)
hakaru 図 67(261)
hakaru 測 148(668)
hakaru 量 161(734)
hako 箱 268a
hakobu 運 46(157)
HAKU 白 22(37)
HAKU 博 154(695)
HAKU 伯 206a
HAKU 拍 217a
HAKU 泊 218b
HAKU 迫 220a
HAKU 舶 243a
HAKU 薄 272a
haku 吐 203a
haku 掃 240a
hama 浜 233b
HAN 半 40(129)
HAN 坂 75(304)
HAN 板 76(305)
HAN 反 113(492)
HAN 飯 154(696)
HAN 犯 186(859)
HAN 判 187(860)
HAN 版 187(861)
HAN 帆 204a
HAN 伴 206a
HAN 班 233b
HAN 畔 233b
HAN 般 235b

HAN 販 244a
HAN 搬 256a
HAN 煩 257b, 281b
HAN 頒 260b, 281b
HAN 範 268a
HAN 繁 272a
HAN 藩 275b
hana 花 23(43)
hana 鼻 114(496)
hanareru, hanasu 離 276a
hanashi, hanasu 話 45(151)
hanasu, hanatsu 放 117(512)
hane 羽 205b
hara 原 56(205)
hara 腹 258b
harau 払 199b
hare, hareru 晴 68(265)
hari, haru 張 150(675)
hari 針 236b
haru 春 33(91)
hashi 橋 53(193)
hashi 端 263a
hashira 柱 70(278)
hashiru 走 36(105)
hata, hatake 畑 75(302)
hata 旗 89(371)
hata 機 89(373)
hataraki, hataraku 働 112(488)
hatasu 果 127(560)
hate 果 127(560)
HATSU 発 75(303)
HATSU 髪 265b
hatsu 初 100(428)
haya, hayai 早 35(104)
hayai 速 105(453)
hayashi 林 45(150)
hedataru, hedateru 隔 260b
HEI 平 78(315)
HEI 兵 157(712)
HEI 陛 188(867)
HEI 丙 197a
HEI 併 213b
HEI 並 219b
HEI 柄 224b
HEI 閉 245a
HEI 幣 266b
HEI 弊 266b
HEKI 壁 270a
HEKI 癖 275a
HEN 返 78(316)
HEN 変 116(509)
HEN 辺 157(713)
HEN 編 157(714)
HEN 片 197a
HEN 偏 237a
HEN 遍 253b
herasu, heru 減 170(775)
heru 経 134(596)
HI 皮 76(307)
HI 飛 113(493)
HI 悲 113(494)
HI 費 114(495)
HI 比 154(697)
HI 非 154(698)
HI 肥 154(699)
HI 否 187(862)
HI 妃 203b
HI 批 210a
HI 彼 216a
HI 卑 221b
HI 疲 234a
HI 秘 234a
HI 被 236a
HI 碑 262b
HI 罷 268b, 281b
HI 避 272b
HI 披 279a
hi 日 17(11)
hi 火 17(13)
hi 灯 280b
hibiki, hibiku 響 278a
hidari 左 18(18)
hieru, hiyasu 冷 122(535)
higashi 東 39(121)
hikaeru 控 240a
hikari, hikaru 光 29(72)
HIKI 匹 195b
hiki, hiku 引 46(156)
hikiiru 率 190(878)
hikui 低 150(677)
hima 暇 256b
hime 姫 230a
HIN 品 77(311)
HIN 貧 156(705)
HIN 浜 233b
HIN 賓 269a
hiraku 開 49(171)
hiratai 平 78(315)
hirogaru, hirogeru, hiroi, hiromaru 広 57(211)
hiro(u) 拾 100(425)
hiru 昼 70(279)
hiru 干 194b
hirugaeru, hirugaesu 翻 276b
hisashii, hisashiku 久 131(582)
hisomu 潜 267b
hitai 額 164(748)
hitasu 浸 233b
hito 人 21(30)
hitoshii 等 111(484)
hitotsu 一 15(1)
HITSU 必 114(497)
HITSU 筆 155(701)
HITSU 匹 195b
HITSU 泌 218b
hitsuji 羊 205b
HO 歩 42(136)
HO 保 158(716)
HO 補 188(868)
HO 捕 232a
HO 浦 233a
HO 舗 268b
ho 帆 204a
ho 穂 268a
HŌ 方 42(138)
HŌ 包 117(511)
HŌ 放 117(512)
HŌ 法 117(513)
HŌ 報 158(717)
HŌ 豊 189(870)
HŌ 芳 211b
HŌ 邦 212b

HŌ 奉 215a
HŌ 宝 215b
HŌ 抱 216b
HŌ 封 222b
HŌ 胞 227a
HŌ 倣 229a
HŌ 峰 230b
HŌ 砲 234a
HŌ 崩 239a
HŌ 訪 244a
HŌ 飽 260b
HŌ 縫 272a
HŌ 俸 279b
hodokosu 施 224a
hogaraka 朗 232a
hoka 外 26(56)
hokori, hokoru 誇 259a
HOKU 北 42(139)
homare 誉 259b
hōmuru 葬 251b
HON 本 24(45)
HON 奔 215a
HON 翻 276b
hone 骨 237b
hono-o 炎 219a
hori 堀 280a
horobiru, horobosu 滅 257a
horu 彫 239b
horu 掘 240a
hoshi 星 67(264)
hosoi 細 58(218)
hossuru 欲 190(876)
hosu 干 194b
hotoke 仏 157(711)
hōzuru 奉 215a
HYAKU 百 41(130)
HYŌ 表 76(309)
HYŌ 氷 114(498)
HYŌ 俵 155(702)
HYŌ 票 155(703)
HYŌ 標 155(704)
HYŌ, *hyōsuru* 評 187(863)
HYŌ 拍 217a
HYŌ 漂 262b

—I—

I 意 46(155)
I 衣 83(341)
I 以 83(342)
I 囲 83(343)
I 位 83(344)
I 医 84(345)
I 委 84(346)
I 易 124(545)
I 胃 124(546)
I 移 124(547)
I 異 162(738)
I 遺 162(739)
I 依 213a
I 威 222b
I 為 225a
I 尉 239a
I 偉 246a
I 違 260a
I 維 263a
I 慰 266b
I 緯 271b
i 井 194b
ICHI 一 15(1)
ICHI 壱 163(740)
ichi 市 59(222)
ichijirushii 著 183(843)
ie 家 25(53)
ikaru 怒 223a
ike 池 37(110)
IKI 域 238b
iki 息 105(454)
ikidōru 憤 266b
ikioi 勢 103(441)
ikiru 生 21(34)
IKU 育 84(347)
iku 行 29(73)
iku～ 幾 247b
ima 今 31(81)
imashime, imashimeru 戒 209b
imo 芋 206a
imōto 妹 78(319)
imu 忌 209b
IN 音 25(50)
IN 引 46(156)
IN 印 84(348)
IN 員 84(349)
IN 院 85(350)
IN 飲 85(351)
IN 因 124(548)
IN 姻 222a
IN 陰 245a
IN 隠 265a
IN 韻 277a
ina 否 187(862)
ine 稲 263a
inochi 命 118(519)
inori, inoru 祈 219b
inu 犬 28(66)
ireru, iri 入 40(125)
iro 色 33(94)
iru 居 132(586)
iru 射 230b
iru 鋳 269b
isagiyoi 潔 168(767)
isamashii 勇 119(524)
ishi 石 23(44)
ishizue 礎 275a
isogashii 忙 204a
isogu 急 52(186)
ita 板 76(305)
itadaki 頂 245b
itami, itamu 痛 250b
itaru 至 174(796)
ito 糸 31(83)
itonami, itonamu 営 163(741)
ITSU 逸 244b
itsutsu 五 16(5)
itsuwaru 偽 238a
iu 言 93(392)
iwa 岩 50(178)
iwai, iwau 祝 142(635)
iyashii, iyashimeru 卑 221b
izumi 泉 224b

—J—

JA 邪 212b
JAKU 弱 62(236)

JAKU 若 220a
JAKU 寂 238b
JI 耳 20(26)
JI 字 32(86)
JI 時 32(87)
JI 地 37(111)
JI 次 60(227)
JI 寺 60(228)
JI 自 60(229)
JI 事 61(230)
JI 持 61(231)
JI 治 108(468)
JI 示 139(622)
JI 似 140(625)
JI, *jisuru* 辞 140(626)
JI 児 175(801)
JI, *jisuru* 侍 213a
JI 滋 249b
JI 慈 256a
JI 磁 263a
JI 璽 276a 282b
~*ji* 路 123(540)
JIKI 直 109(472)
JIKU 軸 253a
JIN 人 21(30)
JIN 神 66(257)
JIN 臣 102(436)
JIN 仁 179(820)
JIN 刃 193a
JIN 尽 205a
JIN 迅 206b, 281a
JIN 陣 237a
JIN 尋 247a
JITSU 日 17(11)
JITSU 実 61(233)
JO 女 21(32)
JO 助 64(248)
JO 序 142(638)
JO 除 177(813)
JO 如 203b
JO, *josuru* 叙 224a
JO 徐 231a
JŌ 上 19(20)
JŌ 乗 65(251)
JŌ 場 65(252)
JŌ 星 67(264)
JŌ 成 102(439)
JŌ 静 103(442)
JŌ 定 109(474)
JŌ 常 143(642)
JŌ 情 143(643)
JŌ 条 178(817)
JŌ 状 178(818)
JŌ 丈 193a
JŌ 冗 195a
JŌ 城 222a
JŌ 浄 225a
JŌ 剰 238a
JŌ 盛 242a
JŌ 畳 250b
JŌ 蒸 258b
JŌ 嬢 270b
JŌ 錠 273a
JŌ 譲 277b
JŌ 醸 277b
JŌ 壌 280b
JOKU 辱 236a
JU 受 63(240)
JU 授 175(803)
JU 需 175(804)
JU 就 176(807)
JU 寿 208b
JU 儒 270a
JU 樹 271a
JŪ 十 17(10)
JŪ 住 63(244)
JŪ 重 64(245)
JŪ 拾 100(425)
JŪ 従 176(808)
JŪ 充 202a
JŪ 柔 224b
JŪ 渋 241b
JŪ 銃 264b
JŪ 獣 271b
JŪ 縦 272a
JŪ 汁 279a
JUKU, *jukusuru* 熟 267b
JUN 順 100(427)
JUN 準 142(637)
JUN 純 177(810)
JUN 巡 204a
JUN 旬 204b
JUN 盾 226a
JUN 准 229b
JUN, *junzuru* 殉 233a
JUN 循 247b
JUN 潤 267b
JUN 遵 269b, 282a
JUTSU 術 142(636)
JUTSU 述 176(809)

— K —

KA 火 17(13)
KA 下 19(21)
KA 花 23(43)
KA 何 25(51)
KA 夏 25(52)
KA 家 25(53)
KA 化 47(163)
KA 科 47(164)
KA 荷 48(165)
KA 歌 48(166)
KA 加 86(356)
KA 貨 86(357)
KA 仮 126(559)
KA 果 127(560)
KA 河 127(561)
KA 過 127(562)
KA 価 127(563)
KA 課 127(564)
KA 可 163(744)
KA 佳 213a
KA, *kasuru* 架 224b
KA 華 235b
KA 菓 243b
KA 嫁 255b
KA 暇 256b
KA 禍 257b
KA 寡 261a, 281b
KA 箇 263a, 281b
KA 渦 280b
KA 個 280b
ka 香 228b
ka 蚊 235b
kabe 壁 270a
kabu 株 164(749)
kado 門 43(143)
kaerimiru 省 143(640)

kaerimiru 顧 278b
kaeru 帰 51(182)
kaeru 変 116(509)
kaeru 換 248a
kaeru 替 248b
kaeshi, kaesu 返 78(316)
kagami 鏡 90(378)
kagayaku 輝 269b
kage 陰 245a
kage 影 266b
kagiri, kagiru 限 135(601)
KAI 会 25(54)
KAI 海 26(55)
KAI 回 48(168)
KAI 界 49(170)
KAI 開 49(171)
KAI 絵 49(172)
KAI 改 86(359)
KAI 械 87(360)
KAI 階 87(361)
KAI 快 128(566)
KAI 解 128(567)
KAI, *kaishite* 介 194b
KAI 灰 205a
KAI 戒 209b
KAI 怪 216b
KAI 悔 223b
KAI 皆 225b
KAI 塊 255a
KAI 壊 270a
KAI 懐 271a
kai 貝 48(169)
kaiko 蚕 138(617)
kakageru 掲 240b
kakari, kakaru 係 92(385)
kakeru 欠 134(597)
kakeru 掛 240a
kakeru 駆 265b
kakomu 囲 83(343)
KAKU 画 48(167)
KAKU 角 49(173)
KAKU 客 51(184)
KAKU 覚 87(363)
KAKU 各 128(568)
KAKU 格 128(569)
KAKU 確 129(570)
KAKU 革 164(746)
KAKU 拡 164(747)
KAKU 核 232b
KAKU 郭 244b
KAKU 較 259b
KAKU 隔 260b
KAKU 閣 265a
KAKU 獲 271b
KAKU 嚇 273a, 282b
KAKU 穫 275a
KAKU 殻 280a
kaku 書 33(92)
kaku 欠 134(597)
kakureru, kakusu 隠 265a
kamae, kamaeru 構 172(785)
kambashii 芳 211b
kami 上 19(20)
kami 紙 32(85)
kami 神 66(257)
kami 髪 265b
kaminari 雷 260b
kammuri 冠 221b
KAN 間 26(58)
KAN 寒 50(175)
KAN 感 50(176)
KAN 官 87(364)
KAN 関 88(365)
KAN 館 88(366)
KAN 観 88(367)
KAN 完 129(571)
KAN, ～*kan* 漢 129(572)
KAN 管 129(573)
KAN 慣 129(574)
KAN 刊 165(750)
KAN 幹 165(751)
KAN 勧 165(752)
KAN 歓 165(753)
KAN 干 194b
KAN 甘 200a
KAN 甲 200b
KAN 汗 205a
KAN 肝 211b
KAN 冠 221b
KAN 巻 221b
KAN 看 226a
KAN 陥 237a
KAN 乾 237a
KAN 勘 238a
KAN 患 239b
KAN 貫 244a
KAN 喚 246b
KAN 堪 246b
KAN 換 248a
KAN 敢 248b
KAN 棺 249a
KAN 款 249b
KAN 閑 253b
KAN 寛 255b
KAN 監 267b
KAN 緩 268b
KAN 憾 270b
KAN 還 273a
KAN 環 274a
KAN 簡 275a
KAN 艦 278a
KAN 鑑 278b
kanarazu 必 114(497)
kanashii 悲 113(494)
kane 金 18(16)
kane 鐘 278a
kangae, kangaeru 考 29(74)
kaneru 兼 168(769)
kano 彼 216a
kao 顔 50(179)
kara 殻 280a
karai 辛 212a
karasu, kareru 枯 224a
kare 彼 216a
kari, kariru 借 99(420)
kari 仮 126(559)
kari, karu 狩 225b
karu, karui 軽 92(387)
karu 刈 195a
kasanaru, kasaneru 重 64(245)
kashi, kasu 貸 149(670)
kashikoi 賢 272b
kata 方 42(138)
kata 型 134(595)
kata 片 197a

kata 肩 219b
katachi 形 55(200)
katai 固 93(393)
katai 難 185(853)
katai 堅 246b
katamaru, katameru 固 93(393)
katamukeru, katamuki, katamuku 傾 255a
katana 刀 72(289)
katari, kataru 語 56(209)
KATSU 活 49(174)
KATSU 括 223b
KATSU 渇 241b
KATSU 割 246a
KATSU 滑 257a
KATSU 轄 274b
katsu 勝 65(250)
katsu 且 197a, 281a
kau 買 75(300)
kau 飼 260b
kawa 川 22(39)
kawa 皮 76(307)
kawa 側 148(667)
kawari, kawaru 代 107(463)
kawaru 変 116(509)
kawaru 換 248a
kayou 通 71(281)
kazaru 飾 260b
kaze 風 41(132)
kazoeru, kazu 数 67(262)
KE 家 25(53)
KE 気 26(59)
KE 化 47(163)
KE 景 92(386)
KE 仮 126(559)
KE 懸 277a
ke 毛 43(142)
kegareru, kegasu 汚 205a
KEI 京 27(63)
KEI 兄 54(199)
KEI 形 55(200)
KEI 計 55(201)
KEI 競 90(379)
KEI 係 92(385)
KEI 景 92(386)
KEI 軽 92(387)
KEI 型 134(595)
KEI 経 134(596)
KEI 境 167(761)
KEI 系 168(765)
KEI 敬 168(766)
KEI 刑 202b
KEI 径 216a
KEI 茎 220a
KEI 契 222a
KEI 恵 231b
KEI 啓 238a
KEI 掲 240b
KEI 傾 255a
KEI 携 256b
KEI 継 258a
KEI 慶 266b
KEI 憩 270b
KEI 警 277a
KEI 鶏 277b
KEI 渓 280a
kemono 獣 271b
kemuri 煙 257b
KEN 間 26(58)
KEN 犬 28(66)
KEN 見 28(67)
KEN 県 55(203)
KEN 研 55(204)
KEN 建 93(391)
KEN 件 134(598)
KEN 健 134(599)
KEN 験 135(600)
KEN 券 168(768)
KEN 兼 168(769)
KEN 険 169(770)
KEN 検 169(771)
KEN 絹 169(772)
KEN 憲 169(773)
KEN 権 169(774)
KEN 肩 219b
KEN 倹 229a
KEN 剣 229b
KEN 軒 236a
KEN 圏 246b
KEN 堅 246b
KEN 献 257b
KEN 遣 260a
KEN 賢 272b
KEN 謙 274b
KEN 繭 275b
KEN 顕 276b
KEN 懸 277a
kesu 消 100(429)
KETSU 決 55(202)
KETSU 血 92(389)
KETSU 結 93(390)
KETSU 欠 134(597)
KETSU 潔 168(767)
KETSU 穴 201a
KETSU 傑 254a
kewashii 険 169(770)
kezuru 削 221b
KI 気 26(59)
KI 汽 27(60)
KI 記 51(180)
KI 起 51(181)
KI 帰 51(182)
KI 期 51(183)
KI 季 88(369)
KI 喜 89(370)
KI 旗 89(371)
KI 器 89(372)
KI 機 89(373)
KI 希 130(575)
KI 寄 130(576)
KI 規 130(577)
KI 紀 130(578)
KI 基 166(755)
KI 貴 166(756)
KI 己 170(777)
KI 企 201b
KI 危 202b
KI 机 204b
KI 岐 209a
KI 忌 209b
KI 奇 215a
KI 祈 219b
KI 軌 227b
KI 既 232a
KI 飢 237b
KI 鬼 237b

KI 幾 247b
KI 揮 248a
KI 棋 249a
KI 棄 256b
KI 輝 269b
KI 騎 276b
ki 木 18(15)
ki 生 21(34)
ki 黄 57(214)
KICHI 吉 202b
kieru 消 100(429)
kikoeru, kiku 聞 77(314)
KIKU 菊 243b
kimaru, kimeru 決 55(202)
kimasu 来 44(147)
kimi 君 54(198)
kimo 肝 211b
KIN 金 18(16)
KIN 今 31(81)
KIN 近 54(195)
KIN 均 133(590)
KIN 勤 167(762)
KIN, *kinjiru* 禁 167(763)
KIN 斤 196b
KIN 菌 243b
KIN 琴 250a
KIN 筋 251a
KIN 緊 268a
KIN 謹 274b
kinu 絹 169(772)
kiri 霧 277a
kiru 切 34(99)
kiru 着 70(276)
kishi 岸 50(177)
kisou 競 90(379)
kita 北 42(139)
kitaeru 鍛 274b
KITSU 喫 246b
KITSU 詰 259a
kiwamaru, kiwameru 窮 268a
kiyoi, kiyoraka 清 103(440)
kizamu 刻 214a
kizu 傷 254b
kizuku 築 149(673)
KO 戸 28(69)
KO 古 29(70)
KO 去 52(189)
KO 庫 56(206)
KO 固 93(393)
KO 湖 93(394)
KO 個 135(603), 280b
KO 己 170(777)
KO 故 170(778)
KO 呼 214b
KO 拠 217a
KO 孤 222b
KO 弧 223a
KO 枯 224a
KO 虚 243b
KO 雇 254b
KO 誇 259a
KO 鼓 261b
KO 顧 278b
ko 小 19(24)
ko 子 21(31)
ko 粉 116(507)
KŌ 口 20(27)
KŌ 工 29(71)
KŌ 光 29(72)
KŌ 行 29(73)
KŌ 考 29(74)
KŌ 校 30(75)
KŌ 高 30(76)
KŌ 後 56(208)
KŌ 公 57(210)
KŌ 広 57(211)
KŌ 交 57(212)
KŌ 向 57(213)
KŌ 黄 57(214)
KŌ 幸 94(395)
KŌ 航 94(396)
KŌ 港 94(397)
KŌ 興 132(589)
KŌ 功 136(605)
KŌ 厚 136(606)
KŌ 候 136(607)
KŌ 康 136(608)
KŌ 講 136(609)
KŌ 鉱 137(610)
KŌ 后 171(780)
KŌ 孝 171(781)
KŌ 効 171(782)
KŌ 皇 171(783)
KŌ 耕 171(784)
KŌ 構 172(785)
KŌ 孔 196a
KŌ 巧 199a
KŌ 甲 200b
KŌ 仰 201a
KŌ 好 203b
KŌ 江 205a
KŌ 坑 208b
KŌ 抗 210a
KŌ 攻 210a
KŌ 更 210b
KŌ 拘 217a
KŌ 肯 220a
KŌ 侯 221a
KŌ 恒 223b
KŌ 紅 226b
KŌ 荒 227a
KŌ 郊 228a
KŌ 香 228b
KŌ 貢 236a
KŌ 降 237a
KŌ 控 240a
KŌ 慌 248a
KŌ 硬 250b
KŌ 絞 251b
KŌ 項 254b
KŌ 綱 263b
KŌ 酵 264b
KŌ 稿 268a
KŌ 衡 272b
KŌ 鋼 273a
KŌ 購 274b
KŌ 洪 279b
kobamu 拒 217a
koe 声 34(97)
koeru, koyasu 肥 154(699)
koeru, kosu 越 253a
kogasu, kogeru 焦 250a
kogoeru 凍 229b
koi 来 44(147)
koi, koishii 恋 231b
koi 濃 271a

kokonotsu 九 16(9)
kokoro 心 34(95)
kokoromi, kokoromiru 試 98(416)
kokoroyoi 快 128(566)
kokorozashi, kokorozasu 志 139(623)
KOKU 石 23(44)
KOKU 谷 30(78)
KOKU 国 30(79)
KOKU 黒 31(80)
KOKU 告 94(398)
KOKU 穀 172(786)
KOKU 克 207a
KOKU 刻 214a
KOKU 酷 264b
komakai 細 58(218)
komaru 困 208a
kome 米 42(135)
komeru, komu 込 201b
kōmuru 被 236a
KON 金 18(16)
KON 今 31(81)
KON 根 58(216)
KON, *konzuru* 混 172(787)
KON 困 208a
KON 恨 223b
KON 婚 238b
KON 紺 242b
KON 献 257b
KON 魂 265b
KON 墾 270a
KON 懇 273b
kona 粉 116(507)
konomu 好 203b
korasu 懲 275a
kori, koru 凝 270a
kōri 郡 91(384)
kōri 氷 114(498)
koromo 衣 83(341)
korosu 殺 137(614)
kōru 凍 229b
koshi 腰 258b
kotae, kotaeru 答 73(293)
koto 事 61(230)
koto 言 93(392)
koto 琴 250a
kotobuki 寿 208b
kotonaru 異 162(738)
kotowaru 断 183(841)
KOTSU 骨 237b
kou 請 268b
koyomi 暦 262a
KU 九 16(9)
KU 口 20(27)
KU 工 29(71)
KU 苦 54(197)
KU 宮 89(374)
KU 久 131(582)
KU 区 133(591)
KU 句 133(592)
KU 功 136(605)
KU 紅 226b
KU 駆 265b
KŪ 空 28(65)
kubaru 配 74(299)
kubi 首 62(239)
kuchi 口 20(27)
kuchiru 朽 204b
kuda 管 129(573)
kudaku 砕 226a
kudaru 下 19(21)
kuiru 悔 223b
kujira 鯨 277b
kuki 茎 220a
kumi, kumu 組 35(103)
kumo 雲 24(47)
kumori, kumoru 曇 271a
KUN 君 54(198)
KUN 訓 167(764)
KUN 勲 266a
KUN 薫 272a
kuni 国 30(79)
kura 倉 146(659)
kura 蔵 181(833)
kuraberu 比 154(697)
kurai 暗 45(154)
kurai 位 83(344)
kurasu, kure, kureru 暮 262a
kurenai 紅 226b
kuro, kuroi 黒 31(80)
kuru 来 44(147)
kuru 繰 276b
kurui, kuruu 狂 211a
kuruma 車 32(88)
kurushii 苦 54(197)
kusa 草 36(106)
kusai 臭 227a
kusari 鎖 276a
kusaru 腐 263b
kuse 癖 275a
kusuri 薬 119(521)
KUTSU, *kussuru* 屈 215b
KUTSU 掘 240a
kuu 食 65(253)
kuwa 桑 232b
kuwadate, kuwadateru 企 201b
kuwaeru, kuwawaru 加 86(356)
kuwashii 詳 259a
kuyami, kuyamu 悔 223b
KYAKU 客 51(184)
KYAKU 却 207b
KYAKU 脚 243a
KYO 去 52(189)
KYO 挙 90(375)
KYO 居 132(586)
KYO 許 132(587)
KYO 巨 199a
KYO 拒 217a
KYO 拠 217a
KYO 虚 243b
KYO 距 253a
KYŌ 京 27(63)
KYŌ 教 53(191)
KYŌ 強 53(192)
KYŌ 橋 53(193)
KYŌ 兄 54(199)
KYŌ 共 90(376)
KYŌ 協 90(377)
KYŌ 鏡 90(378)
KYŌ 競 90(379)
KYŌ 興 132(589)
KYŌ 経 134(596)
KYŌ 供 167(760)
KYŌ 境 167(761)

KYŌ 凶 195a
KYŌ 叫 202b
KYŌ 狂 211a
KYŌ 享 213a
KYŌ 況 218b
KYŌ 峡 222b
KYŌ 狭 225b
KYŌ 恐 231a
KYŌ 恭 231b
KYŌ 胸 235a
KYŌ 脅 235b
KYŌ 郷 244b
KYŌ 響 278a
KYŌ 驚 278a
KYŌ 矯 280b
KYOKU 局 53(194)
KYOKU 曲 91(381)
KYOKU 極 91(382)
KYŪ 九 16(9)
KYŪ 休 27(61)
KYŪ 究 52(185)
KYŪ 急 52(186)
KYŪ 級 52(187)
KYŪ 球 52(188)
KYŪ 宮 89(374)
KYŪ 久 131(582)
KYŪ 求 131(583)
KYŪ 救 131(584)
KYŪ 給 132(585)
KYŪ 旧 166(759)
KYŪ 及 193b
KYŪ 弓 194b
KYŪ 丘 197a
KYŪ 吸 203a
KYŪ 朽 204b
KYŪ 泣 218b
KYŪ 糾 226b
KYŪ 窮 268a

—M—

MA 麻 245b
MA, *masuru* 摩 266b
MA 魔 278b
ma 間 26(58)
ma 真 102(438)
maboroshi 幻 196a
machi 町 38(115)
mado 窓 242a
madou 惑 247b
mae 前 35(102)
magaru, mageru 曲 91(381)
magireru 紛 235a
mago 孫 106(458)
MAI 米 42(135)
MAI 毎 78(318)
MAI 妹 78(319)
MAI 枚 218a
MAI 埋 230a
mai, mau 舞 268b
mairu 参 138(616)
majiru, majiwaru 交 57(212)
majiru 混 172(787)
makaseru 任 152(688)
make, makeru 負 77(312)
maki 牧 159(720)
maki, maku 巻 221b
makoto 誠 180(825)
MAKU 幕 255b
MAKU 膜 263b
mame 豆 212a
mamo(ru) 守 99(421)
MAN 万 79(320)
MAN 満 159(721)
MAN 慢 261b
MAN 漫 262b
manabu 学 26(57)
manako 眼 165(754)
maneku 招 177(814)
manukareru 免 213b
marui 丸 193a
masu 増 148(665)
mata 又 192b, 281a
mato 的 110(478)
MATSU 末 118(515)
matsu 待 69(271)
matsu 松 217b
matsuri, matsuru 祭 95(400)
matsurigoto 政 144(646)
mattaku 全 68(267)
mawaru, mawasu 回 48(168)
mayou, mayowasu 迷 159(724)
mayu 繭 275b
mazeru 混 172(787)
mazushii 貧 156(705)
me 目 20(25)
me 芽 86(358)
me 雌 260b
megumi, megumu 恵 231b
meguru 巡 204a
MEI 名 43(140)
MEI 明 43(141)
MEI 鳴 79(321)
MEI 命 118(519)
MEI 迷 159(724)
MEI 盟 189(873)
MEI 銘 264b
mekura 盲 219a
MEN 面 79(322)
MEN 綿 160(725)
MEN, *menzuru* 免 213b
meshi 飯 154(696)
mesu 召 198b
mesu 雌 260b
METSU 滅 257a
mezurashii 珍 225b
MI 味 118(516)
MI 未 189(872)
MI, *misuru* 魅 270b
mi 三 15(3)
mi 実 61(233)
mi 身 66(255)
michi 道 39(122)
michibiki, michibiku 導 151(684)
michiru 満 159(721)
midareru, midasu 乱 206a
midori 緑 121(532)
migi 右 18(19)
mijikai 短 108(466)
miki 幹 165(751)
mikotonori 詔 252b
mimi 耳 20(26)
MIN 民 118(518)

MIN 眠 234a
mina 皆 225b
minami 南 39(124)
minamoto 源 257a
minato 港 94(397)
mine 峰 230b
minikui 醜 274b
minoru 実 61(233)
miru 見 28(67)
misao 操 271a
misasagi 陵 245a
mise 店 71(284)
mitomeru 認 186(855)
MITSU 密 239a
mittsu 三 15(3)
miya 宮 89(374)
miyako 都 72(287)
mizu 水 17(14)
mizukara 自 60(229)
mizu-umi 湖 93(394)
MO 茂 220a
MO 模 262a
mo 喪 246b
MŌ 毛 43(142)
MŌ 望 117(514)
MŌ 盲 219a
MŌ 耗 235a
MŌ 猛 241b
MŌ 網 263b
mochi, motsu 持 61(231)
mochiiru 用 44(146)
modoru, modosu 戻 279a
moeru 燃 153(690)
mōkeru 設 145(653)
MOKU 木 18(15)
MOKU 目 20(25)
MOKU 黙 270b
momme 匁 195a
momo 桃 232b
MON 文 41(134)
MON 門 43(143)
MON 問 119(520)
MON 紋 234b
mono 者 62(235)
mono 物 77(313)
moreru, moru 漏 262b
mori 森 23(41)
moru 盛 242a
moshikuwa 若 220a
mōsu 申 65(254)
moto 下 19(21)
moto 元 28(68)
motome, motomeru 求 131(583)
motoi, motozuku 基 166(755)
MOTSU 物 77(313)
mottomo 最 95(402)
moyasu 燃 153(690)
moyo-oshi, moyo-osu 催 254a
MU 武 156(708)
MU 務 159(722)
MU 無 159(723)
MU 矛 200b
MU 夢 255b
MU 霧 277a
mugi 麦 40(128)
mukae, mukaeru 迎 212b
mukashi 昔 217b
mukau, muku 向 57(213)
muko 婿 247a
mukui, mukuiru 報 158(717)
mune 旨 204a
mune 胸 235a
mura 村 36(107)
muragaru, mure, mureru 群 133(594)
murasaki 紫 242b
muro 室 61(232)
mushi 虫 37(114)
musu 蒸 258b
musubi, musubu 結 93(390)
musume 娘 230a
muttsu 六 16(6)
MYAKU 脈 118(517)
MYŌ 名 43(140)
MYŌ 明 43(141)
MYŌ 命 118(519)
MYŌ 妙 208b

— N —

NA 納 186(856)
na 名 43(140)
na 菜 95(401)
nae 苗 220a
nagai 長 38(116)
nagare, nagareru, nagasu 流 81(334)
nageku 嘆 255a
nageru 投 73(291)
nagusame, nagusameru, nagusami 慰 266b
NAI 内 112(489)
nai, nashi 無 159(723)
naka 中 19(23)
naka 仲 201a
nakaba 半 40(129)
naku 鳴 79(321)
naku 泣 218b
nama 生 21(34)
namari 鉛 260a
nami 波 74(298)
nami 並 219b
namida 涙 233b
NAN 男 36(109)
NAN 南 39(124)
NAN 難 185(853)
NAN 軟 244b
naname 斜 240b
nanatsu 七 16(7)
nani, nan 何 25(51)
naosu 直 109(472)
naraberu, narabini, narabu 並 219b
narau 習 100(426)
nareru 慣 129(574)
naru, nasu 成 102(439)
nasake 情 143(643)
natsu 夏 25(52)
nayami, nayamu 悩 231b
ne 音 25(50)
ne 根 58(216)
ne 値 229a
nebaru 粘 242b
negai, negau 願 88(368)
NEI 寧 261b

nemuri, nemuru 眠 234a
NEN 年 40(126)
NEN 然 105(450)
NEN 念 152(689)
NEN 燃 153(690)
NEN 粘 242b
neru 練 122(539)
neru 寝 255b
NETSU, *nessuru* 熱 113(490)
NI 二 15(2)
NI 児 175(801)
NI 弐 185(854)
NI 尼 199a
ni 荷 48(165)
nibui 鈍 253b
NICHI 日 17(11)
nigai 苦 54(197)
nigeru 逃 228a
nigiru 握 248a
nigori, nigoru 濁 271a
NIKU 肉 74(297)
nikumu 憎 262a
NIN 人 21(30)
NIN 任 152(688)
NIN 認 186(855)
NIN 妊 208b
NIN 忍 209b
niru 似 140(625)
niru 煮 250a
nishi 西 34(96)
niwa 庭 110(477)
niwatori 鶏 277b
no 野 79(323)
NŌ 農 113(491)
NŌ 能 153(691)
NŌ 納 186(856)
NŌ 悩 231b
NŌ 脳 243a
NŌ 濃 271a
nobasu, nobe, nobiru 延 163(743)
nobasu, nobiru 伸 206a
noberu 述 176(809)
nobori, noboru 登 111(483)
noboru 上 19(20)
nochi 後 56(208)
noki 軒 236a
nokori, nokoru, nokosu 残 96(409)
nomu 飲 85(351)
noru, noseru 乗 65(251)
noseru 載 260a
nozoku 除 177(813)
nozomi, nozomu 望 117(514)
nozomu 臨 191(880)
nugu 脱 243a
nuku 抜 210a
numa 沼 218b
nuno 布 156(706)
nuru 塗 255a
nushi 主 62(237)
nusumu 盗 242a
nuu 縫 272a
NYO 女 21(32)
NYO 如 203b
NYŌ 尿 209a
NYŪ 入 40(125)
NYŪ 乳 213a
NYŪ 柔 224b

—O—

O 汚 205a
o 小 19(24)
o 尾 209a
o 雄 254a
o 緒 263b
ō 王 24(49)
ō 黄 57(214)
ō 横 86(355)
ō 央 125(554)
ō 往 126(555)
ō, *ōzuru* 応 126(556)
ō 皇 171(783)
ō 押 216b
ō 欧 218a
ō 殴 218a
ō 桜 232b
ō 翁 235a
ō 奥 247a
obi, obiru 帯 148(669)
obiyakasu 脅 235b
oboeru 覚 87(363)
ochiiru 陥 237a
ochiru, otosu 落 81(330)
odayaka 穏 271b
odori, odoru 踊 264b
odoroki, odoroku 驚 278a
oeru 終 63(241)
ogamu 拝 186(858)
ōgi 扇 231b
oginau 補 188(868)
oi, oiru 老 123(541)
ōi 多 36(108)
oka 丘 197a
okasu 犯 186(859)
okasu 侵 221a
okasu 冒 221b
oki 沖 210b
ōkii 大 19(22)
okiru, okosu 起 51(181)
okonau 行 29(73)
okoru, okosu 興 132(589)
okotaru 怠 223b
OKU 屋 47(161)
OKU 億 126(557)
OKU 奥 247a
OKU 憶 270b
oku 置 108(469)
okureru 遅 253b
okuru 送 68(268)
okuru 贈 275b
omo, omote 面 79(322)
omoi 重 64(245)
omomuki 趣 269b
omote 表 76(309)
omou 思 31(84)
ON 音 25(50)
ON 遠 47(160)
ON 温 47(162)
ON 恩 126(558)
ON 穏 271b
on 御 239b
onaji 同 74(295)
oni 鬼 237b

onna 女 21(32)
ono-ono 各 128(568)
ori, oru 織 143(644)
oriru 降 237a
oroka 愚 256a
oroshi, orosu 卸 214a
oru 折 145(651)
osaeru 押 216b
osameru 治 108(468)
osameru 収 141(631)
osameru 修 141(633)
osameru 納 186(856)
osanai 幼 199b
ōse 仰 201a
oshi, osu 押 216b
oshieru 教 53(191)
oshii, oshimu 惜 239b
osore, osoreru, osoroshii 恐 231a
osore 虞 258b, 281b
osou 襲 278a
osu 推 179(821)
osu 雄 254a
oto 音 25(50)
otoko 男 36(109)
otoroeru 衰 235b
otoru 劣 202b
otōto 弟 71(282)
otozureru 訪 244a
OTSU 乙 192b
otto 夫 115(501)
ou 追 71(280)
ou 負 77(312)
owari, owaru 終 63(241)
oya 親 67(260)
ōyake 公 57(210)
oyobi, oyobu 及 193b
oyogu 泳 85(352)

—R—

RA 裸 259a
RAI 来 44(147)
RAI 雷 260b
RAI 頼 272b
RAKU 落 81(330)
RAKU 楽 81(331)
RAKU 絡 251b
RAKU 酪 260a
RAN 乱 206a
RAN 卵 207b
RAN 覧 274a
RAN 濫 275a, 282b
RAN 欄 277a
REI 礼 82(337)
REI 冷 122(535)
REI 令 162(736)
REI 例 162(737)
REI 励 207b
REI 鈴 260a
REI 零 260b
REI 霊 270a
REI 隷 273b, 282a
REI 齢 275a
REI 麗 277b
REKI 歴 122(536)
REKI 暦 262a
REN 連 122(538)
REN 練 122(539)
REN 恋 231b
REN 廉 255b
REN 錬 273b, 282a
RETSU 列 122(537)
RETSU 劣 202b
RETSU 烈 233b
RETSU 裂 252a
RI 里 81(332)
RI 理 81(333)
RI 利 120(528)
RI 吏 203a
RI 痢 250b
RI 裏 258b
RI 履 266a
RI 離 276a
RIKI 力 44(148)
RIKU 陸 120(529)
RIN 林 45(150)
RIN 輪 121(533)
RIN 臨 191(880)
RIN 厘 222a
RIN 倫 229a
RIN 鈴 260a
RIN 隣 273b
RITSU 立 44(149)
RITSU 律 190(877)
RITSU 率 190(878)
RO 路 123(540)
RO 炉 219a
RO 露 278a
RŌ 老 123(541)
RŌ 労 123(542)
RŌ 郎 228a
RŌ 朗 232a
RŌ 浪 233a
RŌ 廊 247b
RŌ 楼 257a
RŌ 漏 262b
ROKU 六 16(6)
ROKU 緑 121(532)
ROKU 録 123(543)
RON 論 191(881)
RU 流 81(334)
RU 留 161(733)
RUI 類 121(534)
RUI 涙 233b
RUI 累 242b
RUI 塁 247a
RYAKU, *ryakusuru* 略 190(879)
RYO 旅 82(335)
RYO 虜 258b
RYO 慮 266b
RYŌ 両 82(336)
RYŌ 良 121(530)
RYŌ 料 121(531)
RYŌ 漁 132(588)
RYŌ 量 161(734)
RYŌ 領 162(735)
RYŌ 了 192a
RYŌ 涼 241a
RYŌ 猟 241b
RYŌ 陵 245a
RYŌ 僚 261a
RYŌ 寮 266a
RYŌ 療 274a
RYŌ 糧 275a
RYOKU 力 44(148)
RYOKU 緑 121(532)
RYŪ 流 81(334)

RYŪ 留 161(733)
RYŪ 柳 224b
RYŪ 粒 242b
RYŪ 隆 245b
RYŪ 硫 250b
RYŪ 竜 279b

—S—

SA 左 18(18)
SA 作 31(82)
SA 差 94(399)
SA 査 137(611)
SA 佐 207a
SA 砂 226a
SA 唆 230a
SA 詐 252b
SA 鎖 276a
sabishii 寂 238b
sadameru 定 109(474)
sagaru, sageru 下 19(21)
sagasu 捜 232a
saguru 探 240a
SAI 西 34(96)
SAI 切 34(99)
SAI 才 58(217)
SAI 細 58(218)
SAI 祭 95(400)
SAI 菜 95(401)
SAI 最 95(402)
SAI 際 137(612)
SAI 殺 137(614)
SAI 再 172(788)
SAI 災 172(789)
SAI 妻 173(790)
SAI 採 173(791)
SAI 済 173(792)
SAI 砕 226a
SAI 宰 230b
SAI 栽 232b
SAI 彩 239b
SAI 斉 245b
SAI 裁 252a
SAI 催 254a
SAI 債 254b
SAI 歳 257a
SAI 載 260a
saiwai 幸 94(395)
saka 坂 75(304)
sakae, sakaeru 栄 124(549)
sakai 境 167(761)
sakarau 逆 166(758)
sakari 盛 242a
sakazuki 杯 217b
sake, saka 酒 99(422)
sakebu 叫 202b
sakeru, saku 裂 252a
sakeru 避 272b
saki 先 21(33)
SAKU 作 31(82)
SAKU 昨 95(404)
SAKU 策 174(795)
SAKU 削 221b
SAKU 索 235a
SAKU 酢 253b
SAKU 搾 256b
SAKU 錯 273a
saku 咲 222a
sakura 桜 232b
sama 様 80(328)
samatageru 妨 208b
samui 寒 50(175)
SAN 三 15(3)
SAN 山 22(38)
SAN 算 58(219)
SAN 散 96(407)
SAN 産 96(408)
SAN 参 138(616)
SAN 蚕 138(617)
SAN 酸 138(618)
SAN 賛 138(619)
SAN 惨 239b
SAN 桟 279b
sarani 更 210b
saru 去 52(189)
sasoi, sasou 誘 264a
sasu 差 94(399)
sasu 刺 214a
sato 里 81(332)
satoru 悟 231b
SATSU 刷 96(405)
SATSU, *sassuru* 察 96(406)
SATSU 殺 137(614)
SATSU 冊 198a
SATSU 札 200a
SATSU 撮 267a
SATSU 擦 273b
sawa 沢 211a
sawagi, sawagu 騒 276b
sazukaru, sazukeru 授 175(803)
SE 世 67(263)
SE 施 224a
se 背 227a
se 畝 234a
se 瀬 276a
SEI 生 21(34)
SEI 青 22(36)
SEI 正 24(46)
SEI 西 34(96)
SEI 声 34(97)
SEI 世 67(263)
SEI 星 67(264)
SEI 晴 68(265)
SEI 成 102(439)
SEI 清 103(440)
SEI 勢 103(441)
SEI 静 103(442)
SEI 整 103(443)
SEI 省 143(640)
SEI 性 144(645)
SEI 政 144(646)
SEI 精 144(647)
SEI 製 144(648)
SEI, *seisuru* 制 179(823)
SEI 聖 179(824)
SEI 誠 180(825)
SEI 井 194b
SEI 姓 215a
SEI 征 216a
SEI 牲 225a
SEI 盛 242a
SEI 婿 247a
SEI 歳 257a
SEI 誓 264a
SEI 請 268b
SEI 斉 279a
SEKI 赤 22(35)

SEKI 石 23(44)
SEKI 夕 34(98)
SEKI 席 103(444)
SEKI 積 104(445)
SEKI 責 144(649)
SEKI 績 145(650)
SEKI 斥 199b
SEKI 昔 217b
SEKI 析 217b
SEKI 隻 237a
SEKI 惜 239b
SEKI 跡 259b
SEKI 籍 277a
seki 関 88(365)
semai 狭 225b
semaru 迫 220a
seme, semeru 攻 210a
semeru 責 144(649)
SEN 先 21(33)
SEN 川 22(39)
SEN 千 35(101)
SEN 船 68(266)
SEN 線 104(447)
SEN 戦 104(448)
SEN 選 104(449)
SEN 浅 146(655)
SEN 銭 146(656)
SEN 宣 180(829)
SEN 専 181(830)
SEN 占 198b
SEN 染 224b
SEN 泉 224b
SEN 洗 225a
SEN 扇 231b
SEN 旋 240b
SEN 践 259b
SEN 銑 264b
SEN 潜 267b
SEN 遷 269b
SEN 薦 272a
SEN 繊 274a
SEN 鮮 274b
SETSU 切 34(99)
SETSU 雪 35(100)
SETSU 節 104(446)
SETSU 折 145(651)
SETSU, *sessuru* 接 145(652)
SETSU 設 145(653)
SETSU 説 145(654)
SETSU 拙 217a
SETSU 窃 226b
SETSU 摂 256b
SHA 車 32(88)
SHA 社 61(234)
SHA 者 62(235)
SHA 写 98(419)
SHA 舎 140(629)
SHA, *shasuru* 謝 141(630)
SHA 砂 226a
SHA 射 230b
SHA 捨 240a
SHA 斜 240b
SHA 赦 244a
SHA 煮 250a
SHAKU 赤 22(35)
SHAKU 石 23(44)
SHAKU 借 99(420)
SHAKU 釈 175(802)
SHAKU 勺 193a
SHAKU 尺 196a
SHAKU 昔 217b
SHAKU 爵 274a, 282b
SHAKU 酌 279b
SHI 四 15(4)
SHI 子 21(31)
SHI 糸 31(83)
SHI 思 31(84)
SHI 紙 32(85)
SHI 止 59(220)
SHI 仕 59(221)
SHI 市 59(222)
SHI, *shinu* 死 59(223)
SHI 使 59(224)
SHI 始 60(225)
SHI 指 60(226)
SHI 次 60(227)
SHI 自 60(229)
SHI 士 97(410)
SHI 史 97(411)
SHI 司 97(412)
SHI 姉 97(413)
SHI 歯 97(414)
SHI 詩 98(415)
SHI 試 98(416)
SHI 氏 139(620)
SHI 支 139(621)
SHI 示 139(622)
SHI 志 139(623)
SHI 師 139(624)
SHI 至 174(796)
SHI 私 174(797)
SHI 視 174(798)
SHI 詞 174(799)
SHI 資 175(800)
SHI 旨 204a
SHI 伺 206b
SHI 刺 214a
SHI 枝 218a
SHI 祉 219b
SHI 姿 222b
SHI 施 224a
SHI 脂 235a
SHI 紫 242b
SHI 嗣 255a
SHI 雌 260b
SHI 飼 260b
SHI 誌 264a
SHI 賜 269a
SHI 諮 272b
shiba 芝 206a
shibaru 縛 271b
shiboru 絞 251b
shibu, shibui 渋 241b
SHICHI 七 16(7)
SHICHI 質 140(628)
shigeru 茂 220a
SHIKI 色 33(94)
SHIKI 式 98(417)
SHIKI 識 140(627)
SHIKI 織 143(644)
shiku 敷 267a
shima 島 73(292)
shimaru, shimeru 締 268a
shimeru 占 198b
shimeru 湿 250a
shimeru 絞 251b
shimesu 示 139(622)
shimo 下 19(21)

shimo 霜 274b
SHIN 森 23(41)
SHIN 心 34(95)
SHIN 申 65(254)
SHIN 身 66(255)
SHIN 新 66(256)
SHIN 神 66(257)
SHIN 深 66(258)
SHIN 進 66(259)
SHIN 親 67(260)
SHIN 臣 102(436)
SHIN, *shinzuru* 信 102(437)
SHIN 真 102(438)
SHIN 伸 206a
SHIN 辛 212a
SHIN 侵 221a
SHIN 娠 230a
SHIN 振 231b
SHIN 浸 233b
SHIN 針 236b
SHIN 紳 242b
SHIN 診 252a
SHIN 寝 255b
SHIN 慎 256a
SHIN 審 266a
SHIN 請 268b
SHIN 震 270a
SHIN 薪 272a
shina 品 77(311)
shinobu 忍 209b
shio 塩 85(354)
shio 潮 267b
shirabe, shiraberu 調 109(471)
shiraseru, shiru 知 37(112)
shirizokeru, shirizoku 退 182(839)
shiro, shiroi 白 22(37)
shiro 城 222a
shirushi 印 84(348)
shiru 汁 279a
shita 下 19(21)
shita 舌 180(827)
shitagau 従 176(808)
shitashii, shitashimu 親 67(260)
shitau 慕 261b
SHITSU 室 61(232)
SHITSU 失 98(418)
SHITSU 質 140(628)
SHITSU 疾 234a
SHITSU 執 238b
SHITSU 湿 250a
SHITSU 漆 262b
shizuka, shizumaru, shizumeru 静 103(442)
shizumu 沈 210b
SHO 書 33(92)
SHO 所 64(246)
SHO 暑 64(247)
SHO 初 100(428)
SHO, *shosuru* 処 177(811)
SHO 諸 177(812)
SHO 庶 239a
SHO 署 258a
SHO 緒 263b
SHŌ 小 19(24)
SHŌ 生 21(34)
SHŌ 青 22(36)
SHŌ 正 24(46)
SHŌ 少 33(93)
SHŌ 昭 64(249)
SHŌ 勝 65(250)
SHŌ 消 100(429)
SHŌ 唱 101(430)
SHŌ 商 101(431)
SHŌ 章 101(432)
SHŌ 照 101(433)
SHŌ 焼 101(434)
SHŌ 相 105(452)
SHŌ 承 142(639)
SHŌ 省 143(640)
SHŌ 賞 143(641)
SHŌ 性 144(645)
SHŌ 政 144(646)
SHŌ 精 144(647)
SHŌ 象 147(663)
SHŌ 招 177(814)
SHŌ, *shōsuru* 称 178(815)
SHŌ 証 178(816)
SHŌ 井 194b
SHŌ 升 195b
SHŌ 召 198b
SHŌ 匠 202b
SHŌ 床 209a
SHŌ 抄 210a
SHŌ 肖 211b
SHŌ 姓 215a
SHŌ 昇 217b
SHŌ 松 217b
SHŌ 沼 218b
SHŌ 将 230b
SHŌ 症 234a
SHŌ 祥 234b
SHŌ 笑 234b
SHŌ 渉 241a
SHŌ 紹 242b
SHŌ 訟 243b
SHŌ 掌 248a
SHŌ 晶 248b
SHŌ 焦 250a
SHŌ 硝 250b
SHŌ 粧 251a
SHŌ 装 252a
SHŌ 詔 252b
SHŌ 傷 254b
SHŌ 奨 255b
SHŌ 詳 259a
SHŌ 彰 261b
SHŌ 障 265a
SHŌ 衝 268b
SHŌ 償 273a
SHŌ 礁 274a
SHŌ 鐘 278a
SHŌ 尚 279a
SHŌ 宵 279b
SHOKU 色 33(94)
SHOKU 食 65(253)
SHOKU 植 102(435)
SHOKU 織 143(644)
SHOKU 職 178(819)
SHOKU 殖 249b
SHOKU 触 259a
SHOKU 飾 260b
SHOKU 嘱 266a
SHU 手 20(28)

SHU 主 62(237)
SHU 取 62(238)
SHU 首 62(239)
SHU 守 99(421)
SHU 酒 99(422)
SHU 種 99(423)
SHU 修 141(633)
SHU 朱 204b
SHU 狩 225b
SHU 殊 233a
SHU 珠 233b
SHU 趣 269b
SHŪ 秋 32(89)
SHŪ 終 63(241)
SHŪ 週 63(242)
SHŪ 集 63(243)
SHŪ 州 99(424)
SHŪ 拾 100(425)
SHŪ 習 100(426)
SHŪ 収 141(631)
SHŪ 周 141(632)
SHŪ 修 141(633)
SHŪ 宗 176(805)
SHŪ 衆 176(806)
SHŪ 就 176(807)
SHŪ 囚 198b
SHŪ 舟 205b
SHŪ 秀 211a
SHŪ 臭 227a
SHŪ 執 238b
SHŪ 愁 256a
SHŪ 酬 260a
SHŪ 醜 274b
SHŪ 襲 278a
SHUKU 宿 141(634)
SHUKU 祝 142(635)
SHUKU 叔 214a
SHUKU 淑 241a
SHUKU 粛 243a
SHUKU 縮 274a
SHUN 春 33(91)
SHUN 俊 221a
SHUN 瞬 275a
SHUTSU 出 33(90)
SO 組 35(103)
SO 祖 146(657)
SO 素 146(658)
SO 阻 220b
SO 租 234b
SO 措 240b
SO 粗 242b
SO 疎 250b
SO 訴 252a
SO 塑 255a
SO 礎 275a
SŌ 早 35(104)
SŌ 走 36(105)
SŌ 草 36(106)
SŌ 送 68(268)
SŌ 争 105(451)
SŌ 相 105(452)
SŌ 倉 146(659)
SŌ 想 147(660)
SŌ 総 147(661)
SŌ 宗 176(805)
SŌ 創 181(832)
SŌ 双 197b
SŌ 壮 203b
SŌ, *sōsuru* 奏 222a
SŌ 荘 227a
SŌ 捜 232a
SŌ 桑 232b
SŌ 巣 239a
SŌ 掃 240a
SŌ 窓 242a
SŌ 喪 246b
SŌ 葬 251b
SŌ 装 252a
SŌ 僧 255a
SŌ 層 261b
SŌ 遭 264b
SŌ 操 271a
SŌ 燥 273b
SŌ 霜 274b
SŌ 騒 276b
sodateru 育 84(347)
soeru 添 241a
soko 底 110(475)
SOKU 足 20(29)
SOKU 速 105(453)
SOKU 息 105(454)
SOKU 則 148(666)
SOKU 側 148(667)
SOKU 測 148(668)
SOKU 即 207b
SOKU 束 210b
SOKU 促 221a
somaru, someru 染 224b
SON 村 36(107)
SON 孫 106(458)
SON 存 182(836)
SON, *sonsuru* 損 182(837)
SON 尊 182(838)
sonae, sonaeru, sonawaru 備 155(700)
sonaeru 供 167(760)
sono 園 46(159)
sora 空 28(65)
sosogu 注 70(277)
soto 外 26(56)
SOTSU 卒 106(457)
SOTSU 率 190(878)
sou 沿 218b
SU 子 21(31)
SU 主 62(237)
SU 守 99(421)
SU 素 146(658)
su 巣 239a
su 酢 253b
SU 数 67(262)
SŪ 枢 218a
SŪ 崇 239a
suberu 統 151(682)
sudeni 既 232a
sue 末 118(515)
sueru 据 280a
sugata 姿 222b
sugi 杉 279a
sugiru, sugosu 過 127(562)
SUI 水 17(14)
SUI 出 33(90)
SUI 推 179(821)
SUI 吹 208a
SUI 垂 214b
SUI 炊 219a
SUI 帥 223a
SUI 粋 234b
SUI 衰 235b

SUI 酔 245a
SUI 遂 253a
SUI 睡 257b
SUI 穂 268a
SUI 錘 273a
suji 筋 251a
suku 好 203b
suku 透 236a
~suke 助 64(248)
sukoshi 少 33(93)
sukoyaka 健 134(599)
sukui, sukuu 救 131(584)
sukunai 少 33(93)
sumasu, sumu 済 173(792)
sumi 炭 69(274)
sumi 墨 261a
sumu 住 63(244)
sumu 澄 267b
SUN 寸 193b
suna 砂 226a
suru 刷 96(405)
surudoi 鋭 269b
susumeru 勧 165(752)
susumu 進 66(259)
suteru 捨 240a
suu 吸 203a
suzu 鈴 260a
suzushii 涼 241a

—T—

TA 多 36(108)
TA 太 68(269)
TA 他 106(459)
ta 田 23(40)
taba 束 210b
taberu 食 65(253)
tabi 旅 82(335)
tachi 立 44(149)
tadashi 但 206b, 281a
tadashii 正 24(46)
tadayou 漂 262b
taeru 絶 180(828)
taeru 耐 226b
taeru 堪 246b, 281b
tagai 互 194a
tagayasu 耕 171(784)
TAI 大 19(22)
TAI 太 68(269)
TAI 体 69(270)
TAI 待 69(271)
TAI 台 69(272)
TAI 対 107(461)
TAI 隊 107(462)
TAI 帯 148(669)
TAI 貸 149(670)
TAI 退 182(839)
TAI 態 183(840)
TAI 怠 223b
TAI 耐 226b
TAI 胎 227a
TAI 泰 233a
TAI 袋 243b
TAI 逮 244b
TAI 替 248b
TAI 滞 257a
taira 平 78(315)
takai 高 30(76)
takara 宝 215b
take 竹 37(113)
take 岳 216a
taki 滝 257a
TAKU 宅 203b
TAKU 択 210a
TAKU 沢 211a
TAKU 卓 214a
TAKU 拓 217a
TAKU 託 236a
takumi 巧 199a
tama 玉 27(64)
tamago 卵 207b
tamashii 魂 265b
tamawaru 賜 269a
tami 民 118(518)
tamotsu 保 158(716)
TAN 炭 69(274)
TAN 短 108(466)
TAN 反 113(492)
TAN 単 149(671)
TAN 丹 194a, 281a
TAN 担 217a
TAN 胆 227a
TAN 探 240a
TAN 淡 241a
TAN 嘆 255a
TAN 端 263a
TAN 誕 264a
TAN 鍛 274b
tane 種 99(423)
tani 谷 30(78)
tanomi, tanomu 頼 272b
tanoshii 楽 81(331)
taoreru, taosu 倒 229a
tariru 足 20(29)
tashika, tashikameru 確 129(570)
tasukaru, tasukeru 助 64(248)
tatakai, tatakau 戦 104(448)
tatami 畳 250b
tate 縦 272a
tatematsuru 奉 215a
tateru, tatsu 建 93(391)
TATSU, *tassuru* 達 108(465)
tatsu 立 44(149)
tatsu 断 183(841)
tatsu 裁 252a
tattobu, tattoi 尊 182(838)
tawamureru 戯 266b
tawara 俵 155(702)
tazuneru 尋 247a
tazusaeru 携 256b
te 手 20(28)
TEI 体 69(270)
TEI 弟 71(282)
TEI 丁 109(473)
TEI 定 109(474)
TEI 底 110(475)
TEI 停 110(476)
TEI 庭 110(477)
TEI 低 150(677)
TEI 提 184(845)
TEI 程 184(846)
TEI, *teisuru* 呈 208a
TEI 廷 209a
TEI 抵 216b
TEI 邸 220b

TEI 帝 223a
TEI 訂 227b
TEI 貞 227b
TEI 逓 236b, 281b
TEI 堤 246b
TEI 艇 258b
TEI 締 268a
TEI 亭 279b
TEI 偵 279b
TEKI 的 110(478)
TEKI 敵 150(678)
TEKI, *tekisuru* 適 150(679)
TEKI 笛 242a
TEKI 摘 262a
TEKI 滴 262b
TEN 天 38(119)
TEN 店 71(284)
TEN 点 72(285)
TEN 転 110(479)
TEN 典 151(680)
TEN 展 184(847)
TEN 添 241a
TEN 殿 257a
tera 寺 60(228)
terasu, *teru* 照 101(433)
TETSU 鉄 71(283)
TETSU 迭 220b
TETSU 哲 230a
TETSU 徹 266b
TETSU, *tessuru* 撤 267a
TO 土 18(17)
TO 図 67(261)
TO 都 72(287)
TO 徒 111(480)
TO 登 111(483)
TO 斗 196b
TO 吐 203a
TO 途 236b
TO 渡 249b
TO 塗 255a
to 戸 28(69)
TŌ 冬 39(120)
TŌ 東 39(121)
TŌ 刀 72(289)
TŌ 当 73(290)
TŌ 投 73(291)
TŌ 島 73(292)
TŌ 答 73(293)
TŌ 頭 73(294)
TŌ 湯 111(482)
TŌ 登 111(483)
TŌ 等 111(484)
TŌ 燈 112(485), 280a
TŌ 統 151(682)
TŌ 党 184(848)
TŌ 討 184(849)
TŌ 納 186(856)
TŌ 豆 212a
TŌ 到 213b
TŌ 逃 228a
TŌ 倒 229a
TŌ 凍 229b
TŌ 唐 230a, 281a
TŌ 桃 232b
TŌ 透 236a
TŌ 悼 239b
TŌ 盗 242a
TŌ 陶 245a
TŌ 塔 247a
TŌ 痘 250b
TŌ 筒 251a
TŌ 稲 263a
TŌ 踏 269b
TŌ 糖 271b
TŌ 謄 274b
TŌ 闘 276b
TŌ 騰 278b
TŌ 灯 280b
tō 十 17(10)
toboshii 乏 194a
tobu 飛 113(493)
todokeru, *todoku* 届 185(852)
todokōru 滞 257a
tōge 峠 222b
togeru 遂 253a
tōi 遠 47(160)
tojiru 閉 245a
tokasu, *tokeru* 溶 257a
toki 時 32(87)
tokoro 所 64(246)
toko 床 209a
TOKU 読 39(123)
TOKU 特 152(685)
TOKU 得 185(850)
TOKU 徳 185(851)
TOKU 匿 229b
TOKU 督 257b
TOKU 篤 271b
toku 解 128(567)
toku 説 145(654)
tomaru, *tomeru*, *tome* 止 59(220)
tomaru, *tomeru* 泊 218b
tomeru 留 161(733)
tomi, *tomu* 富 187(864)
tomo 友 44(145)
tomo 共 90(376)
tomo 供 167(760)
tomonau 伴 206a
tomurai, *tomurau* 弔 196a
TON 豚 244a
tonaeru 唱 101(430)
tonari 隣 273b
tono 殿 257a
toraeru 捕 232a
tori 鳥 38(117)
toru 取 62(238)
toru 採 173(791)
toru 執 238b
tōru 通 71(281)
toshi 年 40(126)
totonoeru, *totonou* 整 103(443)
TOTSU 突 219b
tou 問 119(520)
TSU 都 72(287)
tsu 津 225a
TSŪ 通 71(281)
TSŪ 痛 250b
tsubasa 翼 274a
tsubo 坪 214b
tsubu 粒 242b
tsuchi 土 18(17)
tsugeru 告 94(398)
tsugi, *tsugu* 次 60(227)
tsugi, *tsugu* 継 258a

tsugunai, tsugunau 償 273a
TSUI 追 71(280)
TSUI 対 107(461)
TSUI 墜 266a
tsuiyasu 費 114(495)
tsukaeru 仕 59(221)
tsukare, tsukareru 疲 234a
tsukau 使 59(224)
tsukeru, tsuku 付 115(502)
tsuki 月 17(12)
tsuku 着 70(276)
tsuku 突 219b
tsukue 机 204b
tsukuri, tsukuru, 造 147(662)
tsukurou 繕 275b
tsukuru 作 31(82)
tsukusu 尽 205a
tsuma 妻 173(790)
tsumeru 詰 259a
tsumetai 冷 122(535)
tsumi 罪 173(794)
tsumori, tsumoru, tsumu 積 104(445)
tsumu 摘 262a
tsumu 錘 273a
tsumugu 紡 235a
tsuna 綱 263b
tsune 常 143(642)
tsuno 角 49(173)
tsunoru 募 246a
tsuranaru, tsureru, 連 122(538)
tsuranuku 貫 244a
tsuri 釣 280b
tsuru 弦 216a
tsurugi 剣 229b
tsutaeru, tsutawaru 伝 151(681)
tsutome 務 159(722)
tsutome, tsutomeru 勤 167(762)
tsutomeru 努 111(481)
tsutsu 筒 251a
tsutsumi 堤 246b
tsutsumu 包 117(511)
tsutsushimu 慎 256a
tsuyoi 強 53(192)
tsuyu 露 278a
tsuzukeru, tsuzuki, tsuzuku 続 106(456)
'suzumi 鼓 261b

— U —

U 右 18(19)
U 雨 23(42)
U 有 119(523)
U 宇 203b
U 羽 205b
ubau 奪 261a
uchi 内 112(489)
ude 腕 251b
ue 上 19(20)
ue, ueru 飢 237b
ueru 植 102(435)
ugoku 動 74(296)
uji 氏 139(620)
ukabu, uku 浮 233a
ukagau 伺 206b
uke, ukeru 受 63(240)
ukeru 請 268b
uketamawaru 承 142(639)
uma 馬 40(127)
umareru, umu 生 21(34)
umaru, umeru 埋 230a
ume 梅 232b
umi 海 26(55)
umu 産 96(408)
UN 雲 24(47)
UN 運 46(157)
unagasu 促 221a
uo 魚 53(190)
ura 浦 233a
ura 裏 258b
urami, uramu 恨 223b
uranai, uranau 占 198b
ureeru, urei 憂 266b
uri, uru 売 75(301)
uruoi, uruosu 潤 267b
urushi 漆 262b
uruwashii 麗 277b
ushi 牛 27(62)
ushinau 失 98(418)
ushiro 後 56(208)
usui 薄 272a
uta, utau 歌 48(166)
utagai, utagau 疑 166(757)
utai 謡 272b
utsu 打 107(460)
utsu 討 184(849)
utsu 撃 267a
utsukushii 美 76(308)
utsuru, utsusu 移 124(547)
utsuru, utsusu 映 224a
utsusu 写 98(419)
utsuwa 器 89(372)
uttae, uttaeru 訴 252a
uyamau 敬 168(766)
uzu 渦 280b

— W —

WA 話 45(151)
WA 和 82(338)
wa 輪 121(533)
WAI 賄 259b
wakai 若 220a
wakareru, wakeru 分 41(133)
wakareru 別 116(508)
wake 訳 189(874)
WAKU 惑 247b
waku 沸 218b
WAN 湾 250a
WAN 腕 251b
warai, warau 笑 234b
ware 我 164(745)
wari, waru 割 246a
warui 悪 45(152)
wasureru 忘 209b
wata 綿 160(725)
watakushi 私 174(797)
wataru 渡 249b
wazawai 災 172(789)
wazurawashii 煩 257b, 281b

— Y —

YA 夜 43(144)
YA 野 79(323)
ya 家 25(53)
ya 屋 47(161)
ya 矢 200b
yabure, yaburu 破 153(692)
yabureru 敗 153(693)
yado, yadoru 宿 141(634)
YAKU 役 79(324)
YAKU 薬 119(521)
YAKU 約 160(726)
YAKU, *yakusuru* 訳 189(874)
YAKU 躍 278a
YAKU 厄 279a
yaku, yakeru 焼 101(434)
yama 山 22(38)
yamai, yamu 病 77(310)
yanagi 柳 224b
yasashii 優 273a
yashinau 養 161(731)
yashiro 社 61(234)
yasui 安 45(153)
yasumu, yasumi 休 27(61)
yatou 雇 254b
yattsu 八 16(8)
yawaragu 和 82(338)
yawarakai 柔 224b
YO 予 120(525)
YO 余 160(728)
YO 預 190(875)
YO 与 194b
YO 誉 259b
yo 四 15(4)
yo 夜 43(144)
yo 世 67(263)
yo 代 107(463)
YŌ 用 44(146)
YŌ 葉 80(327)
YŌ 様 80(328)
YŌ 曜 80(329)
YŌ 洋 120(526)
YŌ 陽 120(527)
YŌ, *yōsuru* 要 160(729)
YŌ 容 161(730)
YŌ 養 161(731)
YŌ 幼 199b
YŌ 羊 205b
YŌ 庸 239a
YŌ 揚 248a
YŌ 揺 248a
YŌ 溶 257a
YŌ 腰 258b
YŌ 踊 264b
YŌ 窯 268a
YŌ, *yōsuru* 擁 271a
YŌ 謡 272b
yobu 呼 214b
yoi 良 121(530)
yoi 宵 279b
yoko 横 86(355)
YOKU 浴 161(732)
YOKU 欲 190(876)
YOKU 抑 210a
YOKU 翌 243a
YOKU 翼 274a
yome 嫁 255b
yomu 読 39(123)
yon 四 15(4)
yoru 夜 43(144)
yoru 因 124(548)
yoru, yoseru 寄 130(576)
yorokobi, yorokobu 喜 89(370)
yoshi 由 80(325)
yoso-oi, yoso-ou 装 252a
yottsu 四 15(4)
you 酔 245a
yowai, yowaru 弱 62(236)
YU 由 80(325)
YU 油 119(522)
YU 輸 160(727)
YU 愉 248a
YU 諭 272b
yu 湯 111(482)
YŪ 右 18(19)
YŪ 友 44(145)
YŪ 由 80(325)
YŪ 遊 80(326)
YŪ 有 119(523)
YŪ 勇 119(524)
YŪ 幽 223a
YŪ 郵 244b
YŪ 猶 250a
YŪ 裕 252a
YŪ 雄 254a
YŪ 誘 264a
YŪ 憂 266b
YŪ 融 272a
YŪ 優 273a
yū 夕 34(98)
yubi 指 60(226)
YUI 遺 162(739)
YUI 唯 238a
yuka 床 209a
yuki 雪 35(100)
yuku 行 29(73)
yume 夢 255b
yumi 弓 194b
yureru 揺 248a
yurushi, yurusu 許 132(587)
yutaka 豊 189(870)
yuu 結 93(390)
yuzuru 譲 277b

— Z —

ZA 座 231a
ZAI 材 95(403)
ZAI 在 137(613)
ZAI 財 173(793)
ZAI 罪 173(794)
ZAI 剤 229b
ZAN 残 96(409)
ZAN 暫 267a
ZATSU 雑 138(615)
ZE 是 179(822)
ZEI 説 145(654)
ZEI 税 180(826)
ZEN 前 35(102)
ZEN 全 68(267)
ZEN 然 105(450)
ZEN 善 181(831)
ZEN 禅 258a
ZEN 漸 262b
ZEN 繕 275b

zeni 銭 146(656)
ZETSU 舌 180(827)
ZETSU 絶 180(828)
ZŌ 雑 138(615)
ZŌ 造 147(662)
ZŌ 象 147(663)
ZŌ 像 147(664)
ZŌ 増 148(665)
ZŌ, *zōsuru* 蔵 181(833)
ZŌ 憎 262a
ZŌ 贈 275b
ZŌ 臓 276b
ZOKU 族 106(455)
ZOKU 続 106(456)
ZOKU 俗 181(834)
ZOKU, *zokusuru* 属 182(835)
ZOKU 賊 259b
ZON, *zonzuru* 存 182(836)
ZU 図 67(261)
ZU 頭 73(294)
ZU 豆 212a
ZUI 随 254a
ZUI 髄 277b
～*zukuri* 147(662)
～*zure* 122(538)
～*zuri* 96(405)